OXFORD
UNIVERSITY PRESS

Great Clarendon Street, Oxford, OX2 6DP,
United Kingdom

Oxford University Press is a department of the University of Oxford.
It furthers the University's objective of excellence in research, scholarship, and education by publishing worldwide. Oxford is a registered trade mark of Oxford University Press in the UK and in certain other countries

First Edition published in 2013
Impression: 2

British Library Cataloguing in Publication Data
Data available

ISBN 978–0–19–966187–9

Printed and bound by CPI Group (UK) Ltd, Croydon, CR0 4YY

The Challenges of Intra-Party Democracy

EDITED BY WILLIAM P. CROSS
AND RICHARD S. KATZ

THE CHALLENGES OF INTRA-PARTY DEMOCRACY

COMPARATIVE POLITICS

Comparative Politics is a series for students, teachers, and researchers of political science that deals with contemporary government and politics. Global in scope, books in the series are characterized by a stress on comparative analysis and strong methodological rigour. The series is published in association with the European Consortium for Political Research. For more information visit www.ecprnet.eu

The Comparative Politics series is edited by Professor David M. Farrell, School of Politics and International Relations, University College Dublin and Kenneth Carty, Professor of Political Science, University of British Columbia

OTHER TITLES IN THIS SERIES

Parliaments and Coalitions
The Role of Legislative Institutions in Multiparty Governance
Lanny W. Martin and Georg Vanberg

When Citizens Decide
Lessons from Citizen Assemblies on Electoral Reform
Patrick Fournier, Henk van der Kolk, R. Kenneth Carty, André Blais, and Jonathan Rose

Platform or Personality?
The Role of Party Leaders in Elections
Amanda Bittner

Political Leaders and Democratic Elections
Edited by Kees Aarts, André Blais, and Hermann Schmitt

The Politics of Party Funding
State Funding to Political Parties and Party Competition in Western Europe
Michael Koß

Designing Democracy in a Dangerous World
Andrew Reynolds

Democracy within Parties
Candidate Selection Methods and
Their Political Consequences
Reuven Y. Hazan and Gideon Rahat

Party Politics in New Democracies
Edited by Paul Webb and Stephen White

Intergovernmental Cooperation
Rational Choices in Federal Systems and Beyond
Nicole Bolleyer

The Dynamics of Two-Party Politics
Party Structures and the Management of Competition
Alan Ware

Cabinets and Coalition Bargaining
The Democratic Life Cycle in Western Europe
Edited by Kaare Strøm, Wolfgang C. Müller, and Torbjörn Bergman

Politics at the Centre
The Selection and Removal of Party Leaders in the Anglo Parliamentary Democracies
William P. Cross and André Blais

Acknowledgements

This volume has its roots in a conversation between the editors at the ECPR general conference in Potsdam. The ECPR has provided many venues for both of us to present our work, and to meet with colleagues, and we appreciate these opportunities.

After agreeing on the need for a comprehensive examination of both the concept and practice of internal party democracy, among the first tasks we set for ourselves was the recruitment of a group of first-rate academics to carry out this examination. If at nothing else, we believe we achieved resounding success at this task. The contributors to this book all have made significant earlier contributions to the study of party politics and this volume benefits greatly from that body of work.

In addition to outstanding scholarship, each of the contributors also brought a professional and collegial approach to the project. This has truly been a team enterprise and the final product is better for it. The group of authors met twice in Ottawa for workshops during which the scope and contours of the study were agreed upon and preliminary drafts of chapters were reviewed and discussed. These gatherings often took on the feel of sophisticated graduate seminars with no shortage of discussion and constructive criticism of each other's work. We are grateful to Thomas Zittel and David Farrell who participated in these meetings and offered much useful advice.

The project was funded through the Hon. Dick and Ruth Bell Chair for the Study of Canadian Parliamentary Democracy at Carleton University and we thank Dr. Ruth Bell for her generosity. We also thank Carleton PhD candidates Joanna Sweet and Scott Pruysers for their administrative support along the way.

As always, the team at OUP has been a pleasure to work with and we look forward to publishing with them again. Lillian Ashworth did the heavy lifting in constructing the index for this volume.

Finally, we thank our spouses, Emma and Judy, for tolerating our dedication to this project over the past several years. We know we are in their debt far beyond our capacity for repayment.

William P. Cross and Richard S. Katz

Contents

Tables and Figures

Abbreviations

ALP	Australian Labor Party
CDU	Christian Democratic Union, Germany
CoE	Council of Europe
D66	Democrats 66, the Netherlands
FDP	Free Democratic Party, Germany
IPD	intra-party democracy
ISSP	International Social Survey Programme
NDP	New Democratic Party, Canada
OSCE	Organization for Security and Cooperation in Europe
PS	Socialist Party, France
PvdA	Labour Party, the Netherlands
PVV	Freedom Party, the Netherlands
QWPA	quasi-women's policy agencies
SMP	single member plurality system
SPD	Social Democratic Party, Germany
UMP	Union for a Popular Movement, France
VLD	Flemish Liberals and Democrats, Belgium
VVD	People's Party for Freedom and Democracy, the Netherlands

List of Contributors

Ingrid van Biezen is Professor of Comparative Politics at Leiden University in the Netherlands.

R. Kenneth Carty is Professor Emeritus of Political Science at the University of British Columbia, Canada.

Sarah Childs is Professor of Politics and Gender at the University of Bristol, United Kingdom.

William P. Cross is the Hon. Dick and Ruth Bell Chair for the Study of Canadian Parliamentary Democracy at Carleton University, Ottawa, Canada.

Anika Gauja is Senior Lecturer in the Department of Government and International Relations at the University of Sydney, Australia.

Richard S. Katz is Professor of Political Science at the Johns Hopkins University in Baltimore, Maryland, USA.

Gideon Rahat is Associate Professor in the Department of Political Science at the Hebrew University of Jerusalem, Israel.

Daniela Romée Piccio (PhD) is Research Associate at Leiden University in the Netherlands.

Susan E. Scarrow is Professor of Political Science at the University of Houston, USA.

Lisa Young is Professor of Political Science at the University of Calgary, Canada.

1

The Challenges of Intra-Party Democracy

William P. Cross and Richard S. Katz

The centrality of political parties to modern democracy was already recognized when Schattschneider (1942: 1) argued 'that the political parties created democracy and that modern democracy is unthinkable save in terms of the parties.... The parties are not therefore merely appendages of modern government; they are in the center of it and play a determinative and creative role in it'. Political scientists have continued to identify parties as key institutions for a healthy democracy, highlighting their roles in the recruitment of candidates, the providing of linkages between government and civil society, the organization of legislatures and the structuring of election campaigns. Beyond observations concerning the importance for democracy of the fact *that* parties do these things, there has also been widespread concern with the *ways in which* parties discharge these responsibilities. In particular, if state-level democracy cannot flourish save for parties, the questions inevitably arise of whether the parties themselves must be, should be, and are internally democratic with respect to their own decision-making practices and distributions of authority or influence.

If these are questions for academic political science, for many of those working to establish democracy in the third (or fourth) wave democracies, the answers are obvious: internal party democracy is either a necessity or a panacea. When the European Commission for Democracy through Law (the 'Venice Commission') issued its *Code of Good Practice in the Field of Political Parties,* it identified 'to reinforce political parties' internal democracy' as 'its explicit aim'.[1] Likewise, the Parliamentary Assembly of the Council of Europe (PACE) has called on member states to 'ensure that the legislative framework promotes the implementation by political parties of internal party democracy principles'.[2] After a workshop on the subject at the Third Assembly of the World Movement for Democracy, 'There was a general consensus at the workshop that the strengthening of internal party democracy is a crucial prerequisite for democratic development in various

[1] <http://www.venice.coe.int/docs/2009/CDL-AD%282009%29021-e.pdf>.

[2] <http://assembly.coe.int/Main.asp?link=/Documents/WorkingDocs/Doc10/EDOC12107.htm>.

countries'.[3] International IDEA has a project on internal party democracy that aims 'to provoke party reform by identifying the challenges facing political parties for them to become more democratic, transparent and effective'.[4] According to the Netherlands Institute for Multiparty Democracy, 'internal democracy' is one of the '"institutional guarantees" that . . . political parties would have to fulfill if they were to effectively meet what is expected of them in a democracy'.[5] Similarly, USAID support for political parties 'emphasizes the need for internal party democracy'.[6]

For many practicing politicians confronting what they see as crises of participation in the longer established democracies, the answers are the same: the way to counter the nearly universal decline of party membership (van Biezen et al. 2012), is for the parties to become more internally democratic. The result has been a wide variety of reforms in party structures and practices—in some cases adopted by internal decisions of individual parties and in others imposed by law (although, of course, in democratic systems the laws are made in elected legislatures, which is to say by representatives of the parties themselves)—to provide for more direct member involvement in the choice of candidates for public office, the selection of the leader(s) of the party, and the formulation or ratification of statements defining the party's policies. Parties often present themselves as being democratically organized both to differentiate themselves from their competitors and as a signal that they are open to participation from all citizens. Rare is the party that admits to being 'undemocratic' in its organization.

While parties and the democracy promotion community may espouse general agreement that internal party democracy (IPD) is a good thing, any survey of parties' internal structures makes it clear that there is no single, agreed upon definition of what it means to be internally democratic. Parties claiming to practice IPD organize and operate in dramatically different ways. Like democracy itself, the definition of IPD is essentially contestable. Is it primarily about participation, inclusiveness, centralization, accountability, or something else altogether? Should the emphasis be on outcomes or on process? For example, if inclusiveness is a key consideration, in terms of candidate selection is the concern about the inclusiveness of the selectorate (those who choose the candidates), or is it about the diversity of the group of candidates ultimately selected? And, who is either group meant to be inclusive of—party members, party supporters in the electorate, the electorate generally?

[3] <http://www.wmd.org/assemblies/third-assembly/workshops/political-parties-and-finance/how-strengthen-internal-party-demo>.

[4] <http://www.idea.int/parties/internal_democracy07.cfm>.

[5] <http://www.nimd.org/documents/I/internal_party_democracy-_state_of_affairs_and_the_road_ahead.pdf>; report written by Augustine Magolowondo.

[6] <http://serbia-montenegro.usaid.gov/code/navigate.php?Id=23>.

There is no obviously correct answer to these questions. First, even when there is agreement about democratic values, the values themselves may be in conflict. For example, there is a significant body of evidence suggesting that processes that strengthen the value of participation can have an adverse impact on the value of inclusion (at least with regard to the inclusiveness of candidate lists—Hazan and Rahat 2010). Second, IPD as an internal value may impede the achievement of the party's external goals. Aside from the frequently cited possibility that giving more power to the party's activists may result in candidates or policy positions that are less able to attract support in the broader electorate (May 1973), thereby increasing the likelihood of government policies that are less to the liking of those activists,[7] there are the examples of left-libertarian or ecological parties in Europe whose insistence on direct member decision making (aside from giving disproportionate power to those members with the stamina to endure interminable meetings) made it impossible to take binding decisions (because they could always be reversed at the next meeting, with a different set of members present) (Kitschelt 1989), or whose abhorrence of hierarchy and insistence on rotation in office denied them both stable and experienced representation. In other words, if democracy, whether intra-party or systemic, is an end in itself, there is no consensus on exactly what that means or how it would be either institutionalized or measured. And if, on the other hand, 'Democracy is a political *method*, that is to say, a certain type of institutional arrangement for arriving at . . . decisions and hence incapable of being an end in itself, irrespective of what decisions it will produce under given historical conditions' (Schumpeter 1962 [1942]: 242), then there may be limits to how much IPD is actually a good thing.

Even parties that generally agree that internally democratic structures are desirable are faced with a series of decisions when operationalizing this principle. In some cases, they are constrained by state imposed party laws that regulate parts of their internal activity. These laws generally are predicated on the ideas that, on the one hand, parties are private associations of citizens who should be free to organize their activities as they choose, but that, on the other hand, they are also powerful actors in politics and potentially subject to capture or perversion by their nominal leaders. Hence, when internal party processes are legally prescribed, it is generally to assure, at a minimum, that the 'members' (somehow defined) are represented in party governing bodies, either directly or through the periodic election of representatives. The German party law, for example, specifies that parties must have: regional branches (art. 7); an executive committee of at least three members, elected at least every two years (art. 11); an assembly, at least half the members of which must be allocated on the basis of membership, with the rest allocated in proportion to votes obtained at the last parliamentary election; party

[7] In other words, the activists might rationally prefer to have less power in a way analogous to the observation of Mancur Olson (1965) that a rational individualist might prefer to be compelled to contribute to the production of public goods which would otherwise be under-provided.

courts of arbitration, whose members must be elected at least every four years, and cannot be 'members of the executive committee of the party or a regional branch, be employed by the party or a regional branch, nor receive regular income from them' (art. 14). In other cases, the law may simply require that the party be internally democratic without specifying what that means, or at the other extreme, it may define the party's internal arrangements in great detail, perhaps going so far as to identify the exact number and functions of its officers and to specify the dates on which they are to be elected. And of course, in still other cases, there may be no legal strictures at all.

Within such legal constraints as are imposed, each political party makes choices regarding how it organizes, reflecting its view of appropriate internal democratic practices, influenced no doubt by its perceived self-interest, and its conception of the political party itself. For example, parties usually decide both the criteria for membership and whether to limit the intra-party franchise in particular areas of decision-making to members, or whether alternatively to permit a broader range of supporters to participate, essentially determining who the party 'demos' is. Some parties restrict formal influence to long-time activists while others invite all partisans to take part in their decision-making. Labour parties may grant formal authority to trade unions while others restrict the internal franchise to party elites. Some parties are heavily reliant upon corporations for their funding while others explicitly reject any corporate contributions. Some may adopt gender and regional quotas for internal decision-making bodies while others choose members of these bodies at-large, and leave the distribution of positions among different categories of individuals entirely to the electors.

Two parties adopting widely different practices may both defend their choices as best reflecting IPD. For example, parties selecting their leader through a one-member-one-vote procedure often argue that this reflects a populist democratic view of equality among members and offers opportunity for expansive participation. Others, deciding to make the choice at a party conference, by delegates chosen to ensure regional and gender balance, argue that this process best respects the democratic values of inclusiveness, representativeness, and collective decision-making. On their face, neither claim is right or wrong; rather each reflects a different understanding of what democracy requires.

Analysis of parties' approaches to IPD is made more complex by their common practice of adopting different practices for different areas of party activity; for example, as parties engage in a variety of activities, the questions of who should be empowered, and in what ways, may have many different answers within a single party. It is not uncommon for a party to decide that one group should have authority over candidate selection, another should choose its leader and a third determine policy positions. Not only do the bodies with decision-making authority differ across activities, so too may the ways in which the members of those bodies are chosen and the 'demos' to whom they are ultimately responsible.

If it is important to understand the internal workings of parties because of the importance of parties to the realization of democracy at the system level, it is also impossible to understand or to evaluate those internal workings without considering the fact that parties are parts of, and enmeshed in, a wider political system. On the one hand, the choices parties make will be influenced, if not necessarily determined, by their environment. The constraints imposed by party laws are examples of one such environmental influence. The type of electoral system, the number of competitive parties, the ideological range of the party system, whether a party is in government or opposition, whether it competes in a federal or unitary state, the degree to which (and the conditions under which) state subventions are available, all might encourage a party to adopt particular approaches to IPD, as indeed might the approaches to IPD taken by other parties in the same political system.

On the other hand, because parties are only parts of the wider system, the underlying idea that the internal democracy of parties is a necessary component of system-level democracy is itself not beyond question. While some theorists argue that real democracy requires that all the institutions of society, including but hardly limited to parties, be themselves democratic, others, such as Giovanni Sartori (1965: 124), are quite clear in their claims that 'democracy on a large scale is not the sum of many little democracies'. Here the basic claim is that the essence of democracy is free choice *among* parties, rather than direct participation *within* parties—based on the further premise that parties are properly understood to be teams of politicians rather than associations of citizens.

In less stark terms, some argue that IPD cannot properly be considered on its own but must be viewed as part of the full range of democratic or participatory opportunities offered a citizen. In this view IPD is but one component of democratic life in a state and it is this full democratic experience that must be considered. IPD can add to the overall democratic experience or it may detract from it depending upon how it is structured. This argument is made most clearly by Hazan and Rahat (2010) who suggest that highly participatory candidate nomination processes may lead to less inclusive and representative groups of candidates. General elections have little opportunity to rectify an inclusiveness problem created through the candidate selection process, as parties, in most systems, are gatekeepers to elected office. On the other hand, general elections can at least partially remedy a participatory shortfall created through more exclusive methods of candidate selection, by maximizing participation in general election voting. The point is that democracy is multifaceted, and some components of it are most easily maximized by the internal workings of political parties and others through general elections. In Hazan and Rahat's argument, inclusiveness in candidate pools and legislatures may be maximized through less participatory party nomination processes, which can be remedied through highly participatory general elections.

The challenge is not only in balancing party and state-level democratic practices but also in prioritizing different democratic impulses within the practice of

IPD. Trade-offs and compromise are inevitable. Parties favouring deliberative decision-making may adopt institutions based on geographic, gender, or even factional representation that guarantee the inclusion of what they view as the important interests or opinions that need to be taken into account, with the objectives of compromise and accommodation 'trumping' direct member participation on a one-member-one-vote basis. Others may not face a need to accommodate widely divergent interests and may instead prefer broadly participatory processes even if these provide little opportunity for collective deliberation. The decision may reflect the character of the party (for example, catch-all versus ideological) or may result from the differences inherent between governing and opposition parties or those operating in a heterogenous versus more homogenous society.

In this sense, IPD cannot be measured in a way that permits a 'scientific' conclusion that one party is more democratic than another—in the same way that it is a mug's game to try to definitively determine whether Germany or Australia or the Netherlands is the most democratic. Rankings of how democratic various countries are depend on the definition they ascribe to democracy and the same is true for IPD. It is an interest in the different approaches parties take to IPD, their rationales for doing so, and the implications of these decisions that animate this book. Accordingly, we are interested in the range of questions parties face in considering whether and how to implement IPD.

SOME OF THE KEY QUESTIONS

Some of the important questions on which we hope to shed light are: what aspects of their internal activity do parties conclude should, and should not, be subject to democratic determination, which democratic values are prioritized in implementing IPD, who is empowered in making party decisions, what are the perceived costs and benefits of different approaches to IPD, and how are these decisions influenced by the context in which a party operates? While not questioning the sincerity of the commitment of parties and politicians to democratic values, we also recognize that IPD is both about the distribution of power and influence within a party, and within the broader society. As such, both internal democratization in general, and the choice of a specific variant of IPD in particular, involve winners and losers. Whose interests are served by what version of IPD?

The first big question is how parties fit into the broader scheme of democratic government. Much of the discussion above concerning IPD stems from the party model/democratic theory of the mass party of integration. In this view, parties are the political arms of well-defined social groups, and politicians—including party leaders—are the agents of those groups, with the members of the groups (archetypically the members of a social class or a particular religion), or at least the members of the group who are sufficiently politically interested to have joined the party, being the principals. Not surprisingly, IPD has a prominent place in the overall understanding of democracy associated with the mass party (Beer 1965; Katz and Mair 1995).

The mass party is not the only party type that has been identified, and indeed most analysts of party organization regard it largely as an historical relic. A variety of types have been suggested to characterize more recent developments in party organizations, including the catch-all party (Kirchheimer 1966), the cartel party (Katz and Mair 1995), the party as public utility (van Biezen 2004), the business-firm party (Hopkin and Paolucci 1999), and the franchise party (Carty 2004). Each of these has its own interpretation of democracy, and its own implications for the proper role and implementation of IPD.

One of the consequences of the widespread perception of IPD as a positive democratic force, and in the minds of some a necessary component of statewide democracy, is the increased attempts by the state to mandate it. Once commonly viewed as strictly private organizations based in civil society, the internal organizational procedures and structures of parties have become increasingly subject to external regulation. In crafting these regulations many states have taken their cue from the classic mass party as a prescriptive model of organization. These regulatory efforts may not rest easily in societies in which the socio-economic structures supporting the mass party are no longer found. Questions of democratic legitimacy may also arise when legislatures and courts become the deciders of how parties should internally organize and conduct their affairs. These can raise concerns relating to state centralization and control over political participation and public life. Diversity in party organizational practices, reflecting prioritization of different democratic norms, perhaps in competition with one another and none *a priori* less valid than another, may be homogenized through these efforts.

As suggested above, one of the central questions a party must consider when implementing IPD is who is the 'demos'—that is, who should have authority in its internal decision making? Although there are exceptions, parties generally attempt to portray themselves as being open and inclusive and thus welcoming of participation from everyone. Most parties are membership organizations and requisites of membership are often minimal—residency, a minimum age, and payment of a small fee. This can vary, however, with some parties requiring a greater commitment to their ideals in return for membership. Significant academic attention has been paid in recent decades to an apparent decline in the number of party members. Some see this as partially reflecting citizen dissatisfaction with parties that they see as being overly hierarchical and not providing sufficient opportunities for their rank-and-file to influence internal decision-making. Accordingly, many of those who view a decline in party membership negatively argue for more robust forms of IPD as a way of providing an increased incentive for party activism. Parties may benefit from a larger membership in a number of ways including:

having a larger base of supporters to draw upon for financial contributions and election campaign volunteers and to legitimize their argument that they have widespread support among the electorate as evidenced by an increasing membership. But this expanded membership may also come with some costs as members can, for example, be a source of policy demands on the party and can constrain the leadership's freedom to manoeuver (Katz 1990).

Regardless of how broadly the demos is defined, one of the fundamental issues parties face in terms of member influence is determining whether their constituency is comprised of individuals or identifiable groups. This question manifests itself in the internal organizational structures of parties through a choice between according all members a free choice and an equal voice in party decision-making, or alternatively guaranteeing particular groups a prescribed level of influence regardless of the immediate preferences of individual members. Group-based representation, whether it is based on trade union membership, age, geography, or gender, challenges notions of popular control based on individual equality. Many parties have struggled with this issue in terms of gender representation, as women continue to be under-represented both in parties' decision-making processes and in the outcomes they produce (in particular, lists of candidates for public office). The question is whether processes and outcomes can in any meaningful way be considered genuinely democratic if they are not fully inclusive of the half of the population comprised of women.

A party's approach towards membership may tell us relatively little about its practice of IPD. While a party that empowers a highly restrictive membership may well not be viewed as practicing robust IPD, the same conclusion may be reached with regard to parties with more expansive memberships that offer them little or no influence in important decision-making. Parties that offer significant influence to supporters who have not chosen to become members may be regarded as even more democratic than those that restrict participation to formal members—or alternatively, they may be seen to be less democratic as organizations themselves precisely because this expansion of the range of participants dilutes the influence of those who are members. The crucial consideration in terms of IPD appears not to be norms of party membership, or even patterns of intra-party participation, but rather who has real authority over what areas of party decision-making.

As suggested above, the answers to this question vary not only among parties but internally for different aspects of party life. We can use the example of leadership selection here. Until well into the second half of the twentieth century, leaders in many parties were said to 'emerge' through processes such as the UK Tories' 'magic circle' in which the outgoing leader, together with a small group of party elites, essentially chose the next leader. This practice has now all but disappeared as most parties agree that some formal 'democratic' process should be followed. There is, however, fundamental disagreement over who should be included. The range is dramatic, with some parties extending the leadership franchise essentially to all of their supporters in the electorate, others to all party members, some only to long time party members, still others to a select group of members in a party conference, and a sizable number restricting formal influence to members of the parliamentary party. In nearly all cases there has been a democratization of the process as even those limiting the vote to MPs now have formal, secret ballots, but the parties' views of who the appropriate demos is for the leadership choice obviously varies.

The same can be said for candidate selection as parties similarly take very different approaches, sometimes leaving the choice to their rank-and-file membership and in other cases having candidates appointed by a central party elite. In this case, the demos question is not just one of scope but also of centralization versus local authority. Parties also differ with some adopting quotas to ensure equitable gender representation in their candidate pool while others reject this approach as placing an artificial restriction on voter choice and a favouring of one group over another. Nearly all parties justify their choices relating to these personnel recruitment issues in terms of advancing democratic norms. The different conclusions they reach, and different practices they adopt, represent a privileging of different democratic priorities. One may favour inclusiveness in the process manifested through the broadest possible selectorate while another privileges democratic deliberation and accommodation best realized through a smaller, representative selectorate. These differences may reflect the democratic needs of particular political communities and may produce very different outcomes.

Similar diversity can be found in approaches to policy development with some seeing this as solely within the purview of the parliamentary party and others as an important function for the extra-parliamentary membership. Differences here often reflect both the internal democratic ethos of the party and its relative proximity to power. Opposition parties, not burdened with the challenges of actually governing or maintaining good relations with coalition partners, may find it easier to empower their extra-parliamentary members in the policy development exercise as they are not faced with the necessary compromises inherent in policymaking across the many interconnected and complicated spheres of contemporary governance. Governing parties also face the 'democratic' question of whether they are meant to represent the views of their activists (perhaps members), their voters, or all citizens. If the answer is the latter, then questions of IPD become more complex as the views of their members can be expected to differ in significant ways from those of the citizenry at large. Similar to candidate selection, the issue arises of whether IPD in terms of policy development is best measured on its own or as a contributing component of the state's overall democratic quality.

As in much of life, the necessity for, and sources of, financial resources underwriting party activity influence who exercises authority in decision-making. This issue relates both to the internal workings of parties and to their place in the broader state-wide democratic apparatus. For example, when parties adopt internally democratic practices based on expanding the inclusiveness of their leadership selectorate, details relating to political financing influence the relative balance of authority within the party. How are candidates financed in these contests that require significantly more expansive (and expensive) campaigns? Are corporate, trade union, and large individual contributions permitted? Are candidates limited in the amounts they can spend in these internal party elections and if so do these limits dampen party building opportunities or do they make them more accessible to all segments of the party regardless of their access to large amounts of resources? For internal contests, parties often make these decisions themselves and the different approaches they take reflect both their democratic ethos and their competitive needs. The regulatory scheme imposed by the state regarding levels of public financing and permissible contributions for general elections also has an impact on IPD as it influences the relationship between parties and civil society. One regulatory approach can result in parties becoming largely dependent on state subventions for their financing, another can encourage parties to seek large numbers of small donations from voters while yet another might encourage the solicitation of large corporate contributions. In considering how these scenarios influence IPD, it is worth recalling the often-repeated observation that 'he who pays the piper calls the tune.'

In each of these aspects of party life there is an important, but sometimes overlooked, distinction between participation and control, and we must be alert to the possibility that party leaders may try to encourage the first without ceding the second. In her study of workplace democracy, Pateman (1970: 69, following Verba 1961) points to the possibility of *pseudo participation*—a feeling of involvement without the substance of decision-making influence—as when employees may question the boss or make suggestions, while the authority to decide still rests firmly at the top. The same might be said about highly participatory but also highly centralized political campaigns. Similarly, to the extent that party congresses operate in practice like the Greek assemblies in Homer, limited to approving or rejecting proposals made by the elite after debate in which only the elite could participate and in any case liable to have their decisions overturned or ignored by the elite, it makes little difference if the delegates are numerous and diverse.

At the other extreme, we must be alert to the fact that oligarchy is only one antithesis of democracy. At another extreme is anarchy. While decentralization/defusion of authority is generally considered to promote democracy (consider, for example, Dahl's idea of 'polyarchy'), if decentralization means that each local branch or party candidate is free to ignore the central party, or if participation in decision-making is expanded beyond party leaders and members to include more passive supporters, or in the limiting case, illustrated by the American open-primary, any citizen who cares to participate, the result may be to render the party as a distinct political entity irrelevant rather than to make it more democratic. While there are many ways in which IPD can be institutionalized, the ultimate questions remain to what extent, how, and in which aspects of party life the members are able to control what their party does.

2

Are Political Parties Meant to Be Internally Democratic?

R. Kenneth Carty

In his pioneering study of *Political Parties*, Maurice Duverger (1954: xv) tells us that any political party is simply 'a community with a particular structure' and that 'modern parties are characterized primarily by their anatomy'. This being the case, a party's democratic character would appear to depend on its formal structure and the fashion in which interested individuals and groups can and do manipulate its parts. Inevitably then, scholars and practitioners have sought to understand the critical distinctions between the different and changing organizational models adopted by parties over time, as well as how these forms have really worked in the hard world of competitive electoral politics.

At its simplest, the intra-party democracy (IPD) question is often posed as 'should the party's leadership determine its policies, or should its mass members or supporters?' (Katz 1997: 38). However there is necessarily more to the issue than that. Besides the determination of policy there are intimately related questions of priority setting, implementation and accountability. What role for members or supporters (or even other citizens) in influencing or controlling them? And beyond policy there are questions of personnel for it may often be, as Trollope once suggested, 'men not measures are, no doubt, the very life of politics'.[1] So what role for members or supporters (or others) in making personnel choices, be they for internal party office or for candidates for public office. These questions lead directly to the problem of just who or what is the party. Katz and Mair's (1993) answer is that modern parties have three distinct faces—the party on the ground, in central office, and in public office. The relationships among the faces define any party as a unique organization and shape the democratic tensions that govern its internal party decision-making and political life.

This is not to say that there is necessarily any easy agreement on the essential democratic character of particular parties or the way that power is organized and

[1] Trollope (in *Phineas Redux*, Ch. XXXI) follows this claim with the observation, equally true of much political science, 'but then it is not the fashion to say so in public places'.

operated within them. Robert McKenzie (1964) writing of British parties in his definitive study subtitled 'The Distribution of Power within the Conservative and Labour Parties' comes to the quite unequivocal conclusion that 'whatever the role granted in theory to the extra-parliamentary wings of the parties, in practice final authority rests in both parties with the parliamentary party and its leadership. In this fundamental respect the distribution of power within the two major parties is the same' (635). By contrast, Samuel Beer's (1965) magisterial account of British politics, cast as 'a study of parties and pressure groups', comes to quite the opposite conclusion arguing 'that in practice as in theory, in the actual distribution of power as in their reigning conceptions of authority, the two parties were deeply opposed' (388).

Both scholars recognized and agreed that these two great British parties had distinctive anatomies and physiologies; their starkly different assessments of the reality of British party politics rested upon their different interpretations of how the country's activists and partisans understood and practiced party democracy. It may be that this difference between the Canadian McKenzie (University of British Columbia and the London School of Economics) and the American Beer (Michigan and Oxford) reflected different scholarly orientations to understanding and interpreting political life: McKenzie giving pride of place to the importance of governing institutions (635), Beer to the role of ideas and political culture (389). However it also reminds us that questions of IPD are not so easily settled.

In pointing to what he calls scholars 'little civil war about "intraparty democracy"' Austin Ranney (see Katz 1997: 38) suggests that our debates are often confused by a failure to recognize that there are (at least) three questions at issue: the actual reality, the practical possibility, and the theoretical desirability of IPD. Thus it may be that McKenzie's focus on immediate practices, and Beer's on the cultural subtleties of these two parties, whose antagonistic relationships long defined British democratic electoral competition, simply left them talking past one another.

A STARTING POINT: TWO BASIC PARTY TYPES

Duverger's starting point in his classic analysis of distinctive party organizations was a recognition that the critical characteristic was the relationship between members and leaders (4); membership was essentially a structural rather than a quantitative question (63). From that insight he elaborated two distinctive party models that have been at the heart of most subsequent analysis of party activity, and which provide very different answers to questions about the desirability, extent or reality of IPD. So we start with his archetypal formulations that describe those polar opposites—the *cadre* and *mass* parties.

Cadre parties are conceived as a rather primitive 'grouping of notabilities for the conduct of elections, conducting campaigns, and maintaining contact with the candidates' (64). Composed of office-seeking politicians, the ideal type cadre party does not want any significant bureaucratic organization (party in central office) nor need a formally organized party on the ground. In this sense pure 'cadre parties have no members' (64) and thus no significant organization that reaches beyond the doors of the Assembly. By definition, a cadre party is composed of insiders—parliamentarians grouped together in their own electoral interest—and while devoted to managing their own supporters, they have no interest in linking them together in an effective wider extra-parliamentary structure. This kind of organization is financed through the personal resources that individual politicians command or access as well as through the patronage resources of the state that they can control.

With no organized membership, and no formal structures binding the supporters of the caucus members together, the issue of IPD is hardly of much concern to the cadre party. For its members in public office there are questions about the extent to which the leadership can discipline the parliamentary caucus, and the management and distribution of patronage, but the essentially transactional relationships between caucus members (and between caucus members and their supporters) makes these less issues of democracy than of personal bargaining within a relatively small and intimate group.

Useful as the cadre party might be as a theoretical construct, Duverger was quick to point out that 'there are few purely cadre parties' that actually match the ideal type—the Radicals of the Third French Republic perhaps being the most obvious (64). In practice most parties of this sort enroll ordinary members in an attempt to identify and build their support base but that membership is not institutionalized in a way that gives the party on the ground any significant or ongoing decision-making influence in the life, work, and financing of the party.

The cadre party's organizational opposite is the party of mass integration which is distinguished by a distinctive membership form (irrespective of size) that casts individual members as 'the very substance of the party, the stuff of its activity' and which provide a 'democratic financing' that frees the party from 'capitalist funding' (63). This makes possible a party controlled by and responsive to a widespread membership, and it necessarily requires a more complex institutional design than those of the simple cadre parties. Thus all three of the distinct faces of mass parties are typically well developed: the members (of the party on the ground) are connected to the party leadership (in public office) through institutions and processes of accountability organized and managed by a bureaucratic cadre of professional partisans (the party in central office). It is the set of relationships that link these different faces that defines its character and legitimates the mass party's claim to be a genuinely representative and democratically accountable institution.

In its inclusive political education and propaganda campaigns, membership conferences to articulate and determine policy, and elections to choose officials and candidates the mass party can function as an internally democratic organization. Yet the very scale of mass parties, with their ambition to enroll large numbers, works against them. Duverger argues that indirect membership—membership acquired by individuals by virtue of belonging to an associated group such as a trade union or an ethnic or religious association—typical of many mass parties 'is not true membership' (77) and frustrates the genuine working of the type. He also admits that leadership while 'democratic in practice' is invariably 'oligarchic in reality' (133). This is to suggest that it is the mass party organizations that are particularly subject to Michels' (1962 [1911]: 365) 'fundamental sociological law of political parties' which asserts that 'it is organization which gives birth to the dominion of the elected over the electors, of the mandatories over the mandators, of the delegates over the delegators. Who says organization says oligarchy'. In that haunting phrase Michels denies the theoretical possibility of a genuinely democratic party.

If the cadre and the mass party models are ideal types, and we can expect to find few, if any, real world parties that correspond to them, then it follows that the accounts they offer of the internally democratic character of individual political parties are at best theoretically suggestive polar opposites. In the case of cadre-style organizations we would expect to find little evidence of significant internal democracy on questions of policy, personnel or money. In parties with mass-style organizations all three aspects ought to be subject to the formal mechanisms of democratic decision-making and accountability. Thus for mass party organizations the issue of IPD turns on how they are constrained by what Duverger called the imperatives of 'practical efficiency' (134) as they engage their electoral opponents.

These party models are not theoretical constructs floating freely of the societies in which they are generated and embedded. Indeed Duverger insists that the very distinction between them 'corresponds to a difference in social and political substructure' (65). In this sense cadre parties are the products of pre or quasi-democratic political regimes with a limited franchise. Suffrage expansion made possible the development of mass parties as a response to the opportunities it offered to previously excluded groups.[2] In this lies the assumption that cadre parties are, by their nature and natural home, parties of the Right while mass parties are the expected product of the Left. Thus Michels focused his attention on

[2] An important exception to this developmental sequence was Daniel O'Connell's (1823) pre-franchise expansion *Catholic Association*, established in Ireland to promote Catholic emancipation (the right of Roman Catholics to sit in parliament). It was a mass-style organization that enrolled and mobilized millions, and was financed by their small contributions. In this it provided the organizational template for the mass parties that would follow decades later across Europe. Though its huge membership legitimated and financed the party's campaigns, the organization made no pretense of being internally democratic—it was deliberately designed to provide a mass base for O'Connell's political agitations. It might be said to have been a case of 'who says oligarch says organization'.

the German Social Democratic party for it was there that theory and principle suggested he should find a thriving IPD. And it is precisely because he did not find it there that he was so convinced that his findings constituted a 'fundamental sociological law'.

Duverger's theoretical cadre-mass dichotomy lurks in the background of both McKenzie and Beer's definitive studies of British party politics. In them they contrast the organizational norms and practices of the Conservatives (implicitly a cadre-style party) with those of its Labour (often regarded as a classic mass party) opponents. McKenzie explicitly confronts Michels' analysis and, while accepting that it appears to account for some Labour party behaviour, he argues that 'it is certainly not an "iron" law' (644). Rather his claim is that British parties have a sophisticated division of labour driven by the constitutional principles structuring Westminster-style parliamentary government. Though Labour while in opposition 'clung to certain "democratic" practices in its internal organization' (412), in office it had to operate like the Conservatives. This left its various organizational parts with separate functions whose roles needed to be recognized and respected by the others. Thus, in practice, the mass party is not a simple hierarchically integrated organization but one with distinct but interdependent elements. In this we can see an intimation of party models that emphasize the 'stratarchical' character of their organizations.

Beer's analysis is deliberately not cast in the theoretical terms of either Duverger or Michels[3] but at the core of his concern is the question as to how the two parties' competing models lead them to understand and practice their politics in a common political system. His conclusion is that they are fundamentally different precisely because Labour exhibited an 'obsessive commitment to intraparty democracy' (388). Its organizational structure may have been legitimated by its class based membership, but at the same time that structure articulated a pluralist culture that shaped its goals and practices in ways that marked it out as morally and practically opposed to its Conservative opponents.

Cast as ideal types, the cadre-mass dichotomy obfuscates any careful consideration of IPD: the cadre model does not provide for it, the mass model adopts it as a central defining characteristic only to surrender its theoretical prospects to Michels. As both McKenzie and Beer reveal, though useful as theoretical straw men, neither fits the political parties of the real world. More useful is the notion that cadre and mass parties may form not a simple dichotomy but the ends of a rather varied and elastic continuum. And this brings us to Duverger's idea of organizational contagion.

[3] Neither name appears in the discussion or the Index, though McKenzie's does.

CONTAGION FROM THE LEFT AND THE RIGHT

The very success of mass parties in mobilizing large numbers of newly enfranchised electors provides them an electoral advantage over their cadre-style opponents. The natural consequence is for the parties of the Right to respond by adopting the same organizational strategies and creating a formal membership base. This membership is designed to help cadre parties legitimate their claims to being democratic instruments, provide personnel and financial resources for their electoral campaigns and mobilization activities, and extend their capacity to reach into the wider society.[4] Despite the creation of bodies like national conferences invested with the trappings of policy debate and consultation, such changes were not intended to alter cadre-style parties' fundamental internal decision-making authority. Those parties' new structures may have the appearance of some degree of IPD but any such mechanisms are either essentially symbolic or tightly controlled. As McKenzie observed of the British Conservative Party's annual conference it 'tended to serve primarily as a demonstration of party solidarity and enthusiasm for its own leaders' (189).

Duverger called this process, by which cadre parties came to adopt some of the organizational forms of their mass party opponents in response to powerful competitive imperatives, the 'phenomenon of contagion from the Left' (xxvii). But at the same time many of the realities of modern electoral campaigning were beginning to transform the mass parties of the Left, a dynamic that Epstein (1967: 257–60) called 'contagion from the right'. Mass parties came to eschew (or at least challenge) their earlier doctrinaire ideological commitments in the search for broader electoral support: the German Social Democrats in their 1959 Bad Godesberg program, British Labour in its intra-party battles over clause IV.[5] They also came to adopt the bourgeois public relations styles of their opponents, depending more on hired professionals and large financial contributors rather than the efforts of individual members. This process was in full swing by the 1960s, a decade Scarrow (2000: 92–5) notes turns out to have been the apogee for party membership numbers in Western Europe.

Taken together these two phenomena, the product of a common competitive dynamic that forces both cadre and mass party organizations to deviate from their pure form, led to the emergence of a new party model—one that Kirchheimer (1966: 184) was to label the '*catch-all* "people's" party'. His catch-all party model departs from the simplicity of the cadre-mass dichotomy. Its alternate theoretical

[4] For a full discussion of the benefits of members to political parties, see Scarrow (1996: 40–6).

[5] These were the intra-party disputes that saw the parties confront their long-standing Marxist commitments. The German SPD opted for a softer social democracy in its 1959 Bad Godesberg convention; British Labour fought a series of internal battles, initiated by party leader Hugh Gaitskell, over whether to keep the clause (IV) in its constitution that called for the nationalization of the means of production.

conceptions of the authoritarian-democratic character of internal party life offers a generally negative portrait of the prospects for IPD.

The catch-all label was an unfortunate choice of terms for Kirchheimer argues that it is important to recognize that such parties 'cannot hope to catch all categories of voters' (186). Constrained by their historic roots, catch-all parties seek to broaden their appeal to a more undifferentiated support base. In the process of doing so they are led to moderate their 'expressive function'—a process often characterized as the 'deideologization' of party life—which contributes to an electoral politics marked by ambiguous and overlapping appeals. Parties of this sort can only operate as efficient electoral machines (their raison d'être) by strengthening their leadership groups (the party in public office) which comes at the cost of meaningful participation by party members. Whatever the Michelian reality of their past practices, Kirchheimer notes that the new catch-all party positively downgrades the 'role of the individual party member, a role considered a historical relic' (190). As catch-all party organizations are not decentralized structures, that avenue for the opening of internal decision-making processes also remains closed.[6] There is no room in this catch-all party type, of which the German and Austrian Social Democrats were held to be classic examples, for any significant IPD.

A slightly different model that emerges out of the same competitive contagion dynamic is Panebianco's (1988) *electoral-professional* party.[7] This model's distinctive feature is its emphasis on the critical impact of the 'professionalization of party organizations' (264). In it Panebianco recognizes the same dominance by personalized leadership, little significant role for party members, and a lack of a strong ideological definition of political life. What is particular to the model is its focus on the central role played by experts and professionals in advancing the party's electoral agenda. These individuals may be responsive to the elites that employ them for specific tasks; they are not accountable to party members in an organization that is structurally inimical to the principle of IPD.

The locus of organizational power in the mass party was the party in central office as it managed the electoral and membership life of the party mediating between the party on the ground and the party in public office. Michels' question was not just how democratic was that process, but also how democratic could it be? The shift to the catch-all model struck at the heart of central office power by simultaneously strengthening the hand of the party in public office and weakening

[6] Epstein (1967: 259–60) notes that this is one significant way in which the parties that practice catch-all politics in Europe differ from those in the United States that are more open. Writing at the same time as Kirchheimer, Epstein doesn't use the latter's catch-all terminology but it seems clear from his comparisons that he has the same party model in mind.

[7] Panebianco seems to claim (in footnote 6 to his chapter (14) that elaborates his model) that the electoral-professional party is equivalent to Kirchheimer's catch-all ideal type. However in the same note he then suggests that the emphasis on its organizational professionalism makes it a different type.

that of the party on the ground. In the case of the electoral-professional model it compounded the challenge by 'contracting out' many of the important electoral management tasks that the central office might have expected to perform. For Panebianco this development constituted a 'crisis of parties' (267–9) and he expected that the de-institutionalized electoral-professional model was inherently unstable and likely to be transitory. He thought three alternatives seemed likely: the dissolution of parties as organizations, the reassertion of traditional mass parties of integration, or some new form created by entrepreneurial political outsiders. As it happened none of those scenarios prevailed.

PARTIES AS PUBLIC UTILITIES

Leon Epstein's (1988) authoritative account of American political parties makes it clear that for decades the US system had taken 'for granted the treatment of parties as state agencies' (155), a practice very different from contemporary practice in other electoral democracies. American parties were, in effect, 'public utilities' whose basic functions of nominating candidates and providing access to the ballot were both privileged and regulated.[8] This wasn't a model that Panebianco or Kirchheimer might have envisioned. But denuded of their ideological weapons, stripped of members, and facing increasing financial campaigning costs, party leaders sought to use the state to defend and protect their well established positions as the system's primary political intermediaries.[9] The result was a new organizational form delineated by Katz and Mair's (1995) *cartel* party model.

Despite Koole's (1996) complaint that the cartel theoretical model is as much one of a systemic phenomenon—a developmental model that culminates in 'cartel democracy'—as a characterization of individual parties, it does contain a distinctive political party organizational form.[10] The cartel party represents the organizational triumph of the party in public office over the other two faces of the organization (Katz and Mair 2002: 122). Professional politicians employ experts to organize capital-intensive electoral campaigns centred on appeals that promise effective management of the state apparatus. To finance these expensive

[8] Carty (1997) argued that Canadian parties could be seen in public utility terms; Carty and Young (2012) suggest that the concept was the animating philosophy of the *Report* of the country's 1991 Royal Commission on Electoral Reform and Party Finance.

[9] Alan Ware (2002) makes much the same point in his argument that the creation of the American direct primary system was the creation of party politicians seeking to institutionalize their organizations rather than the consequence of populist reform insurrections.

[10] In the 20 pages of text the cartel party *per se* gets 3; the rest is focused on the wider questions of the long historical development of party state-society relationships.

campaigns cartel parties depend on state subventions that free them from reliance on interests in, or parts of, civil society.[11]

In this highly managed competition there is little room for intense partisan differences and so battalions of activists to mobilize the faithful are not required. While individual members are recruited to sustain the legitimacy of the leadership, any significant distinction between members and general supporters is blurred (Katz and Mair: 1995: 21). In these parties the necessary cost to the party elites of engaging members is to provide for their direct participation in some internal party decision-making—for instance, in selecting candidates or all-member votes for the party leader.

This dramatic alteration in the role of individual party members would appear to mark the cartel party as the very epitome of IPD. However two aspects of the model suggest that the very opposite is the case. First, popular participation in the cartel party is 'atomistic' with individuals (members or supporters) isolated from one another and engaged in direct personal communication with the party centre in a fashion that inhibits their ability to act in common interest with fellow members (21). This provides the party in public office the ability to manipulate a formally popular decision-making process by ensuring that members' choices are constrained and limited to alternatives acceptable to the existing elite. This dynamic liberates party leaders from the ideological pressures of committed activists while simultaneously legitimating their pragmatic, electorally oriented choices. In this sense the cartel model casts ordinary party members as tools of leaders and the formalities of intra-party decision-making processes become a weapon of elite control rather than of democratic accountability. Echoing Michels, Mair (1994: 17) observes 'democratization on paper may therefore actually coexist with powerful elite influence in practice'.

As well as being manipulated, members in the cartel party are isolated in individual party units that foster a sense of engaged participation through the busy work of locally focused activity. This flows from these parties' decisions to abandon traditional hierarchical organizational structures for 'stratarchical' ones that are characterized by internal unit relationships of interdependence and mutual autonomy. If, in the stratarchical party, members do make decisions, the very fractionalization of the organization means those choices are 'essentially unconcerned with any real input into the national party' (17). Thus, by strengthening the party in public office, the adoption of a stratarchical structure reinforces the non-democratic elements of the cartel party.

For many in Western Europe the age of the cartel party appeared to stifle vigorous partisan life. The response was the proliferation of a wide variety of alternate approaches to organizing competitive parties, often by those on the

[11] It was the changed role of the state in party finance that led van Biezen (2004: 705) to characterize these new cartel party organizations as public utilities, with much the same relationship to the state as parties had in America.

political margins. At one extreme were various Green 'party-movements' determined to resist oligarchic imperatives. Their approach was to resist the institutionalization of leadership in the interest of maximizing participation in the name of grassroots democracy. Tying the hands of the party in public office this way was a strategy ill-suited to effective government participation and most soon came to adopt more traditional structures, albeit ones that emphasized the involvement of members in the parties' personnel and policy decision-making. At the other extreme, personal organizations such as Geert Wilders' Dutch Party for Freedom decided to have no members at all so that the question of internal democracy never really arose. Between these extremes of 'members are all' and 'no members at all' developed a number of other approaches to party-building, many rooted in organizational models drawn from the private sector. Thus the entrepreneurial party, the business firm party, the charismatic party, with Berlusconi's Forza Italia perhaps the most successful of the lot (Hopkin and Paolucci 1999; Paolucci 2006).[12] These organizations are closely tied to the personality of the leader who oversees their internal life, directing a membership much as the owners in a private firm mobilize its work force. Their populist rhetoric provides a thin cover for top-down control that admits of little real party democracy.

MEMBERS AND PARTY MODELS

As Lisa Young (this volume) reminds us, much ink has been spilled in recent decades on the question of declining party membership numbers and what it means for democracy—for IPD as well as the broader health of the wider democratic polity. While sheer size may be important, Duverger's point is that different party models are best contrasted in terms of their distinctive articulations of the place and power of members in a party's organizational structure. With members constituting a party's 'demos' those conceptions reveal the possibility of establishing democratic intra-party relationships.

What is striking about the different basic party models now widely employed to analyze political parties is not their interpretations of the constraints or opportunities shaping the behaviours of members, or the changing institutional dynamics governing modern party life, but the very character of members. The cadre party model denies the existence of members so that even when supporters are formally enrolled in some associational unit they are not considered members in a sense that would vest them with decision-making authority or power. For the cadre model the

[12] This suggests a certain prescience on Panebianco's part, at least with respect to Italian party development.

issue of IPD is essentially moot. Not so the mass party for it conceives of members as the heart of the organization so that individual members are akin to owners who are ultimately responsible for making all key decisions. The democratic problem in such parties is that owners must surrender their prerogatives to a managerial oligarchy if the organization is to prosper.

The catch-all party, whether it has evolved from a cadre past or descended from a mass organization, regards members as a relic of those past forms and conceives of them as organized supporters who are neither to be activated nor offended by the programmatic activity and decisions of the leadership. Panebianco's electoral-professional version of this party type regards them as unorganized, hence its emphasis on the need to use modern professional techniques of electoral mobilization. But organized or not, the nominal members of these types of parties are conceived as supporters to be wooed rather than citizens participating in democratically governed organizations.

A cartel party model sees members as partisans to be manipulated in order to provide the leadership with a patina of democratic legitimacy. To do so the cartel party enhances the range of decision-making opportunities for its members while limiting the real influence of the party on the ground by tightly controlling the alternatives to be chosen and by focusing members on local activities rather than concerns of broader significance. So while the cartel party's intra-party democratic processes are enhanced they are also trivialized and members marginalized.

Katz and Mair's cartel party model contends that stratarchy is employed as an organizational strategy precisely to constrain IPD—to maintain and strengthen the hold of an office-holding elite over party members. However this turns the concept on its head. In his original elaboration of the concept in an analysis of American political parties Eldersveld (1964) argued that it was precisely their stratarchical character that fostered IPD.[13] By their very nature, stratarchical structures lead to 'the proliferation of the ruling group and the diffusion of power prerogatives and power exercise' (9) necessary for healthy internal competition and responsive accountability. On that view stratarchical organization provides a very different, and internally democratic, party model.

STRATARCHICAL PARTY ORGANIZATION AND IPD

The central structural principle of a stratarchical organization is that 'power and authority does not finally rest in a single place, or with any single set of

[13] Curiously, Eldersveld is not cited in the principal statements of the cartel thesis (Mair 1994; Katz & Mair, 1995) which explicitly point to the party's stratarchical structure as key features of the model.

individuals—it is (more or less) broadly shared' (Carty 2004: 9). Organized so its individual units are both interdependent and mutually autonomous, each of the party's organizational units constitutes a potential site for democratic internal competition.[14] Interdependence and autonomy are inevitably locked in an internal tension so that the formal network linking the parts together is itself the focus for ongoing intra-party contestation. Thus the very shape and definition of a stratarchical party is continually being redefined by democratic intra-party competitions.

Stratarchical party structures can take many forms but at their heart is a constitutional bargain that orders the internal relationships between the distinct faces of the party and, more particularly, defines the autonomy and the interdependencies that govern its constituent units.[15] There need be no presumption of how the parts are defined—whether in geographic, sectoral, ideational, communal, or some other terms. That surely depends on the wider socio-political and institutional context as well as the party's own conception of political life. What is critical is that, by guaranteeing the decision-making authority and autonomy of parts of the party, the interdependence of the whole almost ensures that the bargain itself will be the focus of continual and contested debate and negotiation.

Organizational bargains have both formal definitions and informal norms that govern the character of their ongoing operation. Independently, and together, they can be the source of ongoing intra-party division as they constitute the basis for alternate benchmarks against which intra-party practices are assessed. Without shared understandings of how power is organized and exercised on issues of internal party decision-making it is difficult for members of the party to hold the party, and themselves, to acceptable democratic standards.

The Liberal Party of Canada, for a century the dominant player in the country's party system, provides a striking example of the tensions implicit in a stratarchical model of party organization. At the heart of its particular structural arrangement is a political bargain that gives the membership, organized in electoral district associations on the ground, control over personnel decisions—the selection of local candidates and the choice of party leader. Where decisions are to be made, the expectation is that they are the business of open democratic membership conventions. The other half of the bargain assigned the party in public office effective authority over policy decisions. The party's formal constitution hedges

[14] The real autonomy accorded organizational units in a stratarchical party model marks it out as distinct from simple decentralization in which particular party units may be accorded decision-making power on particular subjects but always on the understanding that decisions are subject to acceptance by higher bodies. Thus mass or catch-all parties may be decentralized but they are not stratarchical if their individual components do not have decision-making autonomy.

[15] For a description of the stratarchical form and internal practice of Canadian political parties as cases of 'franchise' systems, see Carty (2002). The comparative democratic character of their internal practices is assessed in Carty and Cross (2006).

this fundamental division of authority with obfuscating checks and balances that allow both members and leaders to trespass on the other's prerogatives.

Party members interested in policy but given no say in articulating it are driven to try and influence it indirectly through their control of personnel decisions. But leadership challenges and contests that drag on over decades are not a particularly transparent or effective way of making policy choices. They confuse the real issues at hand and make it difficult for the party to engage in authoritative policy-making. In this way the facility with which a stratarchy allows internal divisions to be transferred to another site, or transforms them by contesting the appropriate site, undermines the stability and certainty of democratic rule making and can enervate the party's competitive capacity.[16]

For the Liberals to manage their system of stratarchical democracy successfully, members ought to share an understanding of its basic intra-party trade-offs. Recent survey evidence suggests that they may not.[17] Party members were asked if they supported the personnel-policy: party on the ground-party in public office bargain. As illustrated in Figure 2.1 four positions were possible but, at only 10 per cent of the total, those who support the party's core division of power (the 'Covenanters') constitute the smallest group. The largest number of members (the 33 per cent who are 'Opponents') actually opposes both of the principles that define the party's stratarchical arrangement. Another third are 'Populists' unprepared to cede any final decision-making authority to the party elites and the last quarter can be described as the 'Deferentials', apparently prepared to allow their leaders to decide both issues.

The difficulties of intra-party decision-making in this situation are obvious. Individual decisions may not be accepted by significant numbers: if the leadership uses its formal legal prerogative to interfere in an individual candidate selection decision well over half the members may see it as illegitimate, but at the same time (a different) half of the membership feel free to reject some policy position taken by their leaders. Inevitably, challenges to individual decisions threaten the

	Leader has policy freedom	Members determine policy
Members choose candidates	***Covenanters*** 10%	***Populists*** 31%
Leader can appoint candidates	***Deferentials*** 25%	***Opponents*** 33%

FIGURE 2.1 Liberal members' views of the Party's stratarchical bargain

16 Jeffrey (2010) argues that the Liberal leadership contests that plagued the party for two decades from the mid-1980s was in fact a deep policy dispute. The result was to weaken the organization while not confronting the issue that divided it.

17 The data reported here is taken from surveys of national party members conducted by W. Cross and L. Young in 2000.

legitimacy of an inherently fragile system. It may be that this collective ambivalence about appropriate intra-party power relations simply mirrors the authority interdependencies of the party's organization. However, any assessment of the democratic character of the internal life of the party requires a clear statement of how its respective faces relate to one another. In practice, the very lack of clarity and transparency that flows from a stratarchical structure inevitably obscures effective lines of intra-party accountability.

Mair (1994: 15) notes that while 'members might sometimes prove a nuisance... they can also bring tangible, as well as intangible, benefits'. A stratarchical structure provides a membership framework that both defines and confines the place and roles of these members. However it also raises questions as to the identity of the party, making the issue of who constitutes the demos of the party an open issue, shifting over time and varying by the kinds of decisions being taken. Again the Canadian Liberal Party provides a dramatic illustration of the difficulty of identifying a party's demos as it engages in making important internal decisions.

The Liberal's stratarchical arrangement assigns the selection of candidates to party members meeting in local conventions, and has long given members the majority of delegate positions at national leadership selection conventions. Each of these decisions provides an incentive for individuals to join (or renew) their memberships and large numbers often do so. The result is that party membership numbers fluctuate widely from low points in inter-election years through increases in general election years (when a number of electoral district candidate selections will be contested) to leadership selection years when membership numbers in every corner of the party and country quickly increase. Figure 2.2 summarizes membership changes over a four-year period around a general election.[18]

In principle there is but one Liberal Party on the ground made up of the members of local electoral district associations. However these numbers suggests its composition fluctuates wildly, by well over 100 per cent in this short period. (Of course it would be possible to have a set of membership rules that would constrain such variation but that would deny the very openness that makes a

	Member Involvement	*Membership*
Non-election year (1987)	Policy Conventions	150,000
Election year (1988)	Candidate Nominations	280,000
Leadership year (1990)	Leadership Selection	340,000

FIGURE 2.2 The Liberal Party on the ground: three versions

[18] Carty (1991) provides an analysis of the membership cycles of Canadian parties; Figure 2.2 is taken from Carty (2008).

stratarchical model attractive.) In different years the party on the ground discusses and decides different questions—holding policy conventions in non-election years, candidate selection meetings in general election years and leadership conventions when necessary. The result is that there is no single party and it is not at all clear just who, or what, constitutes the party. In effect, different Liberal parties are constantly being created for different decisions, presumably being responsible for them, while all the while attempting to hold their candidates and leaders internally accountable. But if the existence of a different demos for each decision casts the practices of IPD as idiosyncratic episodes, rather than as elements of an ongoing patterned system, then it may be difficult to say much about the state of stratarchical IPD *per se*.

Parties adopt a stratarchical model for their core organizational relationships explicitly to diffuse power throughout their structures in order to provide for greater internal pluralism. In doing so they increase the opportunities for IPD. However much this increases members' participation in individual decisions, the operation of the internal workings of this party model makes clear responsibility and transparent accountability difficult to achieve. The fragmentation of decision-making obscures authority lines; interdependence continually transforms issues across organizational units weakening authoritative decision-making; pluralist practices makes the intra-party processes themselves latent issues in internal conflicts; and fluid memberships confounds any straightforward identification of the boundaries of the party and thus the demos at the heart of a regime of IPD.

Rather than Michels' inevitable oligarchy, stratarchy may result in an organization in which intra-party relationships, and the practices of intra-party politics, are never firmly settled. And if they are so fluid and shifting they may not be genuinely democratic?

PARTY MODELS AND IPD

Although nominally cast as matters of structural anatomy, party models are, at their heart, concerned with the fundamental question of intra-organization democracy. This has meant a focus on the relationship between members and elites: essentially the party on the ground and the party in central office. And the core question asked has been who has real basic power when hard decisions are to be taken.

Michels' central observation is that the very fact of organization makes democratic internal relationships in political parties impossible. Despite their forms and norms theoretically rooted in democratic legitimation, mass parties of integration were inevitably oligarchic. Not surprisingly, more modern party types that have emerged with the transformation of advanced societies' social orders, and the communications technologies that house their electoral processes, have not been able to overturn that 'sociological law'. Indeed catch-all and electoral-professional party models eschew the possibility or even desirability of democratic internal relationships while the cartel model sees the formal practice of IPD mechanisms as a means for elite control of party members and supporters. Stratarchy, embedded in an American faith in the promise of pluralism, provides a model that opens party organizations to multiple points of decision-making but its characteristic fractionalization of the relationships between the two dominant faces of the modern party only makes authoritative, and hence democratic, party decision-making problematic.

This need not be to say that candidates and leaders cannot be chosen in open, competitive contests, policies shaped in democratic exercises, campaigns managed to model a party's commitment to democratic practices, or finances freed from closed influences. It may be only that our simplified models of the core elite-member relationships have yet to find a way to account for the subtle complexities of these processes.

3

Shaping Intra-Party Democracy: On the Legal Regulation of Internal Party Organizations

Ingrid van Biezen and Daniela Romée Piccio[1]

INTRODUCTION

Like so many other aspects of the behaviour and activities of political parties, the internal organizational procedures and structures of parties have become increasingly subject to external regulations. In European systems in particular, political parties have traditionally been understood as primarily private and voluntary organizations. As a consequence, their internal organizational structures and modus operandi has long remained outside the scope of state regulation, which has tended to be limited to the organization of the electoral process as well as, in some countries, the protection of the democratic order from ideological anti-system parties. In recent years, however, the state has increased its propensity to intervene in both the external and internal manifestations of party politics, in that the activities, behaviour, and internal organizational structures are increasingly defined or prescribed by public law. Indeed, the legal regulation of political parties has become more and more customary, to the point that, as Katz has noted, party structures have become 'legitimate objects of state regulation to a degree far exceeding what would normally be acceptable for private associations in a liberal society' (Katz 2002: 90). Many of these regulations were first introduced or were substantially extended in the wake of the introduction of public funding for parties, as the provision of state subventions inevitably demanded a more codified system of party registration and control. Controlling party access to the public broadcasting media has also required the introduction or extension of the system of regulation, which has acted to codify the status of parties and their range of activities (Mair 1998: 167). In addition, the rising levels of popular discontent seem to have

[1] Financial support from the European Research Council (ERC_Stg07_205660) is gratefully acknowledged. This chapter is part of a larger research project on the legal regulation of political parties in post-war European democracies. For more details about the project, see <http://www.partylaw.leidenuniv.nl>.

encouraged the enactment of further party legislation, with the primary focus on the question of how parties ought to operate, both in relation to their environment and their own internal functioning, if they are to fulfil their democratic functions adequately. Finally, an increasing number of guidelines and recommendations are being issued by supra-national organizations, such as the European Union or the Council of Europe, aiming to establish a set of 'good practices' and 'common principles' on party regulation in order to promote greater legislative transparency and clarity of regulation (cf. Piccio 2012).

Despite the substantial increase in the volume and scope of party regulation, however, this phenomenon has received relatively little systematic scholarly attention from political scientists, with the possible exception of Germany, the 'heartland of party law' (Müller and Sieberer 2006: 435). Indeed, the subject of party law continues to be a neglected aspect of research on political parties, with discussions of party law in the scholarly literature usually limited to passing references and lacking a comparative dimension (Avnon 1995). This chapter explores the empirical and normative dimensions of the legal regulation of the internal operation and functioning of political parties, with a particular emphasis on the regulation of internal party democracy (IPD).

STATE REGULATION OF INTERNAL PARTY DEMOCRACY

The legal regulation of the internal organization of political parties is commonly considered as one of the most controversial aspects of party regulation (e.g. Katz 2004: 2–3). The introduction of legal constraints on the internal arrangements and conduct of political parties not only infringes upon fundamental democratic principles such as the freedom of association, but it also deprives political parties of their constitutive nature as private organizational entities, with the possible consequence of transforming them into semi-state agencies, or 'public utilities' (Katz and Mair 1995; van Biezen 2004). In the current climate, in which political parties arguably find themselves in somewhat of a legitimacy crisis, the motto that seems to dominate, including within the parties themselves, is that 'the only cure for democracy is more democracy'. Politicians, policymakers, partisan and non-partisan think tanks as well as international governmental and non-governmental organizations have all been underlining the importance of internal party democracy in recent years. The Venice Commission, for example, although cautioning that the regulation of the internal party organization and functions must be such that it does not 'unduly interfere with the right of parties as free associations to manage their own internal affairs', considers that at least 'some regulation of internal party activities [is] necessary to ensure the proper functioning of a democratic society'.[2] After all, as Teorell rhetorically asks, 'how could we trust party representatives to consider the arguments put forward by opposing groups in the public sphere if they ignore the reasoning of their own members?' (Teorell 1999: 375). Many analysts believe that a greater involvement of the party on the ground in the internal selection and decision-making processes may yield important benefits, because internal democratic procedures may encourage the enrolment of new members, internal democracy provides a sense of grassroots legitimation, and it allows parties to present themselves with a more favourable and 'open' public image (Scarrow 1999b; Scarrow, Webb, and Farrell 2000; Bille 2001; Pennings and Hazan 2001).[3] Possible downsides of (too much) internal democracy, that is, that it may undermine the parties' internal cohesion and efficiency (e.g. Duverger 1954; Wright 1971), and, as a consequence, endanger the representative linkage with its constituency, seem to find much less resonance in current debates.

In a broad sense, party law can be defined as 'the total body of law that affects political parties' (Müller and Sieberer 2006: 435). For any country, the body of party law is derived from a series of related public laws, including (where relevant) a law on political parties, political finance laws, electoral laws, and campaign laws. From the broader perspective adopted here, the body of party law also includes the national constitution. Because the constitutions of the established liberal democracies have tended not to mention political parties, constitutions are not normally considered as a source of party law (Janda 2005). However, as a result of a gradual process of party constitutionalization in the post-war period, the large majority of European democracies today acknowledge the existence of political parties in their constitutions in one form or other (van Biezen 2012). The constitution should therefore also be regarded as a relevant source of party law.

The body of party law broadly conceived regulates a wide variety of aspects related to political parties, ranging from the legal status and definition of parties to issues about their internal organization, mechanisms of candidate selection, their behaviour and activity, party finances, as well as the establishment of a framework of external monitoring and sanctions in order to ensure the parties' compliance with rules and to penalize them if they don't (see also Katz 2004). The focus of the analysis presented here is on the regulation of the internal operation of parties, and on the rules dealing with IPD in particular. These may include, as we shall see

[2] 'Guidelines on political party regulation' by OSCE and Venice Commission. Adopted in October 2010 (par. IX, p. 25).

[3] To be noted, that the adoption of new means of party leadership selection may actually serve *against* the intra-party democracy purpose and does not necessarily amount to the enhancement in the role of party members in the party organization. As Katz and Mair have underlined, membership ballots have an atomizing effect on party members, allowing the party executives to bypass the party on the ground (Katz and Mair 1995). For an application to the cases of the Spanish and British parties, see Hopkin (2001); for the Italian context, see Florida (2009).

below, conditions for the mechanisms by which the public office holders for the party are selected, requirements that the electoral lists of the party are balanced in terms of gender or ethnic composition, or the rights of party members to elect and be elected for internal party offices.

The analysis presented here concentrates on the regulation of internal party procedures in national constitutions and party laws, the two legal sources most likely to concern themselves with matters of internal party affairs. To be sure, the internal functioning of political parties may also be regulated in a number of different acts or laws. As political parties are considered to be private legal entities in most countries, their regulation may fall under the broader Civil Code, for example, or under general laws on associations. As Müller and Sieberer (2006: 440) correctly state, these may contain certain minimal standards of democracy.[4] For the purpose of this chapter, however, we have excluded such pieces of legislation as we are concerned with the rules which exclusively apply to political parties. We also exclude electoral laws. While these may include rules concerning the selection of the parties' candidates for public office, with only a few exceptions (see below) electoral laws generally do not concern themselves with the internal procedures for candidate selection (Pennings and Hazan 2001), leadership selection, or issues of party democracy more generally.

For the purpose of this chapter, the constitution is taken to be that law which is called or commonly referred to as the constitution or basic law, and which is codified in a single document. The party law is taken to be that law which regulates aspects of party activity, organization, and behaviour, and defines itself as a law on political parties or party law. Included in the analysis are all European democracies.[5] The period under investigation spans the entire post-war period, effectively commencing with the first reference to political parties in the 1944 Icelandic constitution and concluding with the constitutions and the party laws in force at the end of 2008.[6]

Table 3.1 provides a chronology of post-war regulation of political parties in national constitutions and party laws. As can be seen, the large majority (N = 28) of post-war European democracies acknowledge political parties in their constitutions in one form or another. In addition, a large number of countries (N = 21) have adopted a specific party law, with the German *Parteiengesetz* adopted in 1967 being the first in post-war Europe. Countries less inclined to formally codify

[4] Under the Dutch Civil Code, for instance, in any association, the Board of Directors is appointed by the members, while all members have the right to participate and to vote in the General Meeting (Civil Code, Book II, art. 37–8).

[5] The countries covered in this research include all European countries which were classified as 'Free' by the Freedom House at the end of 2008, with the exception of smaller states with a population under 100,000. A total of 33 European countries comply with these criteria, i.e. Austria, Belgium, Bulgaria, Croatia, Cyprus, Czech Republic, Denmark, Estonia, Finland, France, Germany, Greece, Hungary, Iceland, Ireland, Italy, Latvia, Lithuania, Luxembourg, Malta, Netherlands, Norway, Poland, Portugal, Romania, Serbia, Slovakia, Slovenia, Spain, Sweden, Switzerland, Ukraine, and the United Kingdom.

[6] Exceptions are the party laws of Austria, Czech Republic, and Portugal for which an earlier version of the law was used. For Bulgaria, Ukraine, Serbia, and Cyprus we used the party laws in force at the end of 2011.

TABLE 3.1 *Chronology of post-war legislation on political parties* [a]

Country	Party constitutionalization	Party law
Iceland	1944	—
Austria	1945	1975
Italy	1947	—
Germany	1949	1967
France	1958	—
Cyprus	1960	2011[b]
Malta	1964	—
Sweden	1974	—
Greece	1975	—
Portugal	1976	1974
Spain	1978	1978
Norway	1984	2005
Hungary	1989	1989
Croatia	1990	1993
Serbia	1990	2009
Bulgaria	1990	1990
Latvia	1991	2006
Romania	1991	1996
Slovenia	1991	1994
Czech Republic	1992	1993
Estonia	1992	1994
Lithuania	1992	1990
Poland	1992	1990
Slovakia	1992	1993
Ukraine	1996	2001
Finland	1999	1969
Switzerland	1999	—
Luxembourg	2008	—
Belgium	—	—
Denmark	—	—
Ireland	—	—
Netherlands	—	—
United Kingdom	n/a	1998
Total	*28*	*21*

[a] Year of approval.
[b] Not included in our quantitative analysis.
n/a = not applicable.

political parties in their national constitutions or to adopt a special party law tend to belong to the group of longer established democracies in Western Europe, which have historically been more reluctant to intervene in party politics and thus possibly infringe upon the democratic freedom of association. Thus it is only in Belgium, Denmark, Ireland, and the Netherlands that parties are not mentioned in the constitution. In a similar vein, most of the countries with a special party law are newly established democracies, that is, democracies that have emerged out of the third wave of democratization, which have adopted such regulatory instruments in the years following the democratic transitions. In fact, Greece is the only new democracy which does not have a party law, although it has codified political parties in the constitution.

NATIONAL CONSTITUTIONS

The requirement that the internal structures and organization of political parties are democratic was first made explicit in the German Basic Law of 1949. Article 21.1 of the Basic Law states:

> The political parties participate in the formation of the political will of the people. They may be freely established. *Their internal organization must conform to democratic principles.* They must publicly account for their assets and for the sources and use of their funds as well as assets. (emphasis added)

Article 21.2 of the Basic Law goes on to stipulate that '[p]arties which, by reason of their aims or the behaviour of their adherents, seek to impair or destroy the free democratic basic order or to endanger the existence of the Federal Republic of Germany are unconstitutional', and assigns the prerogative to decide on questions of unconstitutionality to the Federal Constitutional Court. Hence, the German constitution does not tolerate political parties with purposes or activities antithetical to the democratic constitutional order, a provision which has subsequently provided the foundation for a constitutional ban on the descendants of Nazi and Communist Parties (Kommers 1997).

Mindful of the past, article 21 of the German Basic Law thus gives the state the right to monitor and ban any political party that threatens the democratic order. The origins of this doctrine of 'militant democracy'—that is, the capacity of modern constitutional democracies to defend themselves against political challenges to their continued existence—naturally lie in the fear of repetition of the scenario of the 1930s, when the Weimar regime proved no match against anti-democratic forces. In a narrow sense, the doctrine applies to the external activities of anti-democratic parties or their ideological profile. Understood more broadly, however, it may also apply to the internal organization of parties, on the grounds that a lack of IPD signals a lack of commitment to democratic values *tout court*. This was also the perspective advocated by the German Constitutional Court at the time, arguing in its ruling on the constitutionality of the neo-Nazi *Sozialistische Reichspartei* in 1952 that a logical relationship exists between the concept of a free democratic order and the democratic principles of party organization (Schneider 1957: 536).

The requirement that the internal organization of political parties must be democratic has subsequently been adopted by a number of other countries, enshrining this condition in the constitution first adopted in the wake of the transition to democracy (as in Spain in 1978) or incorporating it in the process of constitutional revision (Portugal in 1997; Croatia in 2000). The stipulation in the Croatian constitution that the internal organization of political parties shall be in accordance with the fundamental constitutional democratic principles (art. 6.2) echoes the general requirement found in the German Basic Law. The Spanish constitution goes somewhat further by demanding that not only the internal structures of parties but also their functioning must be democratic (art. 6). The constitution of Portugal is the most explicit and requires that political parties are governed not only by the principles of transparency, democratic organization and management but also by the participation of all of their members (art. 51.5).

Although the constitutions of Croatia, Germany, Spain, and Portugal are the only ones to explicitly prescribe IPD, in other countries (such as Greece, Italy, and France or the post-communist democracies of Bulgaria, Lithuania, and Poland) the principle of IPD may be considered to be implicitly present in the constitutional requirement that political parties either serve or respect democratic principles or methods (e.g. Tsatsos et al. 1990; Tsatsos and Kedzia 1994). Consider article 49 of the Italian Constitution, for instance, which states that political parties contribute to the determination of national policy 'by democratic method'. The question whether this requirement should not also be understood to apply to the parties' internal organizational functioning has dominated the debates of constitutional lawyers ever since its promulgation in 1948 (e.g. Basso 1966; Calamandrei 1970). While the prevailing interpretation has thus far delimited the 'democratic method' to the arena of *inter*-party competition, scholars are increasingly willing to consider that the constitution also provides a legitimate basis for the legal regulation of *intra*-party democracy.[7] Hence, despite the fact that such constitutional provisions have *de facto* been interpreted almost exclusively in relation to the external activities of political parties, in recent years a shift in doctrine appears to have taken place by which these stipulations are increasingly understood as potentially pertinent to the internal democratic functioning of the parties as well.

Where the German Basic Law limits the extent of state intervention in the internal organizational affairs of the parties to the general requirement that their internal organization conform to democratic principles (and that they must account for their assets and sources of income), the constitutions of some other countries go further in laying down requirements regarding the form and functioning of the parties' organizational structure, even though they are not necessarily explicit about IPD. Constitutions may stipulate requirements for party affiliation, for example, such as age in Greece, the prohibition of dual membership in Portugal

[7] Indeed, it is with a view to the implementation of art. 49 of the Italian constitution that a number of law proposals that aim to the establish minimal requirements for intra-party democracy are currently under examination with the Commission of Constitutional Affairs of the Chamber of Deputies (Piccio and Pacini 2012). On the constitutional grounds for the regulation of internal party democracy in Italy, see Barbera (2008) and Elia (2009).

or, more controversially, citizenship in Ukraine and Estonia. This is a salient issue in the Baltic region in particular, as it essentially deprives the large minority group of stateless Russians, for whom the exacting legal requirements make it extremely difficult to obtain national citizenship, the fundamental political right to organize in political parties. Not only do such requirements deprive the parties of their autonomy to determine their own membership criteria, they also demonstrate that the law can become a powerful instrument in the hands of the state to effectively exclude a significant population group from participating in the democratic process. Constitutions may also include demands regarding the admissible type of organizational structure. This is the case in Croatia, Poland, and Ukraine, where the constitution, in an implicit reference to the communist past, prohibits the organization of parties on the work-floor and prescribes a territorial form of party organization. The relationship between such legal requirements and internal democracy lies primarily in the fact that they explicitly prescribe or implicitly adhere to a particular organizational model. We will examine this in more detail after we first turn to an investigation of the content of party laws.

PARTY LAWS

Party laws inevitably contain a much greater amount of detail on the operation and functioning of political parties than national constitutions. Since the establishment of the first party law in Germany (1967), an increasing number of European countries have followed this example by bringing together the rules applying specifically to political parties in a single legal document, as can be seen in Table 3.1. Indeed, German party law has thus functioned as a model for the legal regulation of political parties in the young democracies of Spain and Portugal established in the 1970s (Müller and Sieberer 2006: 438) as well as in post-communist Eastern Europe (Tsatsos and Kedzia 1994: 334). Others have noted, however, that party laws in Eastern Europe have adopted most of the fundamental provisions contained in the German party law, except for those pertaining to intra-party processes (Kasapovic 2001: 7). In this section we explore the ways in which the party laws across Europe have regulated the internal functioning and structure of party organizations, examining—both quantitatively and qualitatively—the differences and similarities between countries as well as the trends over time.

A quantitative overview

For our first—quantitative—investigation, we have conducted a content analysis of the party laws, coding the different provisions in specific categories of

TABLE 3.2 *Relative emphasis of dimensions of party regulation (%)*

Area of regulation	Magnitude
Extra-parliamentary party	*33.0*
External oversight	31.7
Party finance	20.9
Rights and freedoms	0.9
Secondary legislation	6.3
Electoral party	0.7
Democratic principles	1.4
Identity and programme	1.4
Media access	0.5
Activity and behaviour	3.0
Parliamentary party	0.1
Governmental party	0.1

Note: N = 20.

regulation.[8] For the purpose of this chapter, we are most interested in the regulation of the 'extra-parliamentary party', which is the category that includes provisions on the (extra-parliamentary) organizational structure and functioning of the party, many of which, although not all, are linked to aspects of internal democracy. In this context, we have made a distinction between the external party organization, on the one hand, and the internal party organization, on the other. The former includes provisions related to the external operational activities of political parties, and mainly involves requirements for their formal registration with the relevant authorities, such as the need for deposits, signatures, or the obligation to submit a copy of the party statutes or the party programme upon registration. The latter category is more interesting in the context of this chapter, as it includes provisions related to internal procedures and to the internal organizational structure of the parties. Under this broader rubric, the law may regulate the internal decision-making procedures of political parties, prescribe the internal channels of accountability, define the powers and composition of the internal organs of the party, prescribe the frequency of meetings for party organs, lay down the voting and election procedures, define the rights and duties of party members, stipulate admission requirements for party membership, identify the incompatibility of party membership with other (public) offices or organizations, proscribe the type or form of organizational structure, and so on.

As shown in Table 3.2,[9] the extra-parliamentary party is the most frequent subject of regulation, accounting for 33 per cent of the total provisions in national party laws. Included under this rubric are all references to both the internal and

[8] For details on the categorization of party regulation, see van Biezen and Borz (2012).

[9] Our quantitative analysis excludes the party law of Cyprus, adopted in February 2011.

external party organization, which each contribute in equal measure to this category overall. The second and third most important domains of regulation are those of external oversight (32 per cent) and party finance (32 per cent)—this despite the fact that many of these countries also have separate party finance laws.[10] The overall distribution of the different categories suggests that party laws are primarily about the regulation of the parties' extra-parliamentary organizations, party financing as well as the monitoring of their activities and behaviour—in the form of independent auditing committees, for example, or judicial oversight by (constitutional) courts. Party laws dedicate relatively little attention to a further elaboration of the parties' rights and freedoms of association or speech, or the permissible forms of activity and behaviour, both of which are constitutionally enshrined in the majority of national constitutions of contemporary European democracies.

There is considerable variation between countries with regard to the emphasis the law places on the regulation of the political parties' internal organization, however.[11] This can be seen from Table 3.3, which presents the relative weight of provisions related to the internal party organization in party laws across countries and over time. In countries such as Austria, Finland, Hungary, Norway, and the UK, the party law appears to devote relatively little attention to intra-party organizational procedures and structures. The bulk of the laws in these countries is in fact concerned with the financing of parties and mechanisms of external monitoring and control (Austria, Hungary, and Norway), or with party registration requirements and external control thereof (Finland and the UK).[12] Countries clustered around the mean are Bulgaria, Czech Republic, Croatia, Slovenia, Slovakia, and Ukraine. On the other end of the spectrum, we find countries such as Germany, Latvia, and Portugal, where the references to internal party procedures account for almost one third of the total number of legal provisions. Estonia, Lithuania, Romania, and Spain also rank well above the average magnitude of regulation. More generally, it appears that democracies which emerged out of the third and fourth waves of democratization devote significantly more attention to

[10] Countries that besides a party law also have a specific party finance law are Croatia (adopted in 2006), Finland (1969), Latvia (1995), Lithuania (1999), Norway (1973), Portugal (2003), Romania (2003), Serbia (1991), Slovakia (1992), and the UK (2000).

[11] For an overview on the broader regulatory focus of party laws in Europe, see Casal-Bértoa et al. (2013, forthcoming).

[12] The party laws in Austria, Hungary and Norway are in fact perhaps better regarded as party finance laws. Indeed, the official title of the Austrian party law is the 'Federal Act on the Functions, Financing and Election Campaigning of Political Parties', while in Hungary it concerns the 'Law on the Operation and Financial Functioning of Political Parties'. The Norwegian party law repealed the existing 'Act on Party Finance' and incorporated much of its content. For the UK, we have considered the 1998 'Registration of Political Parties Act' as a party law, and the 2000 'Political Parties, Elections and Referendum Act' as a party finance law. For further details on party regulation in Europe, see Piccio (2012).

TABLE 3.3 *Regulation of the internal party organization, by country (%)*

Country (t_0–t_1)	t_0	t_1	Change
Austria (1975–2003)	3.6 (2)	2.2 (2)	–1.4 (0)
Bulgaria (1990–2009)	10.2 (9)	11.8 (30)	+1.6 (+21)
Croatia (1993–1999)	12.8 (15)	12.8 (14)	0.0 (–1)
Czech Republic (1993–2006)	9.5 (9)	10.5 (17)	+1.0 (+8)
Estonia (1994–2008)	20.0 (12)	21.4 (21)	+1.4 (+9)
Finland (1969–1992)	2.2 (1)	2.0 (1)	–0.2 (0)
Germany (1967–2004)	34.4 (60)	29.9 (91)	–4.5 (+31)
Hungary (1989–2003)	3.7 (3)	4.9 (4)	+1.2 (+1)
Lithuania (1990–2004)	13.1 (13)	25.6 (21)	+10.5 (+8)
Latvia (2006)	30.5 (57)	–	n/a
Norway (2005)	2.8 (2)	–	n/a
Poland (1990–2008)	8.8 (3)	7.6 (17)	–1.2 (+14)
Portugal (1974–2003)	20.3 (14)	33.7 (34)	+13.4 (+20)
Romania (1996–2003)	25.7 (45)	23.3 (42)	–2.4 (–3)
Serbia (2009)	15.4 (22)	–	n/a
Slovakia (1993–2005)	10.2 (9)	11.0 (23)	+0.8 (+14)
Slovenia (1994–2007)	11.8 (19)	12.9 (19)	+1.1 (0)
Spain (1978–2002)	15.6 (5)	21.9 (28)	+6.3 (+ 23)
Ukraine (2001–2010)	16.4 (21)	16.7 (21)	+0.3 (0)
United Kingdom (1998)	2.9 (2)	–	n/a
Mean	*13.5*	*15.5*	+*2*

Note: Figures reported express, in percentages, the relative proportion of the references to the internal party organization in relation to the total number of provisions in the party law as a whole. In parentheses: the raw number of provisions on internal party organization. t_0 = year in which the first party law was adopted; t_1 = amended version of the party law.

the internal party organization than the longer established democracies of the first and second waves, with Germany as the most notable exception.

Table 3.3 also allows us to assess changes over time, by comparing the party law as it was first adopted (t_0) with a more recent version (t_1). As shown in the final column of Table 3.3, the intensity of the regulation of the internal party organization has tended to increase with time. First of all, the average of regulation has increased from 13.5 in the first party laws to 15.5 in their most recent incarnations.[13] Secondly, the tendency towards an increase in the amount of regulation of internal party organizations is visible in virtually all the individual countries, both in relative and in absolute terms. It is particularly evident in the cases of Portugal, Lithuania, and, to a lesser extent, Spain, where both the relative share as well as the absolute number of provisions regulating the internal party organization have increased considerably since the first party law was

[13] N.B. This excludes the party laws of Latvia, Norway, Serbia, and the United Kingdom, where the current version of the party law is also their first. Including these four countries would change the average to 15.0.

adopted. In relative terms, it appears that four countries show a small decline, although the absolute number of provisions remains the same (Austria and Finland) or in fact increases significantly (Germany and Poland); the negative sign here is thus primarily due to an overall increase in the size of the law itself. In absolute terms, only Croatia and Romania record a minor decrease. Our quantitative analysis thus shows that, among the European democracies with a special party law, there is considerable variation in terms of the relative emphasis the party law places on the internal party organization. At the same time, however, there is an unequivocal trend towards more regulation, both over time and across countries.

A qualitative overview

Even though the quantitative data provide a useful indication of the relative emphasis of the regulation of the internal party organization by the different laws, they need to be supplemented with a more qualitative analysis focused on the specific substance of the legislation. In this section we analyse the content of the rules with particular attention to those elements conventionally relevant to internal democracy. For this purpose, we have first of all scrutinized the legal documents for the formal establishment of the general principle of IPD, for instance by legal requirements that the organizational structures of the party or its decision-making processes are internally democratic. Moreover, we have examined the nature of the legal stipulations in relation to key aspects typically associated with IPD, that is the influence of the party membership in the selection of the party candidates for public office, the selection of party leaders, and the formulation of the party policy (Scarrow, Webb, and Farrell 2000; Rahat and Hazan 2001 and 2010; Scarrow 2005). In addition, we have analysed the legal prescriptions for the involvement of the party membership in the selection of the internal organs of representation, such as the party congress or representative assemblies. We have also considered the legal provisions that grant party members the right to challenge internal party decisions or which prescribe the existence of arbitration boards to solve internal disputes. Finally, we have inspected the party laws for the existence of specific voting procedures for internal decision-making and selection processes. The findings are summarized in Table 3.4.

As we can see, a considerable number of party laws makes explicit reference to the various aspects of IPD, leaving, however, the responsibility to the political parties to elaborate specific rules in their internal party statutes. This implies that the legislator has considered the principles of internal democracy important enough to require that they are elaborated in greater detail in the party statutes, while at the same time keeping away from infringing upon their autonomy and freedom of association by not legally prescribing specific directives.

Table 3.4 *Regulation of internal party democracy in national party laws*

Country	Formal principle of internal party democracy	Member role in candidate selection	Member role in leadership selection	Member role in policy formation	Member role in selection of organs of representation	Right to dissent/ internal arbitration body	Voting procedures
Austria	No	No	No	No	No	No	No
Bulgaria	No	No	Statute	Statute	Statute	No	No
Croatia	Yes	No	No	Statute	Statute	No	No
Cyprus	Yes	No	No	No	No	No	No
Czech Republic	Yes	No	Statute	Statute	Statute	Yes	No
Estonia	No	No	No	Statute	Statute	No	No
Finland	Yes	No	No	No	No	No	No
Germany	Yes	Statute	Yes	Yes	Yes	Yes	Yes
Hungary	No	No	No	No	No	No	No
Latvia	Yes	Yes	Yes	Yes	Yes	Yes	Yes
Lithuania	No	No	Statute	Statute	Statute	No	No
Norway	No	No	No	No	No	No	No
Poland	Yes	No	Statute	Statute	Statute	No	No
Portugal	Yes	Statute*	Yes	Yes	Yes	Yes	Yes
Romania	No	No	Statute	Statute	Statute	Yes	Yes
Serbia	No	No	Statute	Statute	Statute	No	No
Slovakia	No	No	Statute	Statute	Statute	Yes	No
Slovenia	No	Statute*	No	Statute	Statute	No	No
Spain	Yes	No	Statute	Yes	Yes	Yes	Yes
Ukraine	No	No	Statute	Statute	Statute	No	No
United Kingdom	No	No	No	No	No	No	No
Defined by law	*9*	*1*	*3*	*4*	*4*	*7*	*5*
Statute	–	*3*	*9*	*11*	*11*	–	–
No reference	*12*	*17*	*9*	*6*	*6*	*14*	*16*

Note: The data refer to the years (T_1) listed in Table 3.3. For Cyprus, 2011. Yes = provision established by law. Statute = intra-party procedures to be regulated by party statutes. No = no reference.

* Although the party law assigns the procedures for candidate selection to the party statutes, it prescribes mechanisms to ensure a gender-balanced representation.

We furthermore observe that almost half of the party laws in Europe establish the principle of IPD, including requirements that the party structures are to be internally democratic or prescribing the direct involvement of the party members in internal decision-making procedures. In some countries, IPD is in fact a legal precondition for the foundation and operation of political parties. In Finland, for example, a political party must guarantee that it respects internal democratic principles and activities in order to be entered in the party register (art. 2.3). In the Czech Republic, 'political parties and movements having no democratic statutes or no democratically elected bodies' may not be established and operate (art. 4.b). In many countries, the stated principle of internal democracy does not necessarily result in further regulation. Nonetheless, we consider the presence of a formally stated principle of internal democracy as an important indication of the underlying normative preferences of the legislator.

Secondly, we investigated whether party laws contain any provisions on the selection of candidates for public office, arguably among the most crucial of the functions performed by political parties (e.g. Dalton and Wattenberg 2000; Bartolini and Mair 2001), if only by 'minimal' definition (Sartori 1976: 63). Alongside the scholarly literature, we can confirm that this process remains a predominantly extra-legal phenomenon (cf. Gallagher 1988; Kasapovic 2001; Barnea and Rahat 2007). In contrast to countries in other regions, such as the US or Israel, candidate selection processes in Europe remain largely within the internal jurisdiction of individual political parties (Pennings and Hazan 2001). Noticeably, countries that are often considered exceptional in Europe for encouraging political parties to adopt relatively inclusive and democratic candidate selection practices (i.e. Finland, Germany, and Norway) do not emerge from our analysis. This is a consequence of the different bodies of party law where such procedures are regulated (the electoral laws for both Finland and Germany, and the Act of Nominations for Norway).[14] As we stated earlier, however, these are exceptional cases given that electoral laws generally do not concern themselves with intra-party candidate selection. Hence, with the exception of the party law of Latvia which establishes the right of party members 'to decide regarding party candidates for election to local government, the *Saeima* and the European Parliament' (art. 29.1.7), no provisions establishing members' influence in the candidate selection procedures appear throughout the European party laws.

The party laws of Germany, Portugal, and Slovenia, make explicit references to candidate selection procedures, but ascribe the competence of regulating these matters to the internal party statutes. This suggests, as we have argued above, that internal party procedures have been considered as important subjects of legislation, while the precise details of the process remain a prerogative of the parties

[14] Section 21 of the German electoral law, for instance, prescribes that the nomination of party candidates be held by the party members' assembly.

themselves. In addition, the party laws of Portugal and Slovenia, in accordance with recent recommendations of the Council of Europe,[15] prescribe that candidate selection mechanisms ensure gender-balanced participation in political activities. Although both laws leave the details of regulation to be established by the party statutes,[16] the establishment of such provisions is an important step in the direction of promoting inclusive—and hence more democratic—candidate selection procedures (cf. Ballington 2004). Noticeably, party laws do not include any prescriptions with respect to the representation of ethnic minorities in candidate selection processes, despite several supra-national recommendations and guidelines in this respect.[17]

With regard to the influence of party members on the selection of party leaders, the formulation of internal party policy, or the composition of internal organs of representation, European party laws contain only a limited amount of regulation. As shown in Table 3.4, only the party laws of Germany, Latvia, Portugal, and Spain include provisions in these domains. These are also the four countries which emerged from our quantitative analysis as those which regulate the internal party organization most intensively.[18] According to the German party law, the membership assembly elects the members of the Executive Committee,[19] determines the composition of other party bodies (art. 9.4), and decides 'on party programmes, statutes, subscription, arbitration procedures, the dissolution of the party and mergers with other parties' (art. 9.3). The Latvian party law contains similarly detailed provisions for the role of party members in internal selection procedures and policymaking. The selection of the party leadership is legally prescribed as a specific right of the party members (art. 29.1), while the competence of electing and recalling the chairperson and other members of the executive board is legally assigned to the membership assembly (art. 33.3 and 34.3). Moreover, the Latvian law assigns to this assembly the competence of making amendments to the party statutes and the party programme (art. 33.3.1) as well as the 'the approval of the pre-election programme for elections to the *Saeima* and the European Parliament'

[15] Increasing women's representation in politics through the electoral system, Recommendation 1899(2010), issued by the Committee of Ministers of the Council of Europe.

[16] Under the Portuguese law, '(t)he statutes shall ensure direct, active and balanced participation by women and men in political activities and the absence of gender discrimination in the access to party bodies and to selection as candidates to stand for the political party' (art. 28). Under the Slovenian law, '(a) Party's statute should determine: . . . the method of ensuring equal opportunities for both sexes when determining candidates in elections' (art. 19.5).

[17] See, for instance, the 'Code of Good Practice in the Field of Political Parties', adopted by the Venice Commission in 2008 [CDL-AD(2009)021].

[18] A law proposal to further elaborate the principle of internal democracy incorporated in the Croatian constitution, specifically aimed at greater transparency in both the financial management of political parties and their internal organization, was ultimately rejected by the parliament during the preliminary discussion (Cular 2004).

[19] We interpreted party leadership more broadly so as to include national executives (see also Scarrow, Webb and Farrell 2000).

(art. 33.3.4). According to the party laws of Spain, party members play similar functions in intra-party dynamics, although they also exercise caution in establishing too much detail, leaving the parties a certain degree of freedom for the further specification of the general rules in their own statutes. Under the Spanish law, the right of the members '(t)o participate in the activities of the party and in the governing and representation bodies, to exercise the right to vote, and to attend the general assembly' must be 'in accordance with the party statutes' (art. 8.2). Similarly, the provision established in the Portuguese party law for the 'holding of internal referenda on political issues that are of importance to the party' (art. 32) finds no further specification in the law itself but refers to the party statutes that 'may provide' for the organization of internal referenda.

Hence, the party laws in some countries include rather explicit prescriptions on the right of party members to participate in the internal decision-making procedures. However, in the large majority of cases, we find that the law leaves the internal selection and decision-making procedures to be elaborated in the party statutes. The party law of Lithuania (2004) may serve as an example of this pattern:

> The Statute of a political party shall indicate: . . . 7) the procedure for establishing branches of the political party, and terminating their activities; 8) the competence, periodicity of a congress (meeting, conference) of the political party, its convening and the decision-making procedure; 9) the collegial management bodies of the political party, their competence, the procedure for electing and recalling them, the term of office of the collegial management bodies, and their decision-making procedure; 10) the procedure for electing and recalling the leader of the political party, his competences and possible periods for which he may be elected. (art. 6.1).

Here, although the law refers to internal procedures for the selection of the party leadership, party policy, and internal party organs, it neither refers to the role that party members ought to play, nor does it prescribe the rules according to which those processes should be conducted. However, this legal rule—requiring a series of electing and decision-making procedures to be laid down in the party statutes—implicitly affirms the importance the legislature has attributed to such internal processes. The requirement that the details are to be specified in the internal party rulings is also relevant in light of the customary condition that party statutes are generally among the necessary documents for the registration of political parties, and hence are a prerequisite for their participation in the political process. Besides, as the Lithuanian example demonstrates, the legal specifications about the content of the party statutes may contain such a large amount of prescriptive detail that they are virtually indistinguishable from direct modes of legislation.

The right to dissent is legally prescribed in seven countries. The right of party members to challenge internal party decisions and the existence of internal arbitration boards for the solution of internal disagreements are considered to be important mechanisms to ensure internally democratic procedures within political parties (Scarrow 2005; Pettitt 2011). In some cases, the law merely stipulates that members have the right to dispute decisions taken by the party (as in Latvia and Spain). Other party laws explicitly require political parties to establish an internal court for arbitration (Czech Republic, Romania, Germany, Portugal). In the two latter cases the laws also specify the terms of their election, their independence, and their incompatibility with the party executive offices. Interestingly, party members in Slovakia may resort to mechanisms external to the party, in that they may ask the courts for reviewing a decision taken by the party body that is considered unlawful or in contradiction with the party statutes (art. 19).

Finally, only five party laws contain rules on the internal voting procedures that political parties ought to adopt for the selection of party leaders and candidates or the process of policy formulation. The regulation of internal voting procedures, which usually implies that parties have to adopt secret and majority voting, is found in the party laws of Germany, Latvia, Portugal, Spain, and Romania. With the exception of the latter, these countries stand out for the relatively intensive regulation of internal party organizations more generally, both in quantitative and qualitative terms.

MODELS OF PARTY DEMOCRACY

When it comes to the underlying norms that guide the content of party laws, it appears that in most countries these are clearly inspired by the model of the classic mass party and its formally bottom-up organizational structure, vertical channels of delegation, and horizontal mechanisms of accountability. This usually implies that legislation compels parties to adopt a territorial organizational structure, comprising several hierarchical organizational echelons from the local to the regional branch up to the national level. The membership organization is considered to be the core foundation of a political party, represented at all organizational levels by a members' or delegates' assembly, composed of or elected by the party membership, and in size principally contingent upon the number of party members; the local and regional assemblies and the national party congress are designated as the supreme decision-making organs of the party at the respective organizational echelons, and entitled to elect the corresponding executive committees; and internal elections and votes are to be conducted on the basis of individual and secret suffrage.

That a mass party conception lies beneath the legal regulation of the parties is also clear from the way in which these laws define the role and purpose of political parties. It is worth quoting the German party law here at length:

> The parties shall participate in the formation of the political will of the people in all fields of public life, in particular by exerting influence on the shaping of public opinion; inspiring and furthering political education; promoting active public participation in political life; training capable people to assume public responsibilities; participating in federal, Land, and local government elections by nominating candidates, exerting influence on political developments in parliament and government; incorporating their defined political aims into the national decision-making process; and ensuring continuous, vital links between the people and the instruments of the state. (art. 1.2)

This clause covers most of the classic functions assigned to political parties—ranging from the articulation and aggregation of interests to the nomination of candidates for public office—and places a strong emphasis on the societal functions typically associated with mass parties firmly anchored in society (furthering political education, promoting active public participation, training future public office holders etc.). A similar participatory perspective on the democratic role of parties emanates from other party laws, such as in Portugal for example, which lists among the many purposes of political parties that they 'promote the training and political preparation of citizens for a direct and active participation in democratic public life' and to 'contribute to the pluralist enlightenment of citizens and to the exercise of their freedoms and rights' (art. 2).

These normative conceptions of party democracy appear to be relatively widespread. They are mirrored also at the supra-national level, where in the last decade or so, organizations such as the Council of Europe (CoE), the Organization for Security and Cooperation in Europe (OSCE) or the European Union have developed an extensive array of rules, regulations, guidelines, and recommendations for political parties. The code of good practice adopted by the Venice Commission,[20] for example, is similarly based on a participatory democratic norm and establishes that decision-making procedures within parties should rely on principles of direct democracy or democratic delegation and that channels of communication should be created between grassroots members and party leaders. It is quite explicit in establishing the educational and training activities that parties must provide, the way the internal organization should be structured, how often such bodies should meet, how the party leaders must be elected, and how the party's finances should be monitored. Hence, in line with much of the scholarly literature (Katz and Mair 1995), both European legislators and policymakers have clearly embraced the mass party as the desirable model.

The fact that the German party law embraces the classic mass party as a prescriptive model of organization was perhaps logical at the time—the *Parteiengesetz* was first adopted in 1967—when the mass party constituted the dominant model of party organization in both empirical and normative terms. By now, of

[20] 'Code of Good Practice in the Field of Political Parties', adopted by the Venice Commission in 2008 [CDL-AD(2009)021].

course, the mass party is clearly out of date, as an ongoing process of party transformation and adaptation has meant that in the established liberal democracies of Western Europe it has given way to alternative forms of organization, such as the catch-all, cartel, and modern cadre parties (Katz and Mair 1995; Kirchheimer 1966; Koole 1996; also see Carty, this volume). In the younger democracies of Southern and Eastern Europe, it is doubtful that mass parties have ever really existed (van Biezen 2003). Nevertheless, the legal regulation of parties seems to suggest that the mass party, despite its near obsolescence in political reality, still constitutes a powerful norm. This implies that the underling normative conceptions of parties and democracy are somewhat out of sync with the opportunity structures for political mobilization in contemporary democracies, with the discrepancies between 'facts' and 'norms' likely to become increasingly wider. Furthermore, the legal prescription of a certain model of party organization effectively reduces the possibilities for parties to experiment with alternative forms of party organization, including those which are potentially better suited to modern societies.

This raises the question on what normative grounds the intervention of the state in the internal affairs of parties can be justified. One possible answer is that the legal prescription of IPD is driven by the need to counteract the inevitable predisposition towards oligarchization of large and complex organizations such as parties, as famously described by Michels' 'Iron Law'. Some scholars therefore argue in favour of 'broadly inclusive internal procedures' which may limit the potential of parties to become dominated by a largely unaccountable leadership (see Gardner 2000). A party like the Dutch PVV (Party for Freedom), for example, which is in essence led by party leader Wilders and lacks a membership basis or indeed a formal party organization, would be unconstitutional in countries such as Germany and against the law in many others, purely on the grounds that it lacked an internally democratic structure.

In addition, a lack of IPD may be seen to facilitate the implementation of undemocratic policies or the materialization of undemocratic political behaviour. The PVV is in fact a case in point, as it occasionally pushes the boundaries of the rule of law, with its (anti-Islamic) views on the verge of violating basic democratic liberties such as the freedom of speech and religion. From this perspective, a lack of internal democracy may be seen to represent, or is seen to be conducive to, a lack of commitment to democratic values and beliefs more generally. Some scholars even consider it to be sufficient grounds for a party ban (Mersel 2006: 97). The strong emphasis on internal democracy in some of the national constitutions and party laws should therefore be understood in the context of safeguarding the democratic order.[21] In the wake of the many second and third wave transitions to democracy, a pivotal role was assigned to the democratic parties in

[21] Cf. also Biezen and Borz (2012) who argue that the dominant mode of party constitutionalization in new and re-established democracies can be best described as 'defending democracy'.

the restoration or establishment of the new regime, with the adjective 'democratic' referring not only to aspects of the parties' behaviour and ideology but also to their internal structures and procedures. Countries where the law insists on IPD in fact take the doctrine of 'militant democracy' a step further by demanding that the parties themselves must reflect a commitment to democratic principles if together they are to form a democratic polity. On that view, parties in a democratic polity must be held to the core conditions of democracy, both externally in their goals and internally in their organizational structures. Accordingly, efforts to guarantee that parties will not disrupt or destroy democratic government should not be confined to the judicial control over their aims and behaviour but also over the party organization itself. Such motivations are likely to be found mainly in new or re-established democracies, where the memory of the past and a concern with the preservation of the new democratic order has led to the creation of strict legal requirements for the democratic behaviour and organization of parties. Countries such as Germany, Spain, Portugal, and Latvia, where regulation of the internal party organization is most pronounced provide cases in point.

In addition, the rationale for imposing a duty of internal democracy on party organizations may centre on a substantive rather than procedural conception of democracy, according to which key democratic values such as representation and participation cannot be realized in the absence of internally democratic parties (Mersel 2006: 96). From an alternative perspective, however, it can been argued that, because parties are not the state, the need for certain democratic values to be realized within the political system does not necessarily require the same values to be realized within each of the existing individual parties. It is, in fact, far from evident that democracy at the system level requires, or is indeed furthered by, parties that are democratic with regard to their internal structures and procedures. As Sartori has famously put it, 'democracy on a large scale is not the sum of many little democracies' (Sartori 1965: 124). While internal democracy may be indispensable from the perspective of certain participatory theories of democracy, there is a significant body of democratic theory that takes an opposite view (see also Katz 2004). Internal party democracy might produce policy choices that are further removed from preferences of the median voter, for example. Moreover, given the continuous decline of party memberships in modern democracies, party members may constitute an increasingly unrepresentative group of citizens, socially and professionally if not ideologically (van Biezen et al. 2012). This makes the outcome of internally democratic procedures restricted to party members less and less likely to represent 'the will of the people'. Furthermore, from a conception of democracy which centres primarily on the maximization of voter choice and political competition, there are no compelling reasons to impose internally democratic structures upon the parties as long as the system guarantees, in Hirschman's terms, sufficiently meaningful 'exit' options (e.g. membership exit or electoral defeat).

From this perspective, it is difficult to identify the interest of the state in so tightly controlling the internal governance of political parties. Such attempts, as

Issacharoff has argued, bring 'the force of state authority deep into the heart of all political organizations', and raise serious concerns about the relationship between political parties and the state. More fundamentally, such impositions threaten to compromise the political integrity of the parties and their organizational independence from the state. 'Political parties play a key role in providing a mechanism for informed popular participation in a democracy precisely because they are organizationally independent of the state' (Issacharoff, 2007: 1460–61). However, as the internal life and the external activities of parties become regulated by public law and as party rules become constitutional or administrative rules, the parties themselves become transformed into semi-state agencies or public service entities, with a corresponding weakening of their own internal organizational autonomy (Bartolini and Mair 2001). In addition, the increased regulation of the internal party organizations implies that the primary locus of accountability is shifted from the internal organs of the party towards external and non-majoritarian institutions of the state. This is demonstrated by the case of Slovakia discussed earlier, where members may appeal to the courts to have internal party decisions reviewed. Ultimately, the legal regulation of parties not only evokes anxieties about the state centralization and control of political participation and public life, but also about the democratic legitimacy of transferring the ultimate decision-making authority on their behaviour and organization from the responsible organs of the party to a non-elected body of judges. This externalizes the channels of accountability from the party leadership to the courts, thereby possibly creating a greater distance with the ordinary party membership in the process.

CONCLUSION

The evidence presented in this chapter suggests that Müller and Sieberer might be right in observing that there is no European country in which political parties are subject to more detailed and explicit regulation than Germany (Müller and Sieberer 2006: 35, 440). However, their assertion that, with only very few exceptions, most other countries do not have specific prescriptions on IPD, has to be slightly nuanced. Our content analysis of constitutions and party laws demonstrates that, first of all, the constitutions of four countries (Croatia, Germany, Spain, and Portugal) contain explicit requirements that political parties are to be internally democratic. The same requirement we find in almost half of the existing party laws in Europe. Moreover, the notion that existing constitutional references should, in addition to their external activities, also be seen to apply to the internal functioning of political parties, has gained increasing traction among legal scholars (cf. Tsatsos et al. 1990; Tsatsos and Kedzia 1994). In addition, supranational organizations such as the Council of Europe have become increasingly more vociferous on the need to regulate matters of IPD.

It thus appears that the internal party organization constitutes an increasingly important feature of party regulation. To be sure, our analysis also shows that the formal codification of the principle of IPD does not necessarily entail a detailed specification of the legal rules on the internal party structures and procedures. Hence, when focusing on those elements that are conventionally associated to IPD, that is, the role of members in the selection of party representatives (candidates, leaders, or internal members) or in the selection of policies, we found that only a few party laws (in Germany, Latvia, Portugal, and Spain) as well as a handful of electoral laws (Finland, Germany, and Norway) establish specific provisions in this respect. In addition, while a larger number of countries prescribe the right for party members to voice their dissent with respect to decisions adopted by the party's leading organs by party law (7 out of 21) and define the voting procedures to be followed in the internal selection or decision-making procedures (5 out of 21), we observed how European party laws tend to assign the prerogative to outline the precise details of intra-party processes to the party statutes, rather than regulating them directly. At the same time, however, we consider the fact that party laws require political parties to establish specific rules on their internal functioning in their own statutes, coupled with the commonly found prerequisite that an application for the formal registration of parties includes a copy of the party statutes, as an important indication of the underlying normative preferences of the legislature. Moreover, we argue that the legal specifications about the content of the party statutes may contain such a large amount of prescriptive detail that they are in effect virtually indistinguishable from direct modes of legislation. In this sense, and given that the extra-parliamentary organization constitutes the most important dimension of regulation in national party laws overall, we would argue that IPD constitutes a significant and increasing area of national regulation.

We have also shown how countries tend to take their cue from the classic mass party as a prescriptive model of organization. Predominant conceptions of modern democracy, according to which political parties are both necessary and desirable institutions, coupled with preferred models of party organization appear to form the basis of increasing levels of state intervention in the internal affairs of the parties, undermining their character as voluntary and private associations. That some of these normative conceptions are rather out of sync with the existing opportunity structures for political mobilization will only counter the effectiveness of party regulation, about which, it should be noted, we know comparatively little. While the central regulation of IPD may be justified according to some theories of democracy, others caution for the unwarranted intrusion of the state upon the organizational autonomy of the parties. At the very least, the increased level of state intervention in internal party politics raises fundamental questions about the democratic legitimacy of transferring decision-making authority from the parties to the judiciary as well as the state centralization and control of political participation and organization.

4

Should We Believe that Improved Intra-Party Democracy Would Arrest Party Decline?

Richard S. Katz

Much of the discussion of intra-party democracy starts from the presumption that citizens should, and do, want to be actively involved and influential within political parties. If this is so, then it is a short step to conclude that declining party membership and participation must indicate some failing on the party side of the equation. If only the parties made membership more attractive, in particular by increasing the quality of internal party democracy, membership would grow and the decline of popular satisfaction with the entire enterprise of partisan politics, as evidenced by opinion polls as well as falling turnout at elections, would be arrested or reversed.

This chapter takes a contrarian view. While not questioning the normative claim that citizens ought to be more involved in the governing of parties, either because IPD is judged to be a good in its own right or because it can be expected to lead to otherwise desirable outcomes (those questions are addressed in other chapters in this volume), I do problematize the idea that declining involvement in partisan politics is especially the fault of the parties, and that therefore it could be reversed by reform of the parties. In particular, by addressing the prior question of why citizens might decide to become involved in parties in the first place (Young, this volume, considers the question of why parties might desire members), I suggest that forces largely exogenous to the internal arrangements of the parties have made partisan involvement less attractive to citizens, and so should have been expected to result in declining party membership—as well as to declining party identification, declining turnout in elections, and declining interest in partisan politics as a spectator sport. Moreover, many of the social changes that underlie these forces are themselves widely regarded as desirable, suggesting that they ought not to be reversed, even if that were possible. To the extent that this argument is valid, the conclusion would be that rather than expecting IPD to be a cure that allows things otherwise to return to 'normal', the socio-political environment has changed in ways that compel both political actors and political analysts to adapt to a new 'normal'. In particular, it may be unrealistic to assume that parties, no matter how democratic their internal arrangements may be, can continue to occupy their previously assumed places as the central linkage between citizens and government, or as the primary channel for activity by politically engaged citizens.

WHY BE INVOLVED WITH PARTIES?

The logical first step in considering why citizens might be disengaging from parties is to ask why they might have engaged in the first place. This obviously is a very complex question, but in simplified terms, we can offer at least eight possible answers.

The first answer investigated by studies of party members (e.g. Seyd and Whiteley 1992; Whiteley, Seyd, and Richardson 1994) is that party membership is a prerequisite to making a *career in politics*, in particular to selection as a candidate or to obtaining a job like assistant to an MP or as a member of some politically appointed board. If this were to have been a significant source of party membership, then the increasing willingness of some parties to nominate new or non-members might be a contributor to declining membership. This stimulus, however, has been relevant only for a tiny minority of party members (e.g. less than one-third of one per cent of respondents to Seyd and Whiteley's 1992 (74) survey of Labour Party members, and only 1.4 per cent of those in Whiteley, Seyd and Richardson's 1994 (96) study of Conservative Party members, cited these as their most important reason for joining the party). A recent survey of young (18–25-year-old) party members in six countries suggests that careerist motivations are particularly strong among this age group (Bruter and Harrison 2009a), but they remain a small minority of party members. Moreover, to the extent that they do become career politicians, one could ask whether they would favour IPD as the empowering of the ordinary members relative to the professionals (i.e. themselves), or whether their increased participation in party governance should be interpreted as an increase in IPD. Overall, while careerist motivation cannot be dismissed entirely—for example, Sundberg (1986) suggested that differences in membership trends between Denmark and the other Scandinavian parties could be explained in part by the lesser availability in Denmark of local office—its impact on temporal trends would depend on decreasing attractiveness or decreasing availability of such personal rewards over time within individual political systems.

A second possible answer is a generalization of the first. People may be motivated to join parties by the belief that party membership is a prerequisite for *receiving political patronage*—or simply for obtaining a job in publicly owned enterprises or in the state bureaucracy. Hopkin (2006), for example, refers to the 'strictly partisan allocation of jobs in the state-run postal service or railways' in Italy, while Müller (1989) reports similar practices in Austria. Alternatively, they may believe that membership will in some way result in more sympathetic treatment by the authorities (e.g. Zariski 1972).

A third possibility is the party membership analog of the *simple rational choice/* Downsian explanation for voter turnout: the potential member calculates his/her expected utility under a variety of scenarios (for voting, these scenarios are the expected policy results of the electoral victory of each potential party or coalition; for party membership, they would be expected policy outcomes brought about either through the electoral success or changes in the policy stance of each party) and then acts (votes or joins a party) so as to maximize his/her expected utility *discounted by the probability that the action will bring about the desired outcome* (specifically on voting, see Downs 1957: 36–50). The problem of course is that no matter how success is defined, be it party victory (inclusion in government) or a shift in party policy or in party image, the probability that a single individual's action even in the most internally democratic of parties will bring that happy state of affairs into being is essentially zero. Within the strictly individualistic framework of the classical rational choice model, the question is, as Whiteley, Seyd, and Billinghurst (2006: 74) drawing on Olson (1965) observe, why anyone joins parties at all.

If one relaxes the assumption that voters are capable of making realistic estimates of the utilities and probabilities in the simple rational choice explanation, then a fourth possibility, which I will identify as *subjective rational choice*, might be considered. The potential member makes the same calculations as with the simple rational choice model, but the 'numbers' that go into the calculations are wrong. On one hand, the person may over-estimate the utility differences among potential outcomes. On the other hand, and more likely if party membership is to be explained in these terms, the person may over-estimate the probability of his/her own individual action having a perceptible impact on the outcome. While this retains the methodological individualism of simple rational choice, as well as the nominal emphasis on perceived utilities and probabilities, in reality the meaning of 'perceived' shifts decisively; where in the simple rational choice model, perceptions are assumed to be sufficiently grounded in reality that they can be estimated by the analyst as reality plus a modest random error term, in the subjective rational choice model attention shifts from the rational processing of more-or-less accurate information to the non-rational development of potentially, or even certainly, inaccurate beliefs.

The fifth possibility is to retain the assumption that perceived utilities and probabilities are reasonably accurate reflections of reality, but to replace the individualism of the simple and subjective models with an orientation toward groups. In this case, which I call *social rational choice*, the key variable is not the probability that the individual potential party member's actions will make a difference, but the probability that the collective actions of some group with which the individual identifies will make a difference. The expectation of party membership in this model depends on two variables. First the potential member must believe that the ties binding the group together are sufficiently strong for an expectation of solidarity to make sense; the threshold for this may be far short of an expectation of unanimity, and indeed for something like party membership an expectation that only a minority of group members will become party members may be sufficient—provided there is no expectation of significant numbers of group members joining some party that is opposed to the one in question. Second, the potential member must him/herself identify with the group sufficiently strongly to identify his/her interests with those of the group—which is to say at a minimum that the potential member favours the party or cluster of parties that s/he expects the group to be supporting.

All of the explanations for party membership listed so far are instrumental—directed at the production of an identifiable outcome, with the likelihood of party membership determined jointly by the degree to which the outcome is valued and the expectation that membership, either of the individual or of some fraction of a group with which the individual identifies, will significantly increase the likelihood that the outcome will be achieved. In the first case, the desired outcome is advancement of the potential member's individual political career; in the second it is receipt of other discretionary personal advantages; in the third, fourth, and fifth cases it is advancement of the potential member's political preferences. In each case, unless there is an expectation that membership will make a difference, these accounts fail to explain why anyone would join a party.

As with voting, however, there are potential explanations for party membership that are independent of the expectation of an immediate impact on outcomes. Perhaps the most obvious (and the sixth in this list) is that party membership is *expressive* rather than instrumental. One joins a party because one agrees with its general philosophy or specific policies and wants to demonstrate this agreement. Some sense of contributing to the ultimate realization of that philosophy or those policies may play a role, but that is secondary to the psychic reward of 'taking a stand' or 'having one's say'.

A seventh, and closely related, explanation would be that party membership is valued as an *expression of social identity*. Analogous to the '*voto d'appartenenza*' (Parisi and Pasquino 1979), membership is an expression of solidarity with the party that is independent of (or possibly the underlying cause of) policy agreement. On one hand, this could be the direct organizational expression of strong party identification: since I am a Liberal (in the sense of 'generally speaking, so you think of yourself as . . . '), it is only appropriate that I join the Liberal party. On the other hand, it could be the political expression of some other social identity: since I am a worker, it is only appropriate that I join the party of the working class. Here the psychic reward is that of 'being a member of the team'.

All of these explanations can be understood to be primarily political. Studies of party membership also suggest an eighth possibility, which might be characterized as a class of *social* explanations for party membership: a venue to socialize with like-minded people, not just with explicit regard to politics, but in talking about sports or having a summer picnic; perhaps (as was once said of rural villages in Norway), the local party headquarters have the best, or only, televisions in town; perhaps they have particularly nice bars or other public social spaces. A variant of this explanation, frequently cited as the most common immediate stimulus to party membership, is simply 'I joined because someone asked me to'. While these motivations may not be strictly apolitical in the sense that they are unlikely to lead to membership in a party with which the member strongly disagrees (and also in the sense that an invitation to join a party may be stimulated by a desire to recruit supporters for a particular aspirant to candidacy or party leadership), they may encourage membership, and perhaps ultimately even commitment through subconscious social pressure, by people who are not initially much interested in politics.

Finally, this list must be supplemented with three observations. First, although the explanations have been listed largely as if they were independent, any particular party member is likely to be motivated by a combination of several of them: the psychic rewards of expression or membership are likely to be stronger if the member also believes that his/her membership will make a difference; social interaction is likely to be more pleasant when with those with whom one shares a cultural and political identity. Indeed, such synergies among explanations for party membership—and by extension for party support generally—lie at the heart of the mobilization strategy of the mass party of integration. At the same time, however, even if (or perhaps because) it is impossible fully to disentangle these explanations, any set of developments that would tend to weaken all of these processes would lead to a strong expectation of partisan disengagement.

Second, the magnitude of reward necessary to generate membership should be expected to vary with the cost. Most simply, high membership subscriptions should discourage membership by all but those who expect the largest material benefits (e.g. the recipients of patronage) or those who expect the largest non-material rewards (e.g. the most deeply committed). In particular, the opportunity to seriously contribute to the shaping of party decisions may be more relevant to the recruitment and retention of activists than the recruitment of 'mere' members, for whom the warm feeling of responding to the membership drive of a party with which they are in vague sympathy may be adequate compensation for a nominal membership fee (and no further involvement).

Third, as with all activities, the likelihood of party membership should be inversely related to the availability of alternative ways of achieving the same objectives. At the most mundane level, as private ownership of televisions expanded, the attractive power of the party hall as a public screening room decreased. At a more general level, higher levels of education, greater leisure time and greater disposable income, more readily available and diverse forms of mass communication, the proliferation of interest organizations, all would be expected to increase the range of alternatives to party that are available to citizens.

WHITHER MEMBERSHIP?

Although the specific mechanisms through which an expectation of party membership is reached vary among these explanations, they can nonetheless be categorized into three (overlapping) groups based on their underlying preconditions. The first category (especially explanations one and two) relies on private and particularistic benefits to the member: jobs, other forms of personal patronage, and favours. The second category (especially explanations three, four, five, and six) relies on the perceived importance of the outcome of interparty struggles. The third category (especially explanations five and seven) relies on a sense of solidarity within social groups and a concomitant sense of hostility or antagonism among groups. It is my contention in this section that each of these preconditions has, in fact, decayed in Western societies over the course of the last fifty or sixty years, leading to the natural expectation that party membership will also have declined—as indeed it has (van Biezen et al. 2012) Moreover, although the processes leading to this decay are in some cases rooted in public policies promoted and enacted by parties (for example, reforms of public recruitment procedures, the growth of the welfare state, and later the widespread acceptance of neo-liberal economic theory), they have nothing to do with the internal organization of the parties. Ironically, although the decline of popular participation in partisan politics, especially with regard to electoral turnout, but extending to declining party membership as well, is often regarded as a problem,[1] the processes that underlie the decline usually are regarded as good.

The first such process is the breakdown of rigid social divisions that was taking place during most of the twentieth century, but which progressed most rapidly over the last forty years or so. This has been obvious along many dimensions. One is the secularization of modern societies. To take an example from the case that was regarded as the archetype of social segmentation along confessional lines, between 1967 and 1986 the share of the Dutch population identifying with the Dutch Reformed Church was cut in half, from 30 per cent to 15 per cent; while the proportion identifying as Roman Catholic only declined from 37 per cent to 31 per cent, the percentage of Catholics attending church at least once a week plunged from 75 to 26. (For additional figures, see Dogan 2001: 105.) Similarly, between 1989 and 2009, mass attendance by Catholics in Germany was cut in half, from 28 per cent to less than 14 per cent (St. Leger 2009); between 1967 and 1992 the proportion of Germans of any Christian denomination saying that they attend church 'every or almost every Sunday' fell from 25 per cent to 10 per cent (Dogan 2002: 143). According to the World Values Survey, the proportion of the

[1] For example, referring specifically to turnout in the 2001 British general election, Whiteley et al. (2001: 786) observe that '[t]he word crisis is often abused in contemporary accounts of politics. But if this is not a crisis of democratic politics in Britain, then it is hard to know what would be'.

population attending religious services once a month or more fell between 1981 and 2000 by 15 per cent in Australia, 11 per cent in Canada, 6 per cent in France, 18 per cent in Ireland, 15 per cent in the Netherlands, 18 per cent in Spain; in Denmark, Iceland, and Sweden, the figure was already below 15 per cent in 1981 (Halman et al. 2008: 210). Even where there is some evidence of increased religious belief, it appears to be 'not in the official, traditional, institutional way, but in a personal, unofficial way' (Halman and Riis 2003: 10).

Perhaps of even greater significance has been the erosion of social class divisions. This is not to say that there are no longer real differences in life experiences based on differences in income, or that aggregate distributions of income and wealth have not become less egalitarian. Rather, it is to point to two trends that have undermined social class as a basis for politics. The first is the shrinking of the industrial working class, the traditional home of class-based politics. For example, the French industrial working class, which represented 51 per cent of the electorate in 1951 was only 30 per cent in 1988 (Dogan 2001: 101). The flip side of this has been the growth of a large self-identified middle class. In 1963, Butler and Stokes (1969: 67) found 32 per cent of the British to identify themselves as 'upper middle', 'middle', or 'lower middle' class; in the 1995 wave of the World Values Survey in Britain, 68.8 per cent identified themselves as 'upper middle' or 'lower middle' class.[2] Moreover, given the prevalence of universal benefits of the welfare state (health care, public education, public pensions) and the rise of mass communications, the differences in life experiences and expectations among all of these classes have become more quantitative (the price of the car or home on which payments are being made) rather than qualitative.

The other trend has been an increase in social mobility. Using a four-class ranking of occupations, Noble shows that 10-year career mobility for British men 1971–81 (45 per cent changing category) was more than twice what it had been for 1953–63 (21.6 per cent) (Noble 2000: 38). Looking at a series of studies over the period from 1949 to 1984, Noble (40) also reports a steady increase in upward intergenerational mobility across the manual-non-manual divide (and a decline in downward intergenerational mobility, accompanying a shrinking of the manual working class overall). Moreover, people who themselves move across the class divide, whether within their own careers or inter-generationally tend to keep their old contacts, thus further eroding the boundary between classes.

It is hard to argue that the resulting lessening of inter-class and inter-confessional hostility is not a good thing. (It is, for example, hard to image any

[2] European and World Values Surveys four-wave integrated data file, 1981–2004, v.20060423, 2006. Surveys designed and executed by the European Values Study Group and World Values Survey Association. File Producers: ASEP/JDS, Madrid, Spain, and Tilburg University, Tilburg, the Netherlands. File Distributors: ASEP/JDS and GESIS, Cologne, Germany.

politician today making the equivalent of Aneurin Bevan's famous 'vermin speech',[3] if only because it would be unlikely to resonate with the audience.) As is widely recognized, however, that these developments also undercut the social basis of the mass party of integration—a party model characterized by the mobilization and encapsulation of a *classe gardée*—and by at least a nominal ideological commitment to IPD. It should hardly be surprising that the erosion of the social basis for the mass party of integration has undermined that model of party organization, and that the decline of the mass party model in turn has meant that fewer people are in fact mobilized and encapsulated under the umbrella of party organizations.

More specifically, while class and religious prejudices generally are regarded as bad, weakening those divisions should have a direct negative impact on participation motivated by, or dependent on, social ties, in particular social rational choice or identity-based participation. Indirectly, by fostering the conditions assumed by the simple Downsian model of party/electoral behaviour (or alternatively, by the catch-all model of party), and therefore encouraging parties to moderate their positions or to converge toward the first preference of the median voter, these trends should reduce participation based on policy differences (all of the rational models) as well. The increased cognitive mobilization, economic security, and leisure time that have been a part of this process should have a negative impact on partisan participation by broadening the range of alternatives open to citizens—although they might also increase the number of citizens who cross the threshold required even for relatively passive party membership.

The second general explanation of partisan decline stems from the increasing tendency for political debate to revolve around questions of competence and efficiency rather than ideology. Perhaps this is best exemplified by the 1999 Tony Blair/Gerhard Schroeder statement, *The Third Way/Die Neue Mitte* (for example, 'social conscience cannot be measured by the level of public expenditure. The real test for society is how effectively this expenditure is used'; 'within the public sector bureaucracy at all levels must be reduced, performance targets and objectives formulated, the quality of public services rigorously monitored'), but goes hand-in-hand with the moderation of party policies brought about by the processes just discussed, as well as by the fiscal constraints imposed by the failure of revenue to keep up with obligations.[4] Government in general, and the rule of a specific party or coalition in particular, is legitimated by the (economic) quality of

[3] 'No amount of cajolery, and no attempts at ethical or social seduction, can eradicate from my heart a deep burning hatred for the Tory Party. So far as I am concerned they are lower than vermin' (Speech on 3 July 1948 at the Bellevue Hotel, Manchester).'

[4] Ironically, the success of the welfare state in ameliorating interclass differences has been a large contributor to this problem. Improvements in health care, expansion of universal education, and provision of old age pensions all have meant that an increasing share of the population is supported by a decreasing share that are economically productive, even under conditions of full employment. See Blyth and Katz (2005).

its outputs rather than by the (democratic) quality of its inputs. Decisions in many fields are delegated to bodies that are not directly accountable at the ballot box (bureaucratic or specialized agencies; independent central banks; courts), that are deliberately insulated from partisan politics, and that are justified or evaluated with reference to professional and technocratic standards. With regard to elected officials, attention increasingly is focused on questions of personal (and often relatively petty) honesty and virtue (e.g. not using a government credit card for private purchases, even if the bill is to be paid with private funds; not sending a staff person on a personal errand, even if it is to allow the official to perform public duties more effectively; not using air miles accumulated on government travel for private holidays—all things commonly done in the private sector) rather than ideas and values.

This shift in emphasis has been reflected in political party manifestos. Three categories of 'quasi-sentences' coded by the Comparative Manifestos Project reflect this relatively policy-free attitude toward politics: 'governmental and administrative efficiency', 'political corruption', and 'political authority'. Table 4.1 shows the average of the total proportion of manifesto quasi-sentences that fell into these categories for the mainstream (Social Democratic, Liberal, Conservative, and Christian Democratic) parties for three time periods: 1950–70, 1971–95, and 1996–2005. In all but one (Ireland) of the fifteen countries considered, this proportion has gone up, in some cases quite dramatically. And, of course, to the extent that parties are not emphasizing policy differences—whether because they choose not to call attention to real differences, or because the constraints of

TABLE 4.1 *Mean percentage of mainstream party manifesto quasi-sentences concerning honesty, authority, and efficiency*

	1950–70	1971–95	1996–2005
Australia	6.30	7.41	19.49
Austria	2.23	11.89	7.41
Belgium	4.50	7.76	11.26
Canada	3.62	3.274	4.63
Denmark	1.65	3.29	7.18
Finland	3.57	6.83	8.83
Germany	8.75	6.23	9.58
Great Britain	3.08	4.29	15.35
Ireland	15.43	11.66	7.57
Italy	3.32	16.72	20.84
Netherlands	2.22	6.84	8.86
New Zealand	2.02	3.98	4.93
Norway	1.06	2.11	2.91
Sweden	0.88	1.53	1.32
United States	6.59	5.99	12.65

Source: Comparative Manifesto Project.

fiscal reality and prior commitments mean that the actual differences are minimal—policy-oriented motivations for party membership are reduced.

Again, it is hard to argue against efficiency and honesty, but at the same time they undercut many of the incentives for citizens to become involved in party politics. Most obviously, the emphasis on bureaucratic neutrality and personal rectitude reduces the value of patronage and other individual or group incentives for partisan involvement. On the one hand, an obsession with personal rectitude can lead to acceptance of the use of the exposé as a norm of professional journalism, and use of criminal law as a partisan weapon (see for example Ginsberg and Shefter 2002), making the seeking of public office less attractive (indeed, when the accusations and convictions concern arcane technical legal requirements or resurrect minor indiscretions that are otherwise long forgotten, the seeking of public office may simply look like a trap for the unwary), and thereby decreasing the incentives to become involved in party politics as a stepping stone to office. On the other hand, the reduction in patronage appointments, and in the capacity for discretionary favours, even of relatively little economic value (British 'honours', for example), reduces that incentive for party activity as well. In emphasizing technique over questions of preference, the citizen is marginalized from political decisions and the expert—whether in the bureaucracy, or the private sector, or the party itself—is privileged. Again, the incentives for party activity that are rooted in the desire to affect policy are reduced in value—policy is, after all, made elsewhere. A steady stream of accusations, whether justified or not, contributes to a general perception of partisan politics as an unsavoury business—hardly a desirable social outlet, or an activity through which one would express a positive identification.[5]

Closely related to this is the third general explanation—increasing acceptance of the model of consensus democracy (Lijphart 1984, 1999), and the values that underlie it, as superior to the majoritarian model and its associated values. An indicator of this is the increasing use of the idea that a politician or political campaign is 'too partisan'[6] as a criticism, or conversely the use of 'non-partisan' or 'bi-partisan' as a positive attribute. The core value of the consensus models, as the name implies, is decisions that are acceptable to the vast majority of the

[5] As the theory of cognitive dissonance minimization suggests (Festinger 1962), if one of the links in the triad of self-party politics 'object of identification' is negative, then one of the other links should be as well. If we assume the self-'object of identification' link to be positive and self-party politics link to be negative (party politics is unsavoury), then the perceived link between party politics and the 'object of identification' should be negative. But in that case, the expression of social identity can hardly be a motive for party involvement.

[6] Perhaps the clearest example would be former-President Jimmy Carter's observation in early October 2004 that the presidential campaign had become 'too partisan'. The headlines in the Toronto Star of 17 December 2007, 'Ottawa too partisan on emissions', or the Brandon (Manitoba) Sun online edition of 14 March 2011, 'Federal ads too partisan: critics' are somewhat less extreme (what could be more extreme than thinking that an election campaign should not be partisan?) examples from Canada.

citizens—ideally, to all of them—in preference to decisions that are desired by a majority and imposed on the minority. Institutionally, this means division and separation of powers, oversized and minority cabinets, strong and independent courts and central banks—on the one hand, many veto players and many impediments to the winner of a single general election straightforwardly imposing its/his/her will in public policy, and on the other hand, many decisions delegated to technocrats and justified with reference to their expertise and professional norms.

Some constraints on majorities of the moment clearly are necessary if peaceful democratic government is to persist. As with efficiency and honesty, it is hard to argue against competence or to suggest that it would be a good thing if those who supported the losers in elections were actively dissatisfied with democracy.[7] Nonetheless, one unintended consequence may be to undermine incentives for participation in party politics. The implications of privileging technical expertise over private interest and preferences, and of striving to minimize the differences in satisfaction as between winners and losers, should be obvious. Even if one believes in a single common interest, the first suggests that the ordinary citizen has little beyond passive acceptance to contribute to achieving it. And whether or not one believes in a common interest, the second implies that it makes little difference who wins the political contest. Beyond this, the multiplication of veto points means that even if it would make a difference who won, if someone could win, real victory itself will be somewhat illusory. The probability that a citizen's political activity will alter the substantive outcome is reduced, because the partisan activities of citizens in general do not control outcomes, which are instead determined by nonpartisan experts and sheer policy inertia (e.g. Rose and Davies 1994). Even if one's activity did have an impact on outcomes, the difference in utility between the alternatives is minimized (for ordinary citizens, if not necessarily for politicians who can enjoy the personal rewards of office). Simple, social, and subjective rational choice incentives for partisan participation are, thus, all undercut. Indeed, to the extent that this analysis is accurate, one might legitimately ask why anyone would do other than take William Butler Yeats' advice in the poem 'The Old Stone Cross':

> So stay at home, and drink your beer
> And let the neighbours' vote

The final explanation is the widespread acceptance of neo-liberalism as the dominant economic paradigm. This implies that the market is always rational and efficient, and hence that any government intervention in the economy must be

[7] See, for example, Lijphart (1999: 286–7) for the argument that minimizing the difference in 'satisfaction with democracy' (the way democracy works in your country, which is arguably more a measure of policy output satisfaction that it is a measure of satisfaction with regime type—see Linde (forthcoming) and the sources cited therein) is a good thing.

inefficient. In particular, it means a commitment to limiting the size of government and the scope of government regulation. Because they were leaders of parties of the moderate left—parties formerly associated with the alternative of social democracy—the other elements of the statement by Tony Blair and Gerhard Schroeder cited above provide clear examples of the triumph of this paradigm:[8]

> The ability of national governments to fine-tune the economy in order to secure growth and jobs has been exaggerated. The importance of individual and business enterprise to the creation of wealth has been undervalued.
>
> Public expenditure as a proportion of national income has more or less reached the limits of acceptability.
>
> Companies must have room for manoeuvre to take advantage of improved economic conditions and seize new opportunities: they must not be gagged by rules and regulations
>
> Product, capital and labour markets must all be flexible.

More recently, there is the emphasis placed by the governments of Germany, the United Kingdom, Canada, and the United States on fiscal austerity (in particular, debt reduction) not withstanding widespread growth of un- and underemployment caused by the financial crisis of 2008.

For the purposes of explaining trends in party membership or other partisan activity, it does not matter tremendously whether the economic claims embodied in the neo-liberal view are true or not. What does matter is that their general acceptance by politicians of all major parties means that what have traditionally been some of the most important concerns of precisely the citizens who form the pool from which party members are drawn—unemployment and inflation—are removed from the realm in which parties are expected to make a difference. But yet again, if the parties do not take different positions, or any positions at all, on matters of importance to citizens, the policy-based rationales for party membership or other party activity are diminished.

ALTERNATIVES TO PARTY

The assumption that citizens should be actively involved in parties, which should themselves be internally democratic in their organizations and decision-making practices, is rooted in a combination of the 'parliamentary party government' model of democracy (Katz 1986, 1987; Rose 1974) and the 'mass party' model of party (Duverger 1954; Beer 1969; Sartori 1976—also see Carty, this volume).

[8] For the full text, and a critique, see <http://web.inter.nl.net/users/Paul.Treanor/drittemitte.html>, accessed 27 May 2011.

Together, they lead to the conventional principal-agent model of democracy (e.g. Strøm et al. 2003: ch. 1): voters are the ultimate principal, using elections to hire and fire parties (in particular, the party in public office—see Katz and Mair 1993) as their agents to make and implement policies on the basis of their pre-election manifestos or well-identified ideologies; simultaneously, the party on the ground is the principal of the party in public office (with the party in central office supervising the party in public office on behalf of the party on the ground); the winning party in public office (the parliamentary party), or coalition, as principal installs a cabinet as their agent; and finally, the cabinet as principal employs the state apparatus (bureaucracy, etc.) as its agent to govern. Hence, with the exception of the problem that the party in public office appears to have two masters—the electorate and its own party on the ground—there is an unambiguous chain of delegation and accountability from the citizens to their government and administration.

In this stylized model, citizens have two points of access to the policy-determining process. On one hand, they can contribute to the formulation of the policy package put forward by the party of which they are members. On the other hand, they can endorse (support with labour and financial contributions, as well as with their votes) one of the policy packages put forward by the parties. In fact, however, citizens have numerous other ways in which to participate in political life beyond those afforded by party membership and electoral participation, and to the extent that these alternatives appear more effective or less costly than participation in or through parties, they may be expected to 'crowd out' partisan activity with no real cost to democratic quality.

As observed long ago (e.g. Almond and Powell 1978 [1966]: ch. 8), one of the functions of political parties is interest aggregation—that is, the formulation through processes of compromise and accommodation of a limited number of policy packages among which voters could make a meaningful choice, and which, after further compromise and accommodation, would become the basis for government policy. As a compromise, it is unlikely that the policy package of a party will fully satisfy any, let alone every, party member or supporter. If the party programme were the final word on policy, then active involvement in its formulation would be centrally important to any politically involved citizen, and if parties were free to make policies exactly as they might like, this would imply a demand to empower the party's members. Neither of these conditions is the case, however, even for single party governments, let alone coalitions. On the one hand, regardless of who is empowered to make decisions within a party, those decision-makers must be attentive to the desires or demands of myriad interests outside of the party's formal boundaries. These include not only groups that might provide electoral support but also those that have the capacity to shape public opinion or to more or less vigorously support the party's electoral opponents. On the other hand, once in office a government must take account not only of the policies articulated by the party or parties it represents, but also the interests of groups with a capacity to aid or to obstruct the implementation of policy decisions.

The key point, in the terms of the functionalist paradigm, is that these groups are primarily interest articulators rather than interest aggregators; each group needs to take positions on only a limited range of questions, and collectively they offer a range of positions on those questions. Hence the individual supporter is forced to compromise his or her own preferences on any particular question to a much lesser degree—and by 'mixing and matching' groups active in different policy areas the individual can support a package of policy proposals that roughly approximates his or her preferences on all of them. This kind of targeted political action, however, implies costs to the supporter.

One set of costs involves time and money. Just as nominal party membership is likely to be inexpensive and undemanding in terms of effort, so too is nominal support of an interest group—and indeed many groups provide tangible benefits to their members (reduced admission charges at museums; free road service for motorists; special interest magazines) that exceed those benefits that are obviously available to party members.[9] To seriously try to influence the course of public affairs through such groups is likely to demand far more time and money, but then so too does serious party work. The most significant difference, however, is that activity through narrowly focused groups allows the citizen to concentrate his or her money and effort on those issues that are of greatest personal concern, where activity through party necessarily involves a level of dilution of effort by the inclusion of questions that are of lesser concern.

A second set of costs is psychic—the dissonance induced by being compelled to support policies with which one is not fully in agreement. This is largely avoided by the capacity to participate 'à la carte' that working through focused interest groups affords. Here, parties are at a clear disadvantage.

The third set of costs is embodied by the cognitive demands of connecting with and evaluating groups. As has been argued in supporting the idea of party identification, party provides a powerful shortcut to structuring one's relationship with the political world. For those with lower levels of 'cognitive mobilization', the simplification that party provides may even be a prerequisite to involvement, as well as limiting the dissonance costs. Those who are cognitively mobilized—including those who potentially would be party activists—are more likely to be able to 'pay' this cost, and therefore to have the option of political engagement that is not based on party membership.

Taken together, these considerations suggest that party membership will be relatively more attractive to politically interested citizens (and it must be noted that some sense that politics is interesting and important is generally a prerequisite for

[9] Although, as Lisa Young points out in the next chapter, some parties are beginning to use similar selective incentives to encourage party membership.

both partisan and extra-partisan involvement[10]) to the extent that there is an overarching ideology shared by citizen and party that means policies across apparently disparate policy areas are nonetheless logically connected, and to the extent that the citizen lacks the sophistication and other resources necessary for more differentiated involvement through channels other than party. Again, societal developments that may have, indirectly, been the result of party (governmental) policies like expanded educational opportunities and that raise questions—for example those associated with post-material values (e.g. Inglehart 1977)—that cross-cut the dominant left-right ideological dimension, but which have nothing to do with party organization *per se*, lead us to expect declining party involvement.

CONCLUSION

To the extent that parties exercise important political power, understanding the way in which they are governed will continue to be important to understanding democratic politics. Moreover, it should hardly be surprising if at least a significant proportion of those who are party members demand that they be given a major role in the governing of their party. From these observations, two questions arise.

The first is whether the empowerment of party members—that is, making the governance of the parties themselves more democratic—is essential to the democratization of the political system in which those parties operate. While that question has not been the subject of this chapter, it is important at least to note that it is a subject of some contention, both normatively (e.g. the conflict between theorists such as Pateman [(1970)] or Barber [(1984)] on the one hand and Sartori [(1965: 124—'democracy on a large scale is not the sum of many little democracies')] on the other) and empirically (e.g. Rahat et al. 2008). One aspect of this question would be whether the nearly universal decline in party membership is therefore a cause for concern with regard to the future of democracy.

The second question, and the one addressed in this chapter, is whether the decline in party membership should be attributed to failures by the parties and thus could be reversed by reform of the parties. While not giving a definitive answer, this chapter has suggested that there are good grounds to believe that party membership decline has been largely exogenous to decisions concerning party organizational structures and practices: that the decline has been a by-product of social changes that neither can—nor in most cases should—be reversed. If this is so, the conclusion may be that the identification of democracy with a straightforward conception of party government may need to be abandoned, as indeed one

[10] The exception would be involvement that is purely in response to social pressure or incentives.

might argue it already has been, as ideas of catch-all (Kirchheimer 1966), electoral-professional (Panebianco 1988: 262–7), franchise (Carty 2004), and cartel parties (Katz and Mair 1995) have displaced the mass party of integration as the dominant model for students of party, and as pluralist, consensus, and deliberative models of democracy have displaced simple majoritarianism among democratic theorists.

5

Party Members and Intra-Party Democracy

Lisa Young

The era of the mass party—if it ever truly existed—is clearly over. Party membership numbers are dwindling, and systematic studies of party members make it clear that the remaining members are relatively inactive in party life, and often unrepresentative of the party's electorate in both ideological and, more consistently, demographic terms. A small number of newly formed parties have achieved electoral success without a membership base, asserting that democracy takes place in the competition between parties rather than within the structures of party organizations. The boundary between party member and supporter has blurred, with supporters performing many of the traditional functions of members and—in some cases—acquiring the privileges members once enjoyed exclusively.

This chapter examines these trends and the ways in which parties' leaderships have responded to the exogenous changes that Katz examines in chapter 4 (this volume), and argues that parties' continued efforts to attract members is indicative of a perception that members are necessary to legitimize the party in democratic competition. Although membership numbers have declined, it is not evident that this has created a crisis of legitimacy for parties. Public demands for internally democratic parties appear to be satisfied by relatively permeable party structures that offer interested individuals the possibility of joining and influencing the party; the number of individuals who take advantage of the possibility is less significant.

WHAT IS PARTY MEMBERSHIP?

In *Political Parties*, Duverger devotes much of a chapter to the thorny question of what constitutes a 'member' of a political party, and how political scientists should distinguish among members, adherents, supporters and militants. Duverger's conception of a 'member' bears little resemblance to the contemporary meaning: for Duverger, membership in a mass party 'means in the first place completing and signing a membership form' which signals the member's psychological commitment to the party and willingness to offer financial support. 'To pay your subscription regularly, to pay a high rate of contribution that entails some sacrifice, such acts bear witness to the strength of the bonds that unite the member to the party. But they also reinforce the bonds: one's devotion to a community, like one's devotion to a fellow creature is proportional to the sacrifices one makes for it' (74).

Duverger's conception of party membership—which may have been romantic even when he wrote *Political Parties*—bears little resemblance to the obligations and conceptions of party membership in the contemporary era. As Richard S. Katz notes in chapter 4 (this volume), the number of individuals motivated to join political parties has declined sharply since Duverger's time for reasons unrelated to the parties themselves. Parties effectively define the parameters of membership, reflecting an internal calculus weighing costs against benefits for potential members. For Duverger's mass party, the privileges associated with party membership were sufficient to entice potential members to make the 'sacrifices' associated with paying regular dues and volunteering time for the organization. The exogenous changes that Katz outlines have fundamentally altered this calculus: the privileges associated with traditional party membership are insufficient to attract all but the most dedicated group of party loyalists or careerists. Parties have consequently altered the calculus, reducing the cost of membership on the one hand, and increasing apparent privileges of membership on the other.

The first dimension of this altered calculus is greater openness in eligibility for membership: relatively few parties place significant restrictions on who can join the organization. For most parties in established democracies, any individual eligible to vote in state elections is eligible for party membership. Some parties permit certain un-enfranchised individuals to join: they offer membership to youth not yet at voting age or immigrants who have not yet attained citizenship. This has been common practice for several Canadian political parties, which extend membership privileges to teenagers or immigrants who have not yet attained citizenship. Although the trend in defining party membership is towards openness, considerable variation remains. Sandri and Pauwels (2010: 1250–1) studied the membership openness of parties in Belgium and Italy, and found parties ranging from complete openness (requiring new members simply to pay a fee) to restrictive conditions, in which each application for membership is carefully investigated by several levels of party organization to ensure that members belong to no other party, follow party principles and conduct themselves in a manner consistent with the party's ethos. Notably, the party falling into this latter category, the *Alleanza Nazionale*, is an extreme right party with a limited membership.

A second dimension is that most parties make relatively modest demands on their members. Membership fees are low and voluntarism is, in fact, voluntary. There is compelling evidence, both from Whiteley's (2010) analysis of the ISSP data and from surveys of party members conducted in several democracies (Cross and Young 2004; Gallagher and Marsh 2004; Pedersen et al. 2004; Seyd and

Whiteley 2004), that the majority of party members are inactive. The plurality, and often the majority, of party members surveyed report spending no time on party affairs in a typical month, and attended only a small number (or no) meetings in a typical year. Where survey data of party members are available, they point to declining activism among party members. In surveys of party members conducted in the UK, Denmark, and Norway, party members were more likely to report that their involvement in the party had declined, rather than increased, over the prior five years (Seyd and Whiteley 2004: 358–9).

Moreover, party membership is often transitory rather than an enduring commitment. Citizens join parties to avail themselves of the privileges of membership such as voting in a leadership contest and then allow their membership to lapse. Whiteley (2010: 4–5) finds that former party members outnumber current party members in many countries and concludes that this may be a sign of declining membership. It may, however, also reflect a tendency toward transitory membership—many citizens have joined or been recruited into parties for a leadership or other internal contest, but have not maintained membership beyond this event. As parties move toward plebiscitary models, in which they enfranchise members to select candidates and vote on leadership choices, they create incentives for individuals to join the party to influence the outcome of these votes, but struggle to keep them as long-term members.

A third dimension of the altered calculus is an apparent effort by many parties to enhance the inducements to membership, both by empowering members to participate in key decisions about leaders and candidates, and in finding other incentives to offer. As Cross and Rahat note in chapters 7 and 9 (this volume), the general trend is towards party primaries in which members can vote directly. In doing so, parties have succeeded in bringing in waves of short-term members willing to pay a nominal fee in order to exercise one of these privileges of membership. Having lost many of the traditional incentives to membership, as Katz notes in chapter 4 (this volume), parties struggle to replace them. The British Conservative Party's membership webpage illustrates this, telling prospective members that, on joining, they will 'decide who represents the Party in local, general, and European elections; vote in elections for the Party Leader and in your local Association's AGM; Attend Party Conferences. In addition, you'll receive access to our Affinity Programme, which provides great discounts on a wide range of products.' The Conservatives mention no obligations of membership, beyond a £25 annual fee. The British Conservatives' offering of consumer discounts as an incentive to membership speaks to the very limited incentives parties can offer members during the lengthy periods between intra-party plebiscitary votes.

Although parties have altered the calculus of costs and benefits of membership, some have simultaneously reduced the exclusivity of membership by allowing party supporters to participate in activities that were once reserved for members. This has long been the case for major parties in the United States, where state regulation has given registered party supporters the ability to vote in primaries.

Some parties elsewhere are moving to emulate this: notably, the Liberal Party of Canada in 2012 created a formal category of 'supporter' which allows individuals who do not hold a party membership to vote in the party's leadership contest. In practical terms, the difference between 'members' and 'supporters' is limited. Individuals who have taken out a party membership in order to vote in a primary may have as minimal a psychological commitment to the party as the supporters of another party that permits supporters to vote in these contests. In either case, attachment to the party may be shallow, and involvement is likely to be short-lived. The blurring of the boundary between members and supporters raises important questions for research: are there systematic differences between the two groups in their attachment to the party, their orientation toward politics or their degree of activism? Do supporters become members and members lapse into supporters, or are these two groups distinct from one another? Until research gives an empirical understanding of these two groups, the full significance of the blurring of these two categories cannot be fully understood.

As membership has become a less robust and meaningful concept in most parties, the distinction between members and supporters has become less clear. There are two dimensions to this: first, some parties are offering the benefits traditionally reserved for members to their supporters, by implementing open primaries in which non-members can vote to choose a leader or local candidate. Second, supporters are in some instances more extensively engaged in the life of the party than members. In several established democracies, including the UK, Germany, and Canada, non-members comprise a significant proportion of campaign volunteers (Dalton 1996; Fisher et al. 2011; Cross and Young forthcoming). Likewise, donors outnumber members for many parties and provide a greater share of the party's income.

DO PARTIES WANT MEMBERS?

The question 'do parties want members?' suggests that parties are not membership organizations in an essential way; that there is an identifiable party separable from the membership. The party, in this conception, is the party leadership—the leader, the parliamentary party, and the professionals who surround the leader and maintain the routine operations of the party. Because of the availability of political professionals to advise party leaders and maintain the routine operations of the party, and because of the increasingly sophisticated demands associated with this, party leaders' need for party members as volunteers has declined (Scarrow 2000). Pollsters have largely supplanted local party notables who once would have reported to leaders on public opinion on the ground; sophisticated advertising campaigns have reduced the importance of local door-knocking efforts; even local knowledge about which families are likely party supporters has been replaced by centrally-maintained databases tracking voting inclinations. Candidates and parties are able to recruit supporters as temporary campaign workers, sometimes outnumbering party members (Fisher et al. 2011).

Compounding this, members of the party elite may perceive members to be a liability to the party in its pursuit of electoral success. For a party focused on electoral success, 'extensive participation of members in formulation of politics and personnel selection tends to be counter-productive, as it reduces the efficiency and flexibility of a party's organization' (Seisselberg 1996: 718). This is a lesson that the leaders of advocacy groups have learned: the common organizational form for these groups is a staff-led model, with supporters (who show their support through financial contributions), rather than members. This model gives the leaders of these groups the ability to pursue the advocacy strategy they perceive to be the most efficacious, with few external constraints on their strategic choices (Young and Everitt 2004).

In certain partisan contexts, particularly in parties prone to internal factionalism, empowering members or enlarging membership boundaries brings with it the risk of fostering internal conflicts (Sandri and Pauwels 2010: 1254). In these cases, the party leadership may perceive its membership structure to be a liability, but factional leaders or challengers to the leadership will likely position themselves as the champions of members' rights.

Relatively open membership structures, when combined with formal power for members, expose party elites to significant risk. The Progressive Conservative Party in the Canadian province of Alberta allows individuals to purchase a party membership for $5 on the day of the party's leadership contest and then vote for the party's leader. Because the party forms the government (and has done so for the better part of four decades), this practice allows eligible voters who have no prior connection to the party to elect a new Premier for the province, and opens the process to potential interference from political opponents. Why would a party's elite expose itself to such a significant risk? The very openness of the process provides a mechanism to achieve some degree of leadership change and some veneer of responsiveness to public wishes to extend the party's governing dynasty.

The parties that have emerged in the past two decades with limited or non-existent membership structures have been those formed as vehicles for charismatic leaders; in such personalistic parties, members are particularly perceived as a potential threat, as they might constrain the leader from pursuing his political agenda. The clearest instance of this is the Netherlands' Party for Freedom, or PVV, which holds 25 seats in the national legislature. The only member of the party is its leader, Geert Wilders (Vossen 2010). Even the other legislative seat holders are not considered party members. Supporters of the party can donate via the party's website, but cannot join as members. The PVV is a relatively young party, so little can be concluded about the potential for a party without members to persist over time, but its initial electoral success does suggest that a party without members can contest elections effectively. It might be more challenging for a party without members to mount an effective election campaign in the context of a single member electoral system which requires organization on the ground in support of individual candidates. A second instance of a party without members, also a vehicle for a high-profile party leader, is the *Forza Italia*, formed in 1993 as a vehicle for Silvio Berlusconi's political ambition. When Berlusconi established the party, it had no provision for membership; rather, supporters formed 'clubs' which mobilized supporters at election time (Paolucci 2006). Seisselberg (1996) described these clubs as the 'endpoint of an extensive hierarchy' charged with shaping the party in the local context and hosting local functions, but exerting no influence over the central party. In 1997, however, seeking democratic legitimation, the party created a membership system. Membership levels remained low, and members were offered few opportunities for involvement or influence in party decision-making (Raniolo 2006).

The decision by *Forza Italia* leaders to create a membership structure, albeit affording members little influence, suggests that under most circumstances party leaders perceive the need for some kind of membership structure that legitimizes the party in the eyes of voters. The relative openness of membership practices in most mainstream parties in established democracies speaks to some enduring value that party elites place on members. Although many major national and international advocacy groups have maintained their member-free, staff-led organizational forms, very few parties have done the same.[1]

Faced with a declining supply of members, most parties have responded by altering the balance between membership entitlements and costs in an effort to reverse declining membership numbers. The general move toward plebiscitary forms of IPD can be understood as a response by party elites to declining membership numbers (Seyd 1999). No longer able to offer significant material incentives to membership, and competing with many other organizations to provide social incentives, parties are left with solidary and instrumental incentives: individuals may join with a view to supporting the party's ideology or policy platform, or they may join in order to influence the outcome of intra-party contests for leadership or nomination. By extending members' ability to influence these intra-party contests, parties are arguably trying to bolster their membership numbers in order to increase their electoral success and improve public perceptions of their legitimacy.

[1] The definition of 'membership' in advocacy organizations is a complex issue in itself. Some organizations, like various national or subnational Automobile Associations, sell 'memberships' which entitle the member to benefit from various services, but not to vote on any governance issues. For these types of organizations, advocacy is a secondary function. Organizations that focus primarily on advocacy tend to eschew the terminology of 'membership', focusing instead on 'supporters' who donate to support the cause. Putnam (1995) and others have termed this 'chequebook activism' or 'chequebook membership'.

While parties without members can be electorally viable, they cannot claim to be internally democratic.[2] Members' participation in parties' internal affairs, particularly the selection of leaders and candidates, serves as a check on the party leadership and provides interested citizens with a means of influencing the direction of a party. Parties that conduct their internal affairs in a 'democratic' fashion signal to the public that they have internalized a democratic ethos, arguably adding to their credibility as potential governments or participants in governing coalitions. Mersel (2006: 97) suggests that 'it is arguable that a party that is not internally democratic cannot really be externally democratic; in the long run, the internal agenda and predispositions would be bound to influence the party's external attitudes and activities'. This logic underpins the ban on undemocratic parties in some countries, most frequently those that have experienced authoritarian rule (Mersel 2006; also see van Biezen, this volume). In countries that have not had such experience, public opinion and media scrutiny are the effective checks on parties' commitment to internal democracy. Although no systematic examination has been conducted, it would be fair to say that media scrutiny of parties' internal practices does not produce consistent changes to the party's support in the electorate.

Beyond this legitimizing function, party members are often portrayed in the academic literature as critical conduits linking the party to the broader electorate. This portrait is rooted in the mass party model, characterized by numerically large party memberships representative of the party's electoral base. When party memberships encapsulate significant portions of the electorate and party rules give those groups plausible influence over the determination of party policy and the selection of party leaderships, the idea of IPD coexists comfortably with concepts of broader national democracy, as party members serve as a mechanism of connection and accountability to the party's electorate. Party membership, in this view, is valuable to both the party and to democracy more broadly, as party members 'select and socialize candidates for elective office . . . stimulate citizen participation in politics and . . . provide political education by acting as "ambassadors in the community"' (Whiteley 2009: 253). Although party leaders may recognize the potential political costs of membership, their need for legitimacy outweighs it in most instances.

The extreme examples discussed here—from the single-member PVV to the Alberta PCs—suggest that the particular circumstances of a party will dictate the calculations of the party elite with respect to the value of members and the kinds of powers that should be granted to members. Parties with formal membership structures remain the norm, and create considerable pressure on other parties to

[2] Parties in the United States might be considered an exception to this statement: the two key internal democratic functions—selection of candidates and of the leader—have been removed from the party's control through legislated primaries and caucuses. Nevertheless, American parties have devised means to involve supporters in the selection of party executives, delegates to party conventions and the like.

conform to this expectation. Parties that blur the boundaries between supporter and member and extend membership privileges widely may reduce the value of membership in a traditional sense, but also contribute to public expectations that parties be internally democratic, and therefore in need of members.

HOW MANY MEMBERS DOES DEMOCRACY REQUIRE?

When examining contemporary academic literature regarding party members, the most prominent trend identified across established democracies is a decline in the rate of membership in political parties (Katz, Mair et al. 1992; Whiteley 2009, 2010; Scarrow and Gezgor 2010). We must be cautious in our interpretation of the trend. The starting point, in both normative and empirical terms, for establishing this pattern of decline is often the 'golden age' of party membership in the immediate post-war era. The relatively high rates of party membership in this era were fostered by a complimentarity of the expansion of the contemporary state and parties' need for members during this period (Katz 1990). While it is important to note that this period represents a high water mark in party membership, it is nevertheless the appropriate point of comparison, as it also represents the normative ideal against which the contemporary reality is compared. This was, according to Mair (2005), the period in which the representative and constitutional functions of parties were in harmony, with extensive active memberships fulfilling the representative function of parties and thus legitimizing the role of parties in office.

Many explanations have been posited for a decline in party membership beyond the post-war era. Some focus on parties' declining demand for members as volunteers and financial contributors. The advent of polling, advertising and mass communications has made parties less reliant on members as volunteers, giving parties little incentive to recruit them, except as resources in intra-party contests such as leadership races (Scarrow 2000). Changes in election campaigning, with growing reliance on mass advertising, and automated telephone, e-mail, and social media communication have shifted the balance in campaigns toward more centralized, professionalized campaigning.[3]

A second element of the demand-side explanation relates to parties' increasing reliance on the state for financial support. This trend is widespread in established (and many emerging) democracies, and has clear implications for parties' need for

[3] There is, however, an emerging body of evidence suggesting that local (and largely volunteer-based) campaigning has a significant impact on the outcome of election contests, and Norris (2000) posits a tendency toward 'post-modern' campaigning, in which localized campaign efforts coexist with more professionalized national campaigns.

members as volunteer labour and as a source of revenue.[4] In the most comprehensive cross-national analysis of national rates of party membership available, Whiteley (2010: 2) finds evidence supporting the contention that state regulation of parties contributes to a decline in the propensity toward party membership, noting that parties reliant on the state for funding 'have little incentive to recruit or retain members for financial reasons'.[5] The provision of public funds and the potential to raise funds from a broader range of donors using techniques of direct mail solicitation may also have liberated parties somewhat from their members as a source of financial support.

Other explanations, such as that offered by Katz in chapter 4 (this volume), suggest that the supply of potential party members has dwindled as a function of societal and political change. Civil service and other reforms limited the range of selective incentives parties could offer their members as inducements to join, forcing parties to rely on less compelling solidary incentives (see Seyd and Whiteley 1992; Young and Cross 2002a). Katz (1990: 145) argues that as post-war economic expansion slowed, parties had little choice but to take actions unpopular with their supporters, communal ties eroded, and citizens' political autonomy grew, all contributing to a decline in party membership. In other accounts, post-materialist citizens are uninterested in traditional forms of political engagement such as party membership, preferring instead the more immediate satisfaction of consumer boycotts or advocacy activities. This view is supported (somewhat loosely) by Cross and Young's (2008) study of youth activists in left/center parties and campus advocacy groups: we found that campus activists tended to view parties as ineffective means of achieving desired policy outcomes. The belief that parties are ineffective vehicles for policy change is widely shared in the broader public, and may well contribute to disinclination to join parties. Other observers have noted that disinterested or uninformed citizens have abandoned both voting and party membership. Generational change that is driving down electoral turnout is, not surprisingly, having similar effects on rates of party membership.

Because we lack consistent time-series data measuring parties' memberships, we do not know whether certain types of parties are suffering more precipitous declines in membership than others, or whether the overall trend toward declining membership is fairly consistent across party families. It is also unclear whether parties' moves toward plebiscitary democratic models serve to increase

[4] It must, however, be noted that many accounts of the emergence of state funding (for example Katz and Mair 1995) suggest that parties turn to the state for funds in response to declining ability to raise money and volunteer labour.

[5] This conclusion should be drawn with some caution, however. The variable that shows a consistent inverse relationship with party membership in Whiteley's model is a measure of 'regulatory quality' which refers to the 'ability of governments to formulate and implement effective regulatory regimes'. Whiteley surmises that 'countries that regulate extensively may also over-regulate their party systems'. The more direct measure—a party regulation index constructed from IDEA sources—has a much more modest and often not statistically significant relationship with rates of party membership.

membership, or at least to stem its decline. This type of analysis would require extensive and reliable membership data from the parties themselves, and is likely impossible to obtain. This stands in the way of developing a more nuanced understanding of the differential patterns of decline among parties.

What, if anything, is the significance of the apparent decline in party membership for democracy writ large? Scholars who study parties have, perhaps predictably, tended to view this trend with alarm, although for a variety of reasons. Declining party membership has roughly coincided with a decline in voter turnout, rising cynicism and distrust in politicians, and hollowed-out forms of participation. As Mair (2005) notes, this cross-national trend is remarkable in the uniformity of its direction and its universality across established democracies. To the extent that declining party membership is one of the symptoms of this overall decline, it raises questions about the overall evolution of democratic systems. The gap between non-participating citizens and the political elite grows in the absence of mass political participation, and throws into question our notions of political equality and accountability.

In some accounts, declining voter turnout, increasing partisan volatility and growing cynicism or indifference toward politics are not simply phenomena that have emerged simultaneously with the decline in party membership, but rather are a product of the evolution of political parties from membership-based, participatory organizations into leader-dominated, electorally-focused state-supported entities. This is the case Peter Mair (2005: 21) makes, arguing that what has emerged is a mutually reinforcing process 'in which the citizens stay at home while the [state-dependent] parties become, or seek to become, governors'. While parties' capacity to govern is not impaired by this phenomenon, their legitimacy comes into question: 'Parties may be able to fill public offices, but they may no longer be able to justify doing so' (23). Parties without extensive and active membership bases lack the connections to civil society that justify their competition for office, that legitimize their selection of leaders and that make them genuinely responsive to the electorate in a rich and meaningful way between elections.

Another source of concern regarding declining party membership focuses on the interplay between party membership, on the one hand, and the rise of alternative intermediary organizations like interest groups, on the other. This concern is predicated on the idea that party membership is superior to involvement in alternative intermediary organizations because party membership inculcates more desirable participatory tendencies, notably a propensity to mediate among competing interests rather than articulate a single point of view on a narrow range of issues. Seyd and Whiteley (2004: 363) articulate this concern: declining party membership has the effect of promoting special interest politics at the expense of responsible party government. 'Generally, when parties are weak, special interest groups become strong. Such groups are interested in getting benefits for themselves and passing on the costs of these to the wider society. In contrast, political parties have to be responsible in the sense of explaining how they propose to pay for any benefits which they seek.' Here, the concern is less about disconnection from society or the electorate and more a worry about the kind of public discourse that emerges in a group-dominated political system. Interests are articulated forcefully and convincingly, but the agents of interest aggregation are weak and poorly connected to civil society. This argument presupposes that interest aggregation occurs at the level of party members, although there is some reason to believe that it is more likely to occur within the party's elite.

Alternatively, a strong case can be made that it matters relatively little that 'party density' declines from 7 per cent of the electorate to 5, or some similar shift (Scarrow and Gezgor 2010: 4). Knowing that the majority of these members were relatively inactive, we can conclude that parties did not suffer a devastating loss of volunteer labour or income, so they remain able to discharge their functions at election time. In at least some instances, party supporters are filling the seats vacated by members in the campaign office (Fisher et al. 2011). As mechanisms of linkage to the electorate, party members have arguably become substantially less important, so the disintegration of the linkage function is modest at best. In fact, Allern and Pedersen (2007) suggest that changing forms of internal party organization are enhancing parties' capacity to fulfil their electoral functions, as parties become less constrained by a sense of accountability to their members and their members' policy commitments. They also posit a trade-off between quantitative and qualitative aspects of party organization, suggesting that declining membership may enhance the participatory and deliberative aspects of internal party democracy, as a smaller group of members may enjoy opportunities to engage in more meaningful participatory opportunities. Although party members are fewer in number, they have the opportunity to engage more extensively and meaningfully in party life. (While plausible, this argument ignores the shift toward plebiscitary democracy noted in much of the literature.)

If a decline of some 20 per cent or so in party density is not of critical importance to the legitimacy of parties in the eyes of the electorate, and does not impair parties' capacity to execute their core functions, we are left with the question of whether there is a 'tipping point' in the decline of party membership. Is there some point at which declining party membership becomes critical and parties become illegitimate in the eyes of the electorate? Mair (2005), among others, implies that this point has been reached, that the triumph of the party as public utility marks the point at which the internal organization of the party no longer proffers sufficient legitimacy for parties to make representational claims in the broader political sphere. For those who do not agree that the tipping point has been reached, several questions emerge: How will we know that party membership rates have declined to a critical point? Are the key indicators a decline in public trust of parties, the rise of populist parties and alternative intermediary organizations?

Alternatively, there may be no real tipping point. Perhaps even the relatively small memberships contemporary parties can muster are sufficient to make parties appear connected to the electorate and attentive to democratic norms in their internal operations. Perhaps, in low membership systems, we can see party meetings and leadership and candidate selection contests as a means of reassuring voters that the party has internalized the basic norms of democracy, and understands that leaders must have a democratic mandate, even if it is only from a relatively small group of long-time activists or recruits drawn into the party for that particular contest.

Canada offers an interesting case study in this respect. Canadian scholars generally agree that no Canadian party has ever become a true mass party in the European sense of the term. Rates of party membership have always been low and apparently continue to decline. Cross and Young estimate party density in Canada to be approximately 2 per cent, although this is much lower than what Whiteley (2010) reports based on cross-national survey data.[6] Party democracy, in the Canadian context, has given these relatively small groups of members control over the selection of candidates and party leaders (in the past via a delegated convention, but more recently through direct election or a hybrid of the two). Generally, membership has been a transitory phenomenon, with numbers spiking when nominations and leadership contests occur, and falling sharply in the interim. The notion of intra-party and local party democracy is deeply cherished in the Canadian experience, on the grounds that local control over candidate selection gives members some control over the party. In this regard, the relative permeability of Canadian party organizations is significant, as it offers the possibility that citizens could—if so motivated—access the machinery of IPD to participate in selection of a candidate or party leader.

A similar case can be made with respect to parties in the United States. American parties lack formal membership structures, although they do have activists who participate as party officials, delegates to party conventions and the like. The absence of mass party organization is replaced, in one sense, by the high degree of permeability of the parties in their leadership and candidate selection functions. Primary elections serve as a means for party supporters (or even non-supporters, in the case of open primaries) to vote in candidate and leadership selection contests. This lends legitimacy to the parties' monopoly on public office and, in its own limited way, gives the party roots in civil society. Although there are discontents with parties in the United States and Canada, there is little evidence that these discontents are greater than with parties elsewhere, or that these parties are perceived to be less legitimate political organizations than parties elsewhere.

[6] The Cross and Young estimate was based on parties' reported membership rates, while the Whiteley data derive from mass surveys. The latter source likely overestimates party membership, particularly given the transitory character of party membership in Canada. Moreover, most Canadian political parties are not vertically integrated, so reports of party membership may reflect membership in a provincial political party.

DOES DEMOCRACY REQUIRE THAT PARTY MEMBERS BE REPRESENTATIVE OF THE ELECTORATE?

> *When the [Socialist] party includes among its members the owners of factories and workshops, it may be noticed that these, notwithstanding personal goodwill and notwithstanding the pressure which is exercised on them by the party, have the same economic conflict with their employees as have those employers whose convictions harmonize with their economic status, and who think not as socialists but as bourgeois.*
>
> *Michels, 352.*

If members' participation in democratic intra-party decision-making is a significant form of linkage between citizens and the state, questions emerge surrounding the composition of the party's membership. A case might be made that IPD is more legitimate when party members are demographically representative of the electorate: policies adopted by a party membership that is of higher socio-economic status, or older, than the electorate might, for instance, be unrepresentative of the policies desired by the broader electorate.

Because parties appeal to, and purport to represent, specific segments of the electorate, a more reasonable expectation is that parties' memberships be representative of the party's electoral base. Labour parties would have more trade unionists as members, and centrist parties more affluent professionals. Empirically, evidence abounds showing that party members are not demographically representative of their electorates, and that as party membership rates decline this divergence may be increasing.

Surveys of party members conducted over the past decade and a half have generally found that party members are older, on average, than electors (Cross and Young 2004; Gallagher and Marsh 2004; Pedersen et al. 2004; Seyd and Whiteley 2004). Because these analyses are cross-sectional, they cannot determine definitively whether this is a lifecycle or cohort effect. In a recent article examining changes in the composition of European parties' memberships between the 1990s and 2000s, Scarrow and Gezgor (2010: 8) found that in nine of twelve countries studied, the age differential between party members and the population had grown over time. This is suggestive of a cohort effect, with younger citizens less inclined to join political parties than were their elders at the same age. Certainly, such an effect would echo that found in studies of voter turnout in established democracies. Moreover, there is considerable cross-national evidence of generational change in other political activity, so it is reasonable to make the argument that declining rates of party membership among young people comprise part of the broader trend away from traditional forms of political engagement. Cross and Young's (2008) study of young party members and group activists support this, finding that young party members are considerably more 'traditionalist' than their advocacy group counterparts, tending to rely more heavily on traditional news sources, being mobilized to political action through their family, and learning about the political system through their formal education.

Aging party memberships are a source of concern from two perspectives. First, to the extent that they are a product of a cohort effect, they signal an overall decline in parties' ability to recruit members. Second, the relative absence of young party members suggests that parties are unrepresentative of, and out of touch with, a segment of the electorate. In their study of young party members in six European democracies, Bruter and Harrison (2009b: 1285) conclude that there is a gap between the preferences of each type of young party member and what the literature tells us of their elder counterparts that 'may explain some of the recurrent tensions between a dominant but aging general party membership and a small, dynamic segment of young members, which many older members perceive as arrogant and threatening'. Parties unable to accommodate evolving participatory preferences of even their own young members will likely struggle to engage with younger voters, reinforcing the gap between the electorate and the party leadership.

Beyond these differences in age profile, there is persistent evidence that party memberships are disproportionately male, and somewhat more affluent on average than their electorates (Scarrow and Gezgor 2010). Patterns of pervasive under-representation of groups are a concern, as they are symptomatic of identical patterns of exclusion and under-representation in political life as Sarah Childs points out in chapter 6 (this volume). This is significant in itself, but also arguably from the point of view of IPD, if we understand parties to play a particularly important role in structuring patterns of representation in the broader democratic context. The under-representation of politically salient groups in party membership tends to be replicated in the under-representation of these groups in political elites, including elected office. This in turn may affect policy outcomes and state responsiveness, although the linkage between numeric and substantive representation of interests is notoriously difficult to substantiate.

A related concern is the ideological unrepresentativeness of the party members. The starting point for this discussion is John May's (1973) 'law of curvilinearity'. Employing a rational choice approach, Mays argues that both party elites and voters will be less extreme in their views than non-elite party members. This argument is based on several assumptions about motivation to activism. Members of an elite, or 'leaders' in May's terminology, may be motivated to political activism by a range of inducements, including the desire to hold office, the perquisites that accompany office-holding, and prestige. To the extent that such motivations animate members of a partisan elite, we would anticipate a moderation of views. For partisans without such ambitions, however, the only motivation to activism is ideological commitment. In support of this contention, Mays cites Leon Epstein, who asserts that 'the voluntary and amateur nature of [local constituency associations] ensures that they attract zealots in the party cause, and particularly so at the local leadership level, where there are many routine political chores which only the devoted are likely to perform' (Epstein, cited in Mays 1973: 149). It follows from this that extremists have a greater incentive to participate in party life than do moderates. Mays consequently anticipates a curvilinear relationship between degree of activism within the party and ideological extremism, such that party leaders and 'non-leaders' (occasional and lukewarm party supporters) will be less extreme than 'sub-leaders' (regional and local party office holders, constituency activists, and passive grassroots members).

Empirical studies testing the validity of May's Law have, for the most part, concluded that there is little evidence supporting the proposition. Surveys of American, Austrian, British, German, and Scandinavian party activists have concluded that grassroots activists are generally more moderate than middle-level activists holding regional party executive functions or participating in national party conferences (Kitschelt 1989: 405). Several empirical studies in Britain (Butler 1960; Shaw 1988), Europe (Merkyl 1980; Dalton 1985), and the United States (Miller et al. 1986; Miller 1988; Polsby and Wildavsky 1991) have found that activists in general tend to be substantially more extreme in their attitudes than voters. In their study of Labour activists, however, Seyd and Whiteley (1992) found little evidence of extremism among either active or inactive party members. In her study of British voters, party activists, and elites, Norris (1995) found that on a wide range of issues, opinion was organized in a linear fashion, with party 'leaders' (candidates and MPs), consistently more extreme in their views than party members, who were in turn more extreme than the party's supporters in the electorate. Norris concludes that the most plausible explanation for this phenomenon is that 'politicians willing to face the considerable costs and risks of standing for election have to be strongly committed to party principles' (43). Norris' findings are particularly troubling for proponents of May's theory, as critics have suggested that British and American parties are 'among the few Western democracies where there is some likelihood that the law will be confirmed' (Kitschelt 1989: 420). This assertion is made on the grounds that both countries have two-party systems which force radical ideologues into mainstream parties. Both countries also have highly competitive party systems, a condition that fuels conflict between pragmatists and ideologues. Finally, both have loosely coupled party organizations which make it possible for small radical minorities to exercise a relatively great influence within the party organization (ibid. Kitschelt 1989: 421).

While party members tend to be systematically unrepresentative of their party's electorate in demographic terms, the evidence is less compelling that members are systematically unrepresentative in ideological terms. Coupled with the decline in rates of party membership, patterns of under-representation and ideological extremism might be expected to intensify. Examining precisely these phenomena, Scarrow and Gezgor (2010: 17) find no evidence that declining party membership has led to a radicalization of the membership base, concluding that 'party memberships may be shrinking, but at least so far this has not meant that parties' grassroots are becoming some kind of odd subculture, no longer able to provide legitimacy because they are too different from the rest of society'. Thus, while unrepresentativeness of party memberships remains a source of some concern, its intersection with the decline in rates of party membership does not exacerbate the concern.

CONCLUSION

This review of current trends regarding party membership demonstrates that the character of party membership has evolved over the past several decades, entailing less commitment on the part of members, but also offering greater privileges to members as parties move toward more participatory, plebiscitary forms of democracy. Despite this, party membership is declining, with younger citizens less inclined to join parties than were members of prior generations. Parties' memberships are, consequently, significantly less representative of the electorate in demographic terms. Despite this, there is no systematic evidence suggesting that party memberships are consistently unrepresentative of their party's electorate in ideological orientation. Although the linkage function attributed to party members has undeniably waned, the blurring of the distinction between party members and supporters suggests that supporters may be replacing members in some respects, and that parties' increasing openness to supporters facilitates this.

Over the past two decades, political scientists have significantly added to our understanding of party members, both by surveying members of national political parties, and by locating party members and former party members in mass surveys. As the research agenda moves forward, trying to come to terms with the reasons for and implications of declining rates of party membership will be a significant focus for research. Neither of the research programs noted above is entirely equipped to address some of the key questions that emerge from this trend. If our focus is on change over time, panel studies of party members will be key, as they will help us to identify the motivations driving members to maintain their party involvement or to allow it to lapse. Research designs that can capture both active party supporters and party members will be essential to understanding the distinction between these two categories. These analyses will also better our understanding of how transitory a phenomenon party membership is. Comparative analyses across parties will be important to try to determine whether there are consistent patterns of membership decline across all party families, or whether these are concentrated in certain types of party.

Finally, scholars who study political parties must give more systematic theoretical and empirical attention to the interplay between the quantity and quality of party membership, on the one hand, and the overall health of the political system, on the other. Are democratic deficits greater in countries with declining party membership? If so, is the declining party membership a cause or an effect? Are parties held in higher esteem by citizens when they are permeable to citizen participation? Do citizens' evaluations of parties as institutions correlate in any way with the parties' internal membership practices?

6

Intra-Party Democracy: A Gendered Critique and a Feminist Agenda

Sarah Childs

INTRODUCTION[1]

The extant IPD, and gender and politics literatures have rarely engaged explicitly with each other's concerns. Not only is attention to issues of gender rare within the traditional parties literature, the IPD literature, where it does consider gender, does so mostly in respect of candidate selection and internal party representation. Here, demands for sex quotas are usually found to conflict with greater internal party democracy. At the same time, the focus of much contemporary gender and politics literature has been mostly elsewhere: legislatures. When they do address issues of internal party structures, relations and power, gender and politics scholars do so mostly without drawing on the conceptual frameworks of IPD. This chapter brings these two approaches together and makes them speak to, rather than past, each other, setting out an initial gendered reading of the IPD literature, and outlining future research questions, drawing wherever possible on illustrative empirical studies. It takes as its starting point extant claims about what constitutes IPD, recognizing that there are debates about what this refers to, and the extent to which it exists in practice. It then asks what difference it makes to subject such accounts to a feminist critique. Without pretending to survey and engage with all aspects of IPD, the chapter pulls together concerns shared by gender and politics, and IPD scholars; those which at this point seem the most salient, namely, women's parliamentary representation, women's party structures, and women's influence on party policymaking. In addressing these, the relationship between party and system-level democracy and gender is also necessarily considered.

This 'think-piece' chapter is unlikely to answer all of the questions that feminist scholars might ask of IPD, nor, unlike some other chapters in this volume, can it offer

[1] I'd like to thank Lisa Young and the other IPD workshop members and contributors to this book, especially William P. Cross and Richard S. Katz, as well as Drude Dahlerup, Richard Heffernan, and Joni Lovenduski for comments on earlier drafts of this chapter.

a comprehensive empirical basis for many of the issues and concerns it raises. There is a lack of contemporary, systematic comparative empirical research necessary to test some of the claims that the IPD literature beg when considered from a gendered perspective (at least in terms of what is published in English). Hence, for the most part, the normative, conceptual and empirical questions raised here invite, and would benefit from, subsequent research, of both single case-studies by country and, or party-family experts, as well as broader larger 'n' comparative analysis (Kittilson 2011b). Nor is it possible for a single gender and politics scholar to be fully conversant with research for all of the countries of the world. Indeed, part of the aim of this chapter is to present an initial research agenda for gender and politics as well as party scholars to apply to individual cases. Only once these data, both qualitative as well as quantitative, are built up will broader comparative studies be possible.

GENDER AND POLITICS SCHOLARSHIP: THE 'FEMINIZATION' OF POLITICAL PARTIES

Over the last decade or so, empirical studies of women and electoral politics have focused extensively on women's descriptive representation seeking to explain women's under-representation in legislatures relative to their presence in the wider population (for example, Norris and Lovenduski 1995; Kittilson 2006; Krook 2010). More limited research examines women's presence in executives and cabinets (Curtin 2008: Murray 2010b; Bauer and Tremblay 2011), in part because the numbers of women elected or appointed to these has only recently increased. Turning to more specific questions about the nature of women's inclusion and integration within political parties, there is the now rather dated, but key edited collection, *Gender and Party Politics* (Norris and Lovenduski 1993), and, of course, individual party analyses (most notably Young (2000) on US and Canadian parties and, more recently, Wiliarty (2010) on the German CDU, and Childs and Webb (2012) on the UK Conservative party. Broadly speaking, gendered analysis finds that political parties have 'long ignored women's demands for representation' (Kittilson 2011b).

More than a decade ago Lisa Young (2000) outlined a set of criteria by which a political party's *feminist* credentials could be assessed. Her schema was subsequently augmented (Childs 2008), in light of the acknowledgement that parties may re-gender in different ways. As Table 6.1 shows a *feminized* political party—one that integrates women as political actors and addresses women's concerns (Lovenduski 2005a)—need not, in principle, sign up to a feminist project (of whatever type). Consequently, political parties can be distinguished on the basis of whether they make positive, neutral, or negative responses, along both dimensions of feminization.

This typology suggests that gender and politics research on political parties should investigate the following (a research agenda that goes beyond the limits of,

TABLE 6.1 *Feminization and party types*

	1st dimension		2nd Dimension
	Integration of women parliamentary elites	Integration of women party members	Integration of women's concerns
Responsive Party I (feminist both dimensions)	High/moderate representation; well designed and fully implemented quotas; or absence of obstacles to women's representation	Parity of members; women's organizations are fully integrated into party policy making	Positive and in feminist direction
Responsive Party II (feminist 2nd dimension)	Low representation; absent or poorly designed/implemented quotas	Fewer women members; integrated women's organizations	Positive and feminist
Co-optive Party (feminist on 1st dimension, neutral 2nd)	High/moderate representation; may have quotas	Parity of members; auxiliary women's organizations	Negative (women's concerns are not addressed) or positive, (women's concerns are addressed) but addressed in a neutral direction
Anti-feminist Co-optive Party (feminist on 1st dimension, anti-feminist on 2nd)	High/moderate representation; may have quotas	Parity of members; either anti-feminist women's organizations fully integrated into party policy making or 'auxiliaries'	Positive but in anti-feminist direction
Non-responsive	Low representation; absent quotas	Indifferent to representation of women; auxiliary women's organizations rather than integrated ones	Negative
Anti-feminist Party	Low representation; rejects principle and practice of quotas	Indifferent to representation of women; either anti-feminist women's organizations fully integrated into party policymaking or auxiliary women's organization	Positive in an anti-feminist direction

Source: Amended from L. Young (2000); Childs (2008).

even as it informs, this chapter) (Childs and Webb 2012): (1) the level of women's participation in party structures, including, but importantly not limited to, the parliamentary party. Such enquiries should explore whether the party employs specific mechanisms in both party structures and the parliamentary party to guarantee women's descriptive representation; (2) whether women's participation is substantive across the party's various structures and activities or symbolic and limited to certain forms or places; (3) the nature of the role, remit, and ideology of any women's organizations and, in particular, whether these are integrated formally into the wider party structure and policymaking bodies, and to whom they are accountable, both upwards and downwards; (4) whether a party regards women as a corporate entity capable of being represented (both descriptively and substantively) and if so, whether the party is susceptible to feminist arguments for this. This might include whether the party makes gender-based and/or feminist claims rather than non-gendered, neutral, or anti-feminist claims; and finally (5) the extent to which party policies are gendered and, or feminist.[2] Such research should also establish Kittilson's claim (2006: 41) that parties may find it easier 'to incorporate new ideas' than to 'fundamentally reorganize power distribution' within the party.

WOMEN'S PARTICIPATION AS PARTY MEMBERS

Political party membership is often said to be roughly 50:50, male: female, albeit pyramidal in shape, with fewer women near the top (Lovenduski 2005a; Kittilson 2011b). Overall party membership numbers are, whilst notoriously problematic to confirm (Mair and van Biezen 2001; and Young, this volume) experiencing a clear downward trend across established democracies. It might seem counter-intuitive to suggest, as some gender and politics literature does, that feminist women turned towards political parties, at least in some Western countries in the 1970s and 1980s (Lovenduski and Norris 1993; Young 2000; Lovenduski 2005a; Russell 2005; Kittilson 2011b). Susan Scarrow (1999: 353) maintains that neither candidate sex quotas, nor calls to recruit more women by political parties, have significantly altered the composition of the wider party memberships. Cross-national data from twelve European democracies comparing the 1990s to the early twenty-first century show that men continue to outnumber women in all of the countries of study, as Table 6.2 demonstrates (Scarrow and Gezgor 2010). The differences are all statistically significant in the 1990s, as all are, bar France, in the 2000s. Nevertheless, as the change column indicates, there has been some movement:

[2] What constitutes a 'feminist' policy is taken to be an empirical question.

TABLE 6.2 *Gender and party membership (% male party members compared with the general population)*

	1990s			2000s			
	Party members % male	Popn % male	Diff	Party members % male	Popn % male	Diff	Change
Belgium	63	48	15	60	50	10	–
Denmark	60	49	11	67	50	17	+
France	65	48	17	51	46	5	–
Germany	69	46	23	64	48	16	–
Great Britain	58	48	10	61	46	15	+
Greece	73	48	25	63	43	20	–
Ireland	69	50	19	61	44	17	–
Italy	73	49	24	77	47	30	+
Luxembourg	78	53	25	60	50	10	–
Netherlands	61	49	12	56	43	13	+
Portugal	72	48	24	66	40	26	+
Spain	77	48	29	68	49	19	–

Source: Amended from Scarrow and Gezgor (2010: 831); comparison of ESS surveys from the 2000s with Eurobarometer surveys from the 1990s.

differences in party membership have reduced in half of the countries (Belgium, France, Greece, Germany, Ireland, Luxembourg, and Spain) and increased in the other half (Denmark, Great Britain, Italy, Netherlands, and Portugal). There looks to be no obvious pattern here: it is not as if all the Northern or more established, or social democratic democracies are in one camp, and the Southern, or the more recently democratized, or neo-liberal ones are in the other.

What also remains unclear is why countries have seen changes in the ratio of men and women's party membership: is this because of changes in men's participatory behaviour or is it because of changes in women's participatory behaviour? And what is the nature of the distribution of membership across different political parties? In theory, some parties may have seen changes in one direction, others in the opposite direction. Leftist parties may indeed have seen (feminist) women join, as the gender and politics literature implies. Generational replacement of members—bringing in younger members perhaps with different (read: more feminist) attitudes—may also play a role here, even if the ratio of women to men remains constant and unequal overall. When talking of feminist engagement with electoral politics, Kittilson (2006) finds these women sharing a group identity and a concern for women's representation. Additional comparative research at the level of the individual party members would be most useful in this respect. A recent survey of UK Conservative Party members (Childs and Webb 2012) shows that women party members are more likely to be (liberally) feminist than their male peers, although broader generalizations cannot, of course, be drawn from a single case.

THE PRESENCE AND ROLES OF WOMEN'S PARTY ORGANIZATIONS

A party's women's organization may take different forms, and parties may have more than one. They, include, but are not necessarily limited to: (1) a formal members' women's organization(s); (2) a women's post(s) in the party's voluntary organization; (3) women's posts on particular party structures, especially perhaps, at the party leadership level, such as reserved seats on a national executive committee or party board, or as in a few parties' in respect of the party leader post (where there are male and female co-leaders, for example) or in the leader and deputy leader positions; (4) women's posts in the professional/secretariat of the party; (5) at the elected level there may well be a 'Women's Minister' or Opposition spokesperson, perhaps with associated staff; and (6) and at the legislative level, a women's formal parliamentary caucus or more informal cross-party caucus.

Parties' women's structures have not received much academic attention by gender and politics scholars in recent years, with not much more known beyond their existence (Norris and Lovenduski 1993; Young 2000). One recent study (Kittilson 2011a) of 142 parties in 24 post-industrial countries found that just over one third had some form of women's organization, although the proportion of such parties in an individual country varies considerably, as Table 6.3 shows.

The lack of recent research means little is known about what parties' various women's organizations do, how they are organized, how they relate to the wider party organization or the party in office, either formally or informally (Young 2000 is one early exception), as well as what implications such analysis might have for IPD. In terms of party member women's organizations one might want to ask whether they seek to substantively represent women *as women*—constituting what some call quasi-women's policy agencies (QWPA),[3] or whether they act as 'ladies auxiliaries', engaging in 'political housekeeping', supporting the party in a subordinate and not a 'big P' political fashion? (Young 2000: 134; Childs and Webb 2012) Additional research questions might include: are women constituted as subjects in their own right? Are they the centre of their own conversation? (Campbell's 1987: 283) To what extent are a party's women's organizations institutionalized, officially constituted, secure and well-resourced? What powers do they have? And on what basis do they have these, not least, relative to the party leadership, and other party organizations and bodies? Finally, to whom,

[3] WPAs, according to the United Nations' definition, are those bodies 'recognized by the Government as the institutions dealing with the promotion of the status of women' (E/CN.6/1988/3, para.21, cited in Squires 2006). The concept of QWPA was first developed in the context of RNGs research to discuss women's commissions in political parties in parliamentary systems in post-industrial societies (Mazur 2002: 3).

TABLE 6.3 *Political parties with women's organizations*

Presence of women's organizations (WO)	Countries (number with WO/total number of parties)	Total
All parties	Britain Finland Norway Sweden	4
Some	Australia (3/4) Austria (2/4) Belgium (3/11) Canada (2/4)[4] France (2/6) Germany (3/5) Ireland (4/6)[5] Italy (1/25) Japan (7/8) Netherlands (6/9) New Zealand (1/5) Portugal (1/6) Spain (1/4) Switzerland (5/11)	14
None	Denmark Greece US	3

Source: Kittilson unpublished data (see also Kittilson 2011a). NB Kittilson includes women's networks.

and through what processes or structures, are these women's organizations accountable and responsible—to women party members, women representatives, the party in government, the party in the country?

Crucially for this chapter, such questions are rarely asked in the gender and politics literature, and, therefore, their overlap with questions of IPD is likely to be under-appreciated. Nevertheless, considering the policy impact of parties' women's structures, the literature on women's organizations suggest two possibilities: first, that they engender group identity, and therefore constitute an additional site from which to make gendered demands and, second, and alternatively, that they ghettoize women party members away from mainstream policymaking (Kittilson 2011a citing: Dahlerup and Gulli 1985; Appleton and Mazur 1993; and Leyenaar 2004, relating to France, the Nordic Countries, and Holland respectively; see also Haavio-Mannila et al. 1985). The observation that the historic 'ladies auxiliaries' within parties, at least in some cases, such as the UK, Canada, France, and the Netherlands, are transforming themselves into quasi-women's policy agencies, can, in the absence of new research, only be tentative (Norris

[4] Missing data for the Bloc Québécois.

[5] Missing data for Greens.

and Lovenduski 1993; Cross and Young 2004: 432).[6] To be sure, in the period 2005–10 the UK Conservative Party women's organization for members—the Conservative Women's Organization—albeit ultimately steered by the Shadow Minister for Women via the Women's Policy Group (hence, a representative of the party in public office), participated in the development of new policies for women in advance of the 2010 general election (Childs and Webb 2011). Yet, contrast this with the contention that the era for such party women's organizations is over (Kittilson 2011a: 5). As L. Young (2000, n.d.) writes of the Canadian Reform Party, there was a refusal to recognize women as a group and a trend away from 'measures ensuring the representation of women in party affairs'. Both these cases of conservative parties invite wider comparison, and suggest that analysis must be attentive to geographical, ideological, and temporal dimensions. In sum, much more needs to be known about the form of parties' women's organization(s)—including any looser women's networks (Kittilson 2011a)—as well as their strategies, before deciding upon which account better captures the condition of party women's organizations today.

WOMEN IN SENIOR POSITIONS WITHIN POLITICAL PARTIES

With the focus—popular, media, and scholarly—mostly falling on women MPs and parliamentary candidates, the role of senior party women as party actors is less subject to extensive academic analysis. Yet, it is known that women's greater representation in legislatures is itself likely to reflect women's previous enhanced representation in the higher echelons of political parties (Kittilson 2006: 23; Freidenvall et al. 2006). Across Western Europe the presence of women on party national executive committees has risen in recent times from 15 per cent in 1975 to approximately 30 per cent (Kittilson 2006: 42). These advances may, like improvements in women's parliamentary descriptive representation, reflect the wider use of sex quotas, including the use of reserved places by individual political parties. This was true of the UK Labour Party for example, which prior to the introduction of sex quotas for parliamentary candidates ('All Women Shortlists') introduced internal party sex quotas (Perrigo 1995). Women's consequent greater presence throughout the party in turn assisted the passage of party laws to introduce sex quotas for Parliamentary candidates (Russell 2005).

[6] Kittilson (2006: 45) states that there is no published comparative measure for party women's organizations.

Women candidates and MPs

The overall global trend for women's descriptive representation in national parliaments is upwards, notwithstanding falls in post-communist countries, and individual fluctuations or stagnation within others (Dahlerup and Freidenvall 2011). The global average for women's representation in lower Houses now stands at 19 per cent. In 1997 it was 11.7 per cent. Table 6.4 shows regional percentages for women's presence in 1997 and 2010, again showing increases in all regions, although some show larger increases than others. Note, however, that national figures fail to acknowledge within-country differences (Kittilson 2006; Wangnerud 2009). Women's descriptive representation may well be asymmetric across parties (Campbell and Childs 2010). The greater tendency for parties of the Left to elect higher numbers of women, at least in modern times, is a longstanding observation (see Kittilson 2011b; Dahlerup and Freidenvall 2011), although recent developments, for example in the UK and the US, suggest that right of centre parties are increasing their number of women legislators and candidates; nor is it the case that conservative parties uniformly return low percentages of women MPs (Childs and Webb 2012).[7]

Without rehearsing the extensive gender and political recruitment literature,[8] there is agreement that no one single condition has been found to determine levels of women's descriptive representation in parliaments (Krook 2010). Even the use of sex quotas is no guarantee of higher levels of women's representation, as poorly designed and implemented quotas may have limited effects (Murray 2010a; Dahlerup and Freidenvall 2011). Nevertheless, and despite rarely being recognized as such (Celis et al. 2011), the adoption of sex quotas in more than 100 countries is a key feature of electoral and political change in many democracies

TABLE 6.4 *Women's representation in national parliaments, 1997 and 2010*

Region	Lower house 1997	Lower house 2010	Change
Nordic countries	35.9	42.1	+ 6.2
Europe—OSCE member including Nordic	14.3	22.0	+ 7.7
Americas	13.5	22.5	+ 9.0
Asia	9.7	18.6	+ 8.9
Europe, excluding Nordic	12.3	20.1	+ 7.8
Sub-Saharan Africa	10.8	18.3	+ 7.5
Pacific	12.8	13.2	+ 0.4
Arab states	3.7	9.2	+ 5.5

Source: < http://www.ipu.org> accessed 29 July 2010.

7 <http://www.cawp.rutgers.edu/fast_facts/levels_of_office/documents/cong.pdf>.

8 See, for example, Norris and Lovenduski 1995; Krook 2009; Hughes and Paxton 2008.

over the last decade or so. It is, moreover, worth emphasizing that parties' desire for greater women's representation in parliaments relies upon the acceptance of sex as a basis of group identity, and perhaps therefore, also of group representation (Young and Cross 2002b; see Dahlerup and Freidenvall 2011 for survey data of European parties' views on women's descriptive representation)—though the latter is an empirical question.[9] Furthermore, in a study of Canadian parties, party members, particularly women members, are not found, by any means, to be hostile to central efforts to increase the numbers of women representatives (Young and Cross 2002b: 692). A recent study of British Conservative party members and legislators (Childs and Webb 2012) established that women members are more favourably disposed to such efforts than men, even if they mostly reject measures that seem to them to constitute positive discrimination. That said, the introduction of sex quotas is often associated with intra- and inter-party conflict, most notably over principles of fairness and merit (Baachi 2006), as well as concerns over central party intervention in the selection process (Russell 2005).

The substantive representation of women

Theories of women's substantive representation hold that as women's descriptive representation in politics increases so too does their substantive representation; that women representatives are more likely than men to 'act for' women in politics (Phillips 1995; Mansbridge 1999). Such questions have dominated gender and politics scholarship for more than a decade (Childs and Lovenduski 2012).[10] Traditionally concerned with the role of women MPs, scholars are increasing their attention on executives (Curtin 2008; Murray 2010b; Bauer and Tremblay 2011), whilst other studies have explored the actions of actors beyond parliaments (Weldon 2002). Explicitly acknowledging that no simple relationship exists between women's descriptive and substantive representation (Childs and Krook 2006) much of the literature recognizes multiple mediating factors, and investigates the gendered institutions within which representatives act (Lovenduski 2005a). The intuition that shared gendered experiences underpins substantive representation remains, however, appealing for many feminist scholars

[9] Whether other group identities are considered comparable to sex and warrant political representation is both a conceptual (Phillips 1995; Mansbridge 1999; Dovi 2007) and empirical question. In the UK there is some talk of 'All Black Shortlists' in political circles, although no political party has adopted them; such quotas are more rarely considered for disabled, homosexual or working class groups (Speaker's Conference 2010). See Dahlerup and Freidenvall (2011) for data on the discussion of minority quotas in select European countries.

[10] See, for example, Reingold (2000); Swers (2002); Dodson (2006); Childs (2008); and see also Childs and Lovenduski (2012) and Childs and Krook (2006, 2008) for additional references, although these are not themselves exhaustive.

and activists, and there is some evidence to support such claims, even as many studies add caveats and qualifications, as researchers recognize that representatives may not always be able to act, nor to achieve particular outcomes (Childs and Lovenduski 2012; Franceshet and Piscopo 2008), and that representatives may, whilst sharing a concept of women's issues differ on what constitutes women's interests (Celis and Childs 2012). Despite these qualifications, the central role of legislators remains likely (Lovenduski and Guadagnini 2010). The aforementioned Kittilson (2011a) study directly examines how women MPs, women in party leadership positions, *and* women's party organizations influence party policy agendas and rules (Kittilson 2011a: 66, 78). Three key findings are drawn: (1) women's rising numbers among a party's parliamentary representation, and in its leadership group 'contribute to an emphasis on social justice and to the adoption of sex quotas'; (2) a women's organization proves a significant indicator for the salience of social justice, and for organizing as women within the party; and (3) the effect of women MPs is 'amplified by the presence of a women's organization in respect of welfare state expansion' (Kittilson 2011a: 66). The presence of women as parliamentary representatives and in party leadership positions might both directly bring about substantive representation and indirectly do so via contingent effects, with the former seeing women's presence as an outcome of party characteristics and electoral institutions, and the latter referring to situations when the effect of women leadership and parliamentary women is dependent 'upon the mechanism of party organizational or ideological characteristics' (Kittilson 2011a: 73–4).

ENGENDERING IPD

That political parties have sought to enhance the democratic basis of their internal structures and processes is widely agreed upon in the party literature, even as the consequences of these changes are contested, as chapters by Cross, Rahat, and Gauja, in this volume, discuss. Young and Cross (2002b) talk of the emergence of 'plebiscitary' parties (see also Katz and Mair 2009).[11] In this, political parties are said to be reacting to a decline in conventional political participation and a rise in support for direct democracy (Young and Cross 2002b: 673). Broad agreement is apparent on the following dimensions of IPD:

1. Direct election of party leaders (Scarrow 1999a; Young and Cross 2002b; and Cross this volume)

[11] Young and Cross analyse Canadian parties, though they also cite Seyd's (1999) observations of Germany and the UK.

2. Individual (ratifying and/or consultative) referenda on policy (Scarrow 1999a; Young and Cross 2002b; Heffernan 2007; Katz and Mair 2009) with the attendant downgrading of party conferences and committees from substantive policymaking bodies to leadership showcases (Heffernan 2007; and Gauja, this volume)
3. Vertical (unmediated) political communication, from the centre/leadership downwards, for example via email and electronic polling (Katz and Mair 2009) rather than horizontal communication between areas, regions, and constituencies (Seyd, in Young and Cross 2002b; Heffernan 2007)
4. Refusal to differentiate members by group identity and to reject hierarchical membership (Young and Cross 2002b)
5. Decentralized and democratized candidate selection (Rahat, this volume). This gives a greater role to individual party members (Bille 2001; Rahat and Hazan 2001; Blyth and Katz 2005) through broad based ballots (Katz 2001), albeit in ways that pre-empt local associations (Young and Cross 2002b) and local party activists (Katz 2001; Katz and Mair 2002). Candidate selection may well take the form of primary elections (Baldez 2007; Katz and Mair 2009). Primaries may, in turn, include the participation of non-party members (Katz 2001), arguably taking IPD beyond the party—something that might be termed 'without party democracy' (Stokes 1999; Katz and Mair 2009), and rendering redundant and, or meaningless the distinction between party members and citizens (Bolleyer 2009).

Attention to gender in the mainstream literature on IPD is evident in three main ways. First, and in respect of the dynamics of IPD, parties, are, in addition to reacting to general changes in the 'political market', also responding to a perception of electoral benefits related to capturing the votes of women (and young people)—a prize that might be won if parties, through IPD, attract more members and, most importantly, increase the number of candidates, from these groups (Scarrow 1999b). Secondly, gender plays out in terms of group versus individual party membership. In Young and Cross (2002b)'s representational party there are separate women's organizations and group representation, whereas the plebiscitary party sees women included as *individual* members, rather than as representatives *of* women. Accordingly, one is led to ask whether parties have mechanisms or structures that represent women as a group, either descriptively and, or substantively. Thirdly, and most obviously, is candidate selection—the acid test of IPD for Gallagher and Marsh (cited in Bille 2001: 364; see also Mikulska and Scarrow 2011). Here, sex is explicitly identified as a candidate characteristic that parties seek but it also plays out in arguments that suggest women's descriptive representation conflicts with greater internal democracy, and in the apparent tension between IPD at the party level (the greater inclusiveness of members in the processes of candidate selection) and representativeness at the system level (see Rahat et al. 2008; Rahat, this volume). In other words, if highly inclusive selectorates result in candidates becoming less representative in terms of sex, IPD may need to be limited at the party level, on the grounds of what is good for democracy—women's political presence—at the system level.

The starting point in getting the gender and politics and IPD literatures to speak more directly to each other is the acknowledgement that women look to be more included in political parties, not least in respect of women's parliamentary representation, and in the higher echelons of party leadership, in some cases brought about by the introduction of internal sex quotas and quotas for elected representatives. Yet, for the gender and IPD literatures to be successfully brought together requires something more than this. A fully engendered conception of IPD surely implies both (1) that *women gain power*; and (2) that *women gain power relative to where power lies*. In other words, in answering the question, 'in respect of whom must women have power?' a single shift in women's power relative to their male peers, who historically would have held more, would only be limited. Rather, women need to gain power relative to the (historically and overwhelmingly male) *leadership* for it to really 'count' as a plus on the IPD balance sheet. These dual requirements hold whether one is talking of ordinary party members, activists and, or elected representatives. Consequently, any claim that power has shifted within contemporary political parties from men to women, evidenced on the basis of women's greater presence in parliamentary representation, the upper echelons of political parties, or numerically in terms of party membership, only becomes fully meaningful in IPD terms, when one also reflects on debates about the impact of various IPD reforms on leader, activist, and member relations. To illustrate: take the shift to the direct election of party leaders, one indicator of a more democratic political party. This should count as a 'win' for women *and* IPD, as women are more likely to be amongst the ordinary party members empowered by this diversification of the party electorate away from the party's traditional activist elites (presuming that this measure is not merely symbolic). In contrast, there is little value for IPD in women gaining greater presence in political parties relative to men, at the point of which power becomes either more narrowly concentrated at the top—where, taking the example of leadership election, membership roles in practice merely bolster party leaders.

Three normative questions should help address the intersection of IPD and gendered analyses:

1. If women continue to be under-represented at all levels of the party, including at the top, even when recent gains are noted, can a political party be judged internally democratic? Recall that parity of representation is rare at the parliamentary level and, in the absence of global data, an unlikely feature at other levels within parties, other than perhaps ordinary party membership.
2. If women are included but not integrated, that is, lacking substantive power, can a political party be judged internally democratic? Any answer need not

reject, at the outset, claims that women are more integrated than previously (Lovenduski 2005a).

3. What kinds of power must women members have relative to the party leadership? As individuals or as a group? This relates to questions of whether claims for women's representation (descriptive and substantive) are about women as a group, or women as individuals.

Descriptive representation and sex quotas

Given that women are making gains in respect of descriptive representation in parliament in only some countries and remain under-represented in almost all, the depiction of sex quotas as the *sine qua non of centralization* (after Baldez 2007) is likely to alarm those keen to see parity of women and men's representation. This is not to say that gender and politics scholars are unaware that quotas are often (perceived as) top-down initiatives, even as they reflect women members' 'bottom-up' demands (Childs 2006; Kittlison 2006).[12] Indeed, that quotas act to circumvent selectorate discrimination operating against women is often regarded as fundamental to their *raison d'être*: quotas are often introduced precisely to limit party member/activist/selectorate's unfavourable attitudes towards women seeking parliamentary candidacy (Dahlerup 2011). And studies show that decentralized party organizations cause party centres, where they seek the greater descriptive representation of women, to be less able to implement policies to promote women precisely because they have lower levels of control over their local branches and constituency organizations (Norris and Lovenduski 1993: 13; Kittilson 2006).[13] It may also be true—although the evidence is not absolute here—that some political party leaders advocate sex quotas in order to keep some control over candidate selection (Baldez 2004 but contrast with Russell 2005; Childs 2004).[14] Nevertheless, perhaps what matters more is a perception by local party members that the centre is acting in a centralizing, and, what they regard as, an anti-democratic fashion (Childs and Webb 2012). Either way, further moves to decentralize candidate selection on the grounds of IPD look highly problematic for women's parliamentary representation. Again, evidence, such that there is, suggests that gender and politics scholars are right to be concerned: inclusive selectorates have been found to work against the selection of women candidates (Rahat and Hazan 2001). For example, Baldez's studies (2004, 2007)

[12] According to Dahlerup most quota regulations, especially voluntary party quotas come about after pressure from women 'below' (Private correspondence 2011).

[13] Note that Cross and Blais (2012a) find that of the ten women selected as party leaders in principal Westminster countries none were elected by processes that involved all party members.

[14] The UK Prime Minister Tony Blair was not an advocate of AWS, for example, although as party leader he was very interested in who was selected as representatives for the party, not least in terms of the London Mayor elections and for the post of First Minister of Wales.

show that in Mexico primaries have been employed by parties to negate quota laws—because if a party adopts primaries they are not obliged to use a sex quota—and that selections under primaries are less favourable to the selection of women candidates. Note, however, that in the 2010 UK general election Conservative Party primaries did not appear to work against women (Ashe et al. 2010).

If left alone, party selection processes are unlikely to produce parity of descriptive representation for women and men (Wangnerud 2009), nor will women's presence necessarily or 'naturally' increase over time (Dahlerup and Freidenvall 2011).[15] This begs the question of whether the centre should intervene, and whether this, because it undermines IPD *as traditionally understood*, is an acceptable road to go down. In other words, should IPD trump women's equal descriptive representation? Is the democratic value of the former (at the party level) more important than the democratic value of the latter (at the system level) (Rahat and Hazan 2001)? This question, importantly, contains competing democratic norms—first, of processes and secondly, of outcomes. Accordingly, for example, primaries may offer equality of opportunity in selection procedures, but sex quotas can (qualifications about good design and implementation noted) deliver equality of outcome (Baldez 2007). The case for the democratic value of sex quotas is, in this feminist reading, clear: when well-designed and implemented they guarantee the inclusion of a previously excluded group from our democratic institutions.[16] The introduction of sex quotas usually represents greater formalization and transparency in nominations processes, especially in semi- and non-democratic political systems too (Dahlerup 2011). Furthermore, effective sex quotas clearly empower women in terms of ensuring women's legislative presence. In this way, they have the potential to (formally) re-balance the distribution of power between women and men within parliamentary parties and within parliaments. It is also plausible to suggest, as indicated above, that this—in and of itself—empowers women relative to the party leadership, which hitherto would have been a bastion of male, as well as leadership, power. Accordingly, quotas are not just, as Kittilson (2006: 66) suggests 'an institutionalization of changing attitudes towards women in politics' they may also be an institutionalization of women's power. If this logic

[15] See Norris and Lovenduski (1995) and Dahlerup and Freidenvall (2005) for analysis of the causes of women's under-descriptive representation. The former draw attention to the reciprocity between supply-and demand-side explanations, so that a 'lack' of women seeking selection is in part a reflection of party demand. 'Fast track explanations' point to the 'exclusion' of women by parties who become responsible for women's legislative recruitment, rather than blaming women for neither coming forward nor for being sufficiently credentialized. Dahlerup and Freidenvall's (2010) more recent work confirms, on the basis of a review of extant studies, that when parties have needed to recruit more women to meet quotas they have been able to do so.

[16] Other groups may also warrant descriptive representation and, or quotas, as discussed, for example, by Anne Phillips (1995). In the UK the recent Speaker's Conference (2008–10) formally considered the under-representation of women, black, and minority ethnic groups, and the disabled as well as informally addressing issues of sexuality and class.

is accepted, then the inclusion of women in parliamentary representation may very well constitute an indicator of greater IPD, even if it is not so recognized explicitly by much of the mainstream IPD literature, and even when it runs counter to traditional interpretations of what constitutes democratic candidate selection when it relies on sex quotas.

Group representation

The plebiscitary party's refusal to differentiate between members on the basis of group representation and to reject hierarchical membership looks problematic from a feminist perspective (Young and Cross 2002b). It also finds itself in opposition to an acknowledgement of 'feminist' and, or 'gender conscious' women's organizations existing within political parties, even if—and it is not clear as yet whether this is a universal pattern across political parties—more parties (and women within them) are seeking to integrate women as individual party members.[17] Now, individual representation might be interpreted as a plus on the IPD side but might also be regarded as negative on the gender side of the balance sheet—although there may well be different feminist positions on this. And I am not claiming that women should not be individually represented in political parties. But one might ask why it is that women's group and individual representation is regarded as a zero sum game? (Kittilson (2011: 6) makes the same point.) Demands for group and individual representation might also be affected by ideology, time, and wider political context: parties might experience demands for women's group representation at different times, perhaps related to the form and degree of gender consciousness of its women members. If this is the case, then it is fine to admit that women mobilized for collective representation in the UK Labour Party prior to shifting their demands for more individual representation, both within the party and as elected representatives in the 1980s and 1990s (even whilst retaining some group organizations, not least the Parliamentary Labour Party Women's Group), and at the same time, recognize that women members in the contemporary UK Conservative Party are mobilizing at a later time point, and appear to be seeking both group representation (via the professionalization of their women's organization by which they seek, at least in part, to focus on women's policy) as well as, at the same time, demanding the greater descriptive representation for individual women in Parliament (Childs and Webb 2012). They too have established, since autumn 2011, a parliamentary body 'for women'—the Conservative Women's Forum—although its membership is comprised of women and men Conservative parliamentarians.

[17] Recall that in Kittilson's (2011a) study only approximately one-third of the parties studied had women's organizations.

The mobilization of women party members *as women*, and through structures for the substantive representation of women, feeds into wider discussions of policymaking and IPD. IPD debates suggest that parties have moved away from bottom-up policymaking towards top-down leadership efforts—not least via referenda to which individual party members consent (or not); a broad pattern that looks to dilute members' influence (see Young, this volume). One consequence of such a conclusion for advocates of IPD is to decry this as the antithesis of IPD. In drawing this conclusion, the sex of the now over-powerful leadership is not likely to be considered relevant. Yet sex might indeed matter here. These changes might still constitute an expansion of women's power within political parties. As women make their way up the party's ranks, culminating in senior party, legislative, and executive presence, some of the leadership's power to make policy has been transferred to women leaders (feminist criticisms of gendered institutions notwithstanding; Lovenduski 2005a). While this might be regarded as a negative according to mainstream IPD as power remains within the party leadership, it might be considered more positive for advocates of a re-gendered party politics. To recap: in this account individual party members, both male and female, may only be able to accept policy over which they have little say, as IPD critics maintain, but this may well be more gendered than hitherto, as a result of the role that senior party and elected women play in policy development. Whether this meets, in practice, the requirement of the double shift—from women to men, and between the party leadership and party members—remains a critical empirical question. Admittedly, this argument also presumes that senior women seek to act for women (again an empirical question) but it does not, importantly, presume how they seek to act for women; what their particular conceptions of women's interests are. Of course, this also begs the follow-on question of to whom, and in what ways, senior party women and women elected representatives are accountable—a question that is too often left unanswered in the gender and politics literature. In the two main UK parties accountability is, in the absence of any direct mechanisms, informal and not institutionalized. For example, both parties' women's conferences follow the top-down education model; Ministers for Women (and Opposition spokespersons) are not elected by women party members; nor is the Parliamentary Labour Party's Women's Group nor the Conservative Party Women's Forum.

It is worth adding into the mix, moreover, appreciation of the ways in which 'women's' parts of political parties and women in leadership positions (whether of the parliamentary or voluntary side) might still be acting in some ways as corporate bodies of, and for, women. Take the UK Conservative Party in the 2005–10 period once again. The various women's organizations—the CWO, the Women's Officer, the Vice-Chairman for Women, and the Shadow Minister for Women—were all actively involved in a review of the party's policies for women (Childs and Webb 2012). Their Report helped the party's 2010 general election manifesto be much more competitive on the 'women's terrain' (Campbell and

Childs 2010). In this instance, women within the party look to have mobilized for the substantive representation of women. Hence, they can be considered to have acted as a pressure group (Sainsbury in Lovenduski and Norris 1993: 289) or 'faction', at least according to Boucek's definition (2009: 469): 'the partitioning of a political party . . . into subunits which are more or less institutionalized and who engage in collective action in order to achieve their members' particular objectives'. As a 'competitive faction' (Boucek 2009: 476) party women might more generally be able to improve party performance, policymaking, and IPD as they signal to party leaders 'which policies are acceptable'. All this suggests that reading women's participation in a party's leadership is more complex than mainstream IPD accounts suggest.

CONCLUSION

What if political parties are experiencing a rebalancing of power from men to women? (Russell (2005: 124) talks of a 'major shift'): with more women elected as legislators; greater numbers of women present throughout party structures, especially in their higher echelons; and women's concerns better represented in party policies, perhaps through structures 'for women' and, or separate party women's organizations. Is this an indicator of greater IPD? Or is this phenomenon—a transfer of power from men to women—something other than IPD? Maybe it is a feature of contemporary political parties, and maybe it is meaningful in that it tells us something about changing gender relations within parties and, or within politics and wider society, but says little about IPD. This chapter takes issue with such an interpretation—that these developments have no direct meaning for scholars of IPD—arguing instead for a gendered conception of IPD. This is a normative position and one that invites empirical research. Where one is able to identify a shift of power—between women and men and between party members and party leaders—then a party might be considered to have experienced *gendered IPD*. As advanced above, gendered IPD requires both that women (as the hitherto dominated group) gain power relative to men, *and* that women gain power within political parties relative to where power lies.

Here, I make only three tentative claims in this respect. First, the greater presence of women amongst parties' parliamentary representation represents a shift of power from men to women. The party has become more democratic: a hitherto excluded group is now more included. Women's greater presence also has the potential to effect the distribution of power amongst the leadership, as women leaders gain power that traditionally was the preserve of men. Furthermore, if these women representatives seek to act for women in their party, particularly if they do so in conjunction with the party's women's organizations, their presence may also enhance IPD further through acting as a pressure group on the party's leadership, likely effecting policy concerns and potentially policymaking processes too. Secondly, traditional IPD reforms, other than relating to candidate selection, look likely to enhance the power of women in political parties, either directly or indirectly. Party activists are traditionally male and IPD reforms shift power to other, hitherto less activist members, who, even without a large increase in women party members, likely involve an important shift to women. Moreover, this contention might hold even if party members' influence is reduced relative to the party leadership, because limited participation of women members might be better for women than the previously existing state of affairs; dominance of ordinary women members by activist male members. Nor does it stop these women members seeking greater IPD. Thirdly, although the use of sex quotas in delivering women's greater parliamentary representation is often perceived as an anti-democratic effort according to mainstream IPD literature, this conclusion can and should be contested. Not only is this just one reading of the adoption of sex quotas, it fails to recognize the intersection of party and system-level IPD. A strong case can and should be made that women's parliamentary representation may require a limit on (traditionally understood) IPD for the good of system-level democracy. Without so acting, parties will be anti-democratic in the sense of excluding or descriptively under-representing half the population in its parliamentary representation.

Offering a gendered reading of the IPD literature and an IPD-sensitive reading of the gender and politics literature, this chapter contends that both share overlapping concerns, although they have for too long ignored each other's approaches and insights. It also maintains that IPD has much to offer scholars of gender and politics, even if the latter might well be critical of some of its concepts and conclusions. Importantly too, feminist revisions to traditional conceptions of IPD look to change extant considerations about what constitutes IPD, the effect of processes of IPD to date and, in turn, the health of our political parties and wider democracy. Admittedly, much greater consideration of all aspects of women's participation and representation in political parties, and how these may impact IPD and vice versa, is required before stronger conclusions can be made. Attention to party change is important too (Kittilson 2011b). Even so, what this chapter was tasked with was to reflect upon extant IPD research from a gendered perspective. It would also develop a feminist research agenda. Its more conceptual insights are informed by both extant empirical studies as well as feminist normative arguments from the gender and politics literature. It is up to both sets of scholars to undertake the necessary new research—both conceptual and empirical—to expand upon this first 'cut'.

7

Party Leadership Selection and Intra-Party Democracy

William P. Cross

INTRODUCTION

At its core, intra-party democracy is about the internal distribution of power within a political party. Much criticism in recent years has been levelled at parties for being overly hierarchical. The critique has been that if a political party's activist corps forms a triangle with a broad base of supporters at the bottom gradually narrowing to a single leader at the top, the distribution of formal influence in decision-making is inverse—broad authority enjoyed by the few at the top, with little authority shared among the many comprising the activist base. Further compounding this dilemma is the observation that the closer a political party comes to power (for example joining government), the more likely is a concentration of power among a small elite (Michels 1966).

Recent studies of party organization have suggested an increase in authority in the parties' leadership. Adopting the phrase 'presidentialization of politics', Poguntke and Webb (2005) find that leaders have become more influential in nearly every aspect of party decision-making. In an examination of electoral behaviour, internal organization, and legislative behaviour, they and their contributors systematically find that leaders exercise significant influence over all aspects of party life. Savoie (1999), using the phrase 'governing from the centre' makes a similar case in terms of the setting of policy direction. Perhaps as a reaction to this increased concentration of power at the top of the party pyramid, surveys of rank-and-file activists in many countries report dissatisfaction with the role they play in parties and many have pointed to this dissatisfaction as a possible contributing factor to declining party membership numbers in many contemporary democracies. (See both Young and Katz, in this volume, for a full evaluation of this argument.)

While the question of the appropriate degree of a leader's influence is an intriguing one, it is beyond the scope of this chapter. Instead, this analysis accepts the premise that leaders play a key role in party decision-making and considers the 'democratic' nature of the leader's mandate. As Marsh (1993: 229) observed two decades ago 'since there is little doubt that party leaders are important, their recruitment merits attention'. It is also worth noting that parties occasionally directly elect the prime minister. This occurs when a party in government selects a new leader. A recent example is Gordon Brown's ascension to the prime ministership by virtue of being selected leader of the British Labour Party without the necessity of having first won a general election. The fact that parties are sometimes choosing a head of government adds to the importance of considering democratic norms in leadership selection. The decision is important both to the party as an organization and to the politics of the state. Even when not directly choosing the government's leader, parties are choosing the very few individuals from among whom voters select their government and opposition leaders all of whom inevitably exercise influence over public affairs.

In considering norms of IPD relating to leadership selection, this chapter focuses on three questions: who selects the leader, how competitive are leadership contests, and how and when do leaders' terms come to an end? Because the first question largely determines how much influence rank-and-file party members have in leadership politics, this is the focus of much of the analysis that follows. First, however, it is important to consider the context of party leadership.

IDENTIFYING THE PARTY LEADER

Parties do not all take an identical approach to the question of leadership. In some instances this reflects different institutional arrangements of the polity in which they operate while in others it reflects an ideological predilection. Nonetheless, in almost every party operating in western democracies it is possible to identify a 'leader'. The last significant hold-outs in terms of not having a party leader were some Green parties. At the time of their founding in the 1970s and 1980s, many members of this party family objected to what they saw as leader-centred, hierarchical politics in the mainstream parties (Burchell 2000: 105). As a result, Greens typically rejected the notion of a party 'leader' and instead had different groups within the party charged with responsibility for different aspects of party organization and activity. Eventually, as these parties achieved some electoral success many began to select leaders. For example, while the Australian Greens were formed in 1992, they did not select their first leader (Bob Brown) until 2005. Many of these parties felt that in order to maximize their electoral success and facilitate media attention, they needed to identify some individual as their lead campaigner and principal parliamentarian. There are still a few hold-outs as, for example, the Swedish Greens do not have a leader but rather select two 'spokespersons' to represent the party.

The Swedish Green case points to a different example of parties rejecting a single leadership position. Some parties have adopted dual leadership posts with one reserved for a male and one for a female. Both the New Zealand Green and

Maori parties, for example, have joint male/female leaderships. Some parties also select a leader for campaign purposes while selecting someone else to lead them in government or in the legislature. This is the case in some Belgian parties where 'incompatibility' rules can prevent the person commonly perceived as the leader from heading the party in government (Cross and Blais 2012a).

Notwithstanding these caveats, it is generally possible to identify a leader in political parties. There is typically one leader who sits at the apex of party decision-making. The degree of the leader's influence may vary depending upon the organizational and democratic ethos of the party, but as Poguntke and Webb argue, leaders are generally seeing their authority increase in the many different spheres of party activity. In some instances this results from an increase in formal statutory power granted to the leader and in others it results from a greater willingness on the part of a party's members and elites to follow their leader reflecting the increased prominence (and pre-eminence) of the leader's position.

WHO SELECTS THE PARTY LEADER?

Given the importance the leader plays in party and public decision-making, a crucial component of IPD is who is enfranchised in his/her selection. As illustrated in Figure 7.1, there is great diversity of answers to this question ranging from a small party elite making the choice to all supporters of the party in the electorate. Many have identified a trend in terms of an expansion of the leadership selectorate in recent decades. Gone are the days when the outgoing leader, consulting with a small group of other party notables, can essentially name his successor. This method, that most would today consider democratically deficient, was used as recently as the 1960s in parties such as Ireland's Fianna Fáil, the Japanese Liberal Democrats and the United Kingdom's Conservatives (a process referred to as leadership emergence via the 'magic circle'; Punnett 1992: 26–49). While this method of selection is no longer generally viewed as democratically acceptable, it has been used by some new parties formed around a single leader or a small group of parliamentarians. In these parties, inaugural leaders often emerge by force of their own assumption of the leadership position. Prime examples of this are Silvio Berlusconi in Forza Italia and Winston Peters in New Zealand First. However, if

open primaries	**closed primaries**	**party conferences**	**parliamentary party**	**party elite**
(any interested voter)	(all party members)	(delegates representing party members)	(members of national legislature)	(small group)

FIGURE 7.1. Leadership selectorate by degree of inclusiveness

these parties outlast their founding leader, they are eventually likely to democratize the leadership selection process by formalizing participation of a larger selectorate. Examples of this are the Canadian Bloc Québécois and the Irish Progressive Democrats both of which adopted broad leadership selectorates only after the retirement of their founding leaders Lucien Bouchard and Desmond O'Malley.

At the other extreme are parties that allow anyone in the general electorate to participate in the selection of their leader. This method is most generally associated with the American parties which for more than a century have selected their presidential candidates through processes that include 'primaries'. While primaries initially played a modest role in the overall selection of the parties' lead candidates, the process has evolved to where today they play a definitive role.[1] Individual states set the rules for their primaries, with some adopting 'open' processes in which any interested voter can cast a ballot. Similar 'primaries' have been held in parties in other countries, such as the Italian Democrats which attracted several million voters to their leadership primaries in 2007 and 2009 (Seddone and Venturino 2011). Parties in Argentina are required by statute to hold 'open' primaries for which there is no requirement of party membership. These 'open' processes inevitably raise the question of whether they are in any meaningful way 'intra-party' affairs. While the parties typically exercise some discretion over the contests' rules (though not always) participation open to anyone (including those not previously affiliated with the party) suggests that 'democratization' of party events can, at its extreme, deprive them of their very 'partyness'.

Other contests are considered 'closed' primaries in which only those affiliating themselves with the party can participate. The requirement of party affiliation can either be through party-based voter registration (as in the United States) or through a requirement of formal party membership. The essential point is that only those who have formally expressed their support for a party are able to participate (rather than any interested voter). There are an increasing number of parties that are turning the leadership choice over to their members. Kenig (2009: 241) finds at least one major party broadening its selectorate to include its rank-and-file members in Canada, Denmark, France, Greece, Ireland, Israel, Japan, the Netherlands, Portugal, Spain, and the United Kingdom.

There are important distinctions, in terms of the inclusiveness of the selectorate, among some of the parties belonging to each category. Among those enfranchising their grassroots members, some allow would-be voters to join the party at the moment of voting in the leadership contest while others restrict participation to longer-term members. The different approaches reflect competing views over whether participation in leadership selection is a way of rewarding existing

[1] While the formal choice in the US parties is made at a delegated convention, for several decades now these have largely been pro forma events with the decision effectively made months earlier by primary voters.

members, and benefiting from their views, or of recruiting new partisans to party activity. The Irish Labour Party is an example of a party choosing the first option as it initially restricted participation in its membership votes to those who had belonged to the party for at least 24 months and has only recently reduced this to 18 months. Parties taking this approach argue that including long-term members in the leadership selection process increases the value of party membership and rewards activists who participate in an ongoing way in local party affairs. They also suggest that it is important to seek the counsel of these individuals in selecting the 'best' leader for the party.

The Canadian Conservative and Liberal parties provide an excellent example of the alternative approach. In these parties, the first few months of every leadership contest are devoted to candidates, and their campaigns, recruiting new members for the sole purpose of having them participate in the leadership contest (Cross 2004; Flanagan 2007). In the most open contests, voters can register at the polls simultaneously with casting their leadership ballot. The parties view these contests as opportunities to attract new members who might be converted into activists, and they benefit from the membership fees paid by them. Some Israeli parties have taken a similar approach. Kadima, for example, allowed anyone who joined the party up to six weeks prior to the vote to participate in their 2008 leadership election. While these contests are formally restricted to party members they are closer in many ways to US-style primaries than to those in parties with long membership requirements.

These open membership rules can be controversial as they encourage the participation of those who have not been party activists. Allowing new members, attracted only by the leadership contest, dilutes the voice of the party's committed activists, opens up the possibility of infiltration by those wishing only to meddle in the party's choice and potentially cheapens the value of long-time membership. Those with the ability to marshal large numbers of new party members to the polls become very influential in a party's leadership politics. This is captured by Susser (2008) in her analysis of Kadima's rules which she describes as having 'spawned a system of so-called mega recruiters and vote contractors: people with grassroots connections and influence who undertook wholesale recruitment for the various candidates, promising to deliver blocs of support'. A leading candidate in a Canadian Conservative contest who saw an opponent gaining on him by recruiting thousands of new voters to the party for the sole purpose of voting in the leadership contest, referred derisively to these new recruits as 'tourists' to the party (Stewart and Carty 2002). Many studies find that the large majority of these new recruits do not remain as party members but rather are transients passing through for the sole purpose of participating in the contest (Carty, Cross, and Young 2000).

On the continuum of the expansiveness of the leadership selectorate, the next categorization is selection at a party congress. This method is commonly used among many European parties including principal parties in Germany, Austria, Spain, Romania, and Hungary (see Kenig 2009; Detterbeck 2011; Ennser and

Müller 2011; Barbera et al. 2011; Ghergina and Chiru 2011; and Varnagy and Ilonszi 2011). There are significant differences in the inclusiveness of these processes in terms of the degree of influence a party's grassroots plays in the leadership choice. At one extreme, the party conferences may be small, elite-dominated affairs with participation limited to public and party office holders. More typically, congresses today include delegates who are representative of geographic and sometimes descriptive constituencies within a party. Many parties select delegates to represent local communities and grassroots party members often play a role in their selection. To a limited extent the total number of delegates is indicative of the degree of openness of the selectorate and we find wide variance here. Barbera et al. (2011), for example, report a 300 per cent variance in the number of delegates participating in recent leadership congresses in the Spanish parties.

More important than the size of the party conference making the choice is the question of whether those selecting the conference delegates use this ballot as a proxy for expressing their choice for party leader. The question essentially is whether local party members select convention delegates on the basis of their general status in the party and in doing so fully delegate the leadership choice to them; or, alternatively, delegated candidates indicate which leadership candidate they favour and rank-and-file members consider this information when choosing their conference representatives. At one extreme, conference delegates can be bound in their leadership vote by the expressed desires of their local party members. This was the method used by the Canadian Liberals when they last selected leaders at their party conferences in 2003, 2006, and 2009. Delegates were restricted on the convention's first ballot to voting in accordance with their local members' preference. The New Zealand Green Party in 2005 left this decision to each local party organization instructing local branches that: 'Your electorate will make its decisions on the various candidates . . . and may ask the delegates to vote strictly in accordance with these decisions. Or you may choose to give an indication to the delegates, but allow them freedom to vote differently . . . . How much guidance or leeway delegates have is a decision for each electorate to make' (NZ Green Party n.d.). These examples seem more the exception than the rule as in many cases leaders are chosen at regularly scheduled party congressess (as opposed to specially called leadership conventions) and the selection of delegates is not directly related to the leadership choice. In these parties local members may try to influence the choice by making their preferences known to conference attendees but this is at best an indirect role.

The most restrictive selectorate commonly in use today is the parliamentary party. In these cases participation in the choice is restricted to those members of the party serving in national elected office. While this is the default position in many parliamentary systems, in recent decades there has been significant movement away from this position with a minority of parties now falling into this category (Cross and Blais 2011b). Nonetheless, this method is still used in some major parties such as Labor and the Liberals in Australia and New Zealand's National and Labour parties. In some of the Austrian parties, a central executive committee maintains the authority to select the leader.

There are distinct rationales for each of the selectorates commonly used by parties. Parties restricting the choice to their parliamentarians essentially point to three groups of justifications for doing so. First, they argue that one of the leader's primary responsibilities is heading the party in the legislature, thus it is appropriate that the choice be made by those comprising the parliamentary party. This argument has less saliency in countries such as Belgium where the party leader is not necessarily the leader of the parliamentary contingent perhaps helping to explain why wider selectorates have long been used there. The second argument is that members of the parliamentary party know the potential leadership candidates well and are in the best position to judge their relative merits. Related to this is the belief that the leader's principal task is to lead the party to electoral success. No one has more at stake in ensuring that the party makes the best choice in this regard than members of the legislative caucus whose very livelihood is dependent upon the party's electoral success. Finally, parties sometimes argue that leadership choices can be divisive and highlight factional disputes within a party. Accordingly, some contend that these intramural contests are best dealt with in the privacy of the parliamentary party room rather than being open to the inevitable press scrutiny of a party congress or members' plebiscite (Cross and Blais 2012a).

Related to this last concern is the speed with which the parliamentary party is able to dispatch its obligations. Parliamentary parties are able to remove leaders, and select their successors, within a matter of hours. A prime example of this is the ouster of Kevin Rudd as prime minister and leader of the Australian Labor Party in 2010. With little advance notice, and almost no public knowledge of what was to transpire, the parliamentary party effectively removed Rudd from his position and replaced him with Julia Gillard in a process that in its entirety lasted about 24 hours.

This can be contrasted with the long and drawn-out leadership struggles that take place in parties in which the extra-parliamentary membership is formally involved. The UK Labour Party's travails surrounding the leadership of Gordon Brown, both in his long struggle to wrest the top position away from Tony Blair and then the public efforts of many in the party to remove him prior to the 2010 general election, provide a stark contrast with the Australian case. Labour's leadership turmoil dominated the party's press coverage for several years, and revealed deep schisms within the party as competing groups of parliamentarians and party activists first publicly called for Blair's departure and then suggested that Brown resign.

Those favouring an expanded selectorate make several arguments. First they suggest that a party's legislative caucus is too small and unrepresentative a body to make the choice themselves. In the vast majority of parties the parliamentary group is comprised disproportionately of men and is often geographically unrepresentative—with areas of a party's electoral strength typically over-represented and other parts of the country significantly under-represented. The degree of regional under-representation is related to the choice of electoral system with this occurring most frequently in countries using the single member plurality (SMP) system. For example, this argument was quite persuasive in the decision to expand the leadership selectorate in parties such as the UK Conservatives and Liberals and the Canadian Liberals. In all of these parties, patterns of electoral support, magnified by the SMP electoral system, left large parts of the country unrepresented in the parliamentary group. This has also been an important concern in parties such as Ireland's Fine Gael, where the party's electoral support pattern coupled with the single transferable vote electoral system, produced a parliamentary group with almost no representation from Dublin (Cross and Blais 2012a). This is less a concern in countries with proportional electoral systems in which the major parties regularly achieve some legislative representation from all regions.

Selection at both a party congress and in a membership vote can ensure equitable geographic representation. Most party congresses are comprised of delegates chosen through local party associations ensuring inclusion in the leadership selectorate of representatives of every region. Parties differ in terms of whether each region has equal representation or whether the size of the conference delegation reflects the electoral and organizational strength of the party in each region. Nonetheless, in every case the party easily avoids situations of complete or significant under-representation of entire regions.

In membership votes the most common method is to invite all party members to participate and to simply tally up all votes cast. While these contests inevitably result in greater representation from regions where the party has its largest number of supporters, all regions are to some extent included. Some parties, particularly those in Canada, but also in earlier iterations in the UK Labour and Liberal parties, have adopted rules ensuring that each region has exactly the same influence in the leadership choice regardless of the number of members participating in the vote. This is accomplished by weighting members' votes by constituency and assigning an equal number of votes to each district. The rationale for this is to ensure that all regions of the country have an equal say in the leadership choice. Support for this position has been most enduring in Canada where both governing parties (the Conservatives and Liberals) have enshrined it in their rules. This reflects the deep regional cleavages found in both parties and their brokerage approach to electoral politics. Both present themselves as big-tents able to accommodate different regional interests and thus they ensure that all regions are equitably represented in key party decision-making (Carty, Cross, and Young 2000). This approach also reflects the realities of the SMP electoral system in which elections are won and loss at the electoral district level. Ensuring the importance of each constituency in the leadership choice encourages candidates to run national campaigns and not simply to concentrate on areas of party strength where the largest concentration of members is found.

Manufacturing equitable group representation, be it regional or by gender, comes at the expense of the one-person-one-vote principle. For example, when regional equity is mandated, those voting in constituencies where their party has relatively few members have significantly more influence in the outcome than do those where the party has a large membership. Stewart and Carty (2002) find dramatic differences in voter influence in the 1998 Canadian Conservative contest. In the Ontario riding of Kingston and the Islands, 1,300 voters participated compared with eight in the Quebec riding of Bellechasse-Etchemins-Montmagny-L'Islet. As each electorate was allocated 100 votes towards the national total, each vote cast in Kingston counted as 0.13 compared with 12.5 (or 96 times more) for the Bellechasse voters. One result is that candidates are encouraged to campaign in areas where their party is weak as each vote in these 'rotten boroughs' offers significant electoral premium.

Some American and Canadian parties have long enforced rules requiring that the delegations to their national conventions are comprised of equal numbers of men and women. Delegate selection rules also often include provisions for a set proportion of congress attendees to be members of a party's youth wing. Ensuring this sort of representation is more difficult in membership votes and I am aware of no party that manages to do so. Party members are notoriously old and disproportionately male in most Western democracies (see Young, this volume). The little data that exist on who votes in these contests suggests that the selectorates reflect party memberships generally. The dilemma here is similar to that identified by Hazan and Rahat (2010) in the context of candidate selection. The ability to manufacture a representative selectorate, be it reflecting concerns for region or gender or something else, potentially distinguishes selection at a delegate convention from other methods. Increasing participation, to directly include rank-and-file members in the choice, may come at the expense of not realizing other democratic objectives such as representativeness of the selectorate.

The most significant reason advanced for expanding the leadership selectorate is that the choice is too consequential, both for the party and the polity more generally, to be restricted to a small group of party elites. This perspective reflects changing democratic norms generally calling for more inclusive and participatory public decision-making. This argument has been advanced in the movement away from selection both by the parliamentary party and by party conferences. For example, in the Belgian case, many parties in recent decades have adopted membership-wide votes to replace selection at a party congress. Wauters (2011) and Pilet et al. (2011) point to a desire by rank-and-file party supporters to participate in intra-party decision-making as a factor in these organizational reforms.

In an examination of twenty-six parties in the Westminster systems, Cross and Blais (2012b) find that parties often expand their leadership selectorate after an electoral setback and when in opposition. They argue, consistent with Scarrow et al. (2000), that there is typically an ongoing struggle for influence within parties between the grassroots members and elites (in these cases, typically the party in public office). The elite generally have the upper hand and are unwilling to cede authority. This situation changes after a poor campaign performance when the parliamentary leadership is blamed for the electoral setback. The balance of power shifts in favour of the grassroots and they are often able to wring concessions, such as an expansion of the leadership selectorate, from the party elite. Thus, they find a number of cases in which party activists advocated for long periods for a formal voice in leadership selection with no success while their party was in, or close to, government only to have quick success in winning this concession after the party suffered an electoral defeat. Related to this is an acknowledgement by elites, often reluctantly, that parties in such a weakened state need to revitalize at the local level in order to regain their electoral competitiveness. Expansion of the selectorate is seen as one way of reinvigorating the grassroots.

Some parties have taken a middle ground by trying to capture the best of both approaches in their selection processes. In these cases the party includes its membership in the process but reserves significant influence for the party elite. The principal British parties offer two different illustrations of this. Both parties' leadership selection processes include a universal membership ballot while also reserving significant influence for the parliamentary party. In the case of the Tories, the parliamentary party selects the two final candidates from between whom the members select a leader. This typically results in the parliamentary party holding several ballots to narrow the field to a final two. If parliamentarians are united in their choice, as they were in the selection of Michael Howard in 2003, there is no membership ballot as only MPs are able to nominate candidates. In UK Labour, parliamentarians play a key role both controlling one-third of the leadership vote, and also by serving as gatekeepers to the ballot. Party rules require that as many as 20 per cent of MPs nominate a candidate in order for them to contest for the leadership. In the acclamation of Gordon Brown in 2007, there were at least two others who desired to seek the leadership but were not able to win support from enough parliamentarians to force a contest. Thus the Labour Party process, calling for a vote of the party membership, can be circumvented if MPs are strongly in favour of one candidate and act to deny ballot access to others.

A final variant in terms of defining the leadership selectorate is the formal inclusion of groups from outside the party. In a sense this occurs in open primaries as party membership is not a requisite for participation. It also occurs in some labour-based parties that allocate a share of the vote to their trade union supporters. For example, the Canadian New Democrats have in the recent past reserved one-quarter of the vote in their 'membership' ballot for the trade unions. Similarly, the UK Labour Party divides their leadership votes in three equal parts with one share granted to the trade unions. These rules reflect the special relationship between these parties and the trade unions.

Beyond the definition of the selectorate, the degree of competitiveness is an indication of the democratic health of these contests. The next section considers the amount of choice voters have in these elections.

COMPETITIVENESS OF LEADERSHIP CONTESTS

In considering the nature of IPD in leadership selection it is important to consider the competitiveness of these contests. Party rules may suggest that the contests are wide-open affairs—easily accessible to candidates and a broad selectorate—but this is not particularly meaningful if there is little competition. This is especially true in the many cases in which party elites control access to the leadership ballot. The degree of competitiveness of these contests sheds light on whether members have a real choice or are rubber-stamping a decision made by party elites.

The available evidence on this question suggests that there is considerable variance in rates of competitiveness, measured by both the number of candidates and the closeness of the contest (Kenig 2009b: 244), that may be explained by party and state democratic norms and political culture as well as by a party's formal rules and practices. For example, studies of leadership selection in Belgium, Germany, and Spain all find low levels of competition with coronations being the norm. Barbera et al. (2011) study fifty-eight cases of leadership selection in Spanish party congresses and find only ten with two or more candidates. Similarly in Belgium, while most parties have now selected several leaders through full membership votes, there has been no spike in competitiveness as a majority of these contests have been won by acclamation (Wauters 2010). Detterbeck (2011) finds that in the German case, party elites settle on a favoured choice prior to the party congress that is formally charged with selection. The accepted practice is for the party congress to agree with and legitimize this preordained selection. These cases suggest that a formal expansion of the leadership selectorate may not have any significant effect on IPD if the effective choice continues to be made elsewhere.

In other countries there is a strong tradition of contested leadership contests. For example, in Canada acclamations are almost unheard of. This is true even when the outcome is an absolute certainty, thus some of the contests have been very one-sided, such as the Liberal party's selection of Paul Martin with more than 90 per cent of the vote in 2003. Nonetheless, it was felt by many in the party that it was important that there be a challenger to ensure a vote and to provide legitimacy to the process. Party rules do make a difference here. The threshold for candidacy in the Canadian parties is typically very low—normally requiring only the signature of a few dozen party members and requiring no minimal support from parliamentarians. This can be contrasted with parties such as those in the UK where even in contests with broad selectorates the parliamentary parties control access to the ballot. As discussed above, in both Labour and the Conservatives, recent leaders have been chosen by acclamation precisely because this was the wish of MPs.

In a study of more than 200 leadership contests, Cross and Blais (2012a) consider the relationship between party rules and competitiveness and find only modest effects relating to the type of selectorate used. Broader selectorates tend to have slightly more candidates than contests with narrower selectorates. This might be explained by the likelihood that outcomes may be more predictable in contests restricted to parliamentarians and thus may discourage challenges by long-shot candidates. They further find, however, that these contests are no more competitive in terms of the closeness of the share of the vote won by the top two candidates. Kenig's (2009b) findings are similar in that he reports an increase in candidates with the broadening of the selectorate but a decrease in the closeness of the contest.

Cross and Blais (2012a: 118) do find that tougher removal rules result in more competitive leadership contests which they suggest results from the fact that 'potential candidates have more time to prepare for an eventual contest and/or they believe that another opportunity for the top job may be a long time coming because the elected leader is likely to remain for some time, as it is more difficult to remove him'.

It thus appears that a combination of party and state political culture together with formal party rules influence the degree of competitiveness of leadership contests. This is an instance where party statutes indicating inclusive and open contests are sometimes circumvented by party norms legitimizing selection by consensus of the party elite.

When considering democratic norms and the selection of party leaders, consideration must be given to how frequently voters are able to cast judgement on their leaders and possibly remove them from the position. The next section considers how long leaders serve and how their tenures end.

LEADERSHIP TERMS OF OFFICE

The first consideration regarding the length of a leader's tenure is whether there is a fixed length to the leadership term and the resulting frequency with which whatever group in the party selects the leader is able to exercise its authority. Surprisingly, there is considerable variance not only regarding the length of leadership tenure but also as to whether there is a prescribed term. The holding of regular elections for each public position, at least every few years, is widely accepted as an important democratic norm (Powell 1982; Massicotte and Blais 2000). Term lengths for mayors or presidents may vary from state to state, but in all democratic countries the incumbent holds the position for a fixed term with periodic elections held. Not so for party leadership. There is a divide between parties in which the leader is chosen for a fixed term and those in which he/she is chosen for an indefinite period.

When there is a fixed term, the length varies dramatically with a range from one year to as long as a decade. An example at the short end of this spectrum was the UK Conservative party, which from the 1970s to 1990s allowed for an annual leadership contest. Would-be contestants needed only to collect the support of two MPs (a mover and seconder) to challenge the incumbent at a prescribed time each year. It was in one of these annual events that Margaret Thatcher's leadership (and tenure as prime minister) came to an end in 1990. Similarly, many parties that choose their leaders at annual (or biannual) party congresses hold a leadership vote at each gathering. Austrian parties are typical in this regard as their congresses select leaders for terms ranging from two to four years. Parties in which the parliamentary party selects the leader often hold a scheduled leadership vote once each parliamentary term essentially providing for a three or four-year term depending on the frequency of general elections (the three major Australian parties and New Zealand Labour being examples). The Irish Labour party holds a membership vote for the leader's post every five years. Some parties provide for a longer term when their leader is serving in government. The UK Liberal Democrats' leader normally has a five-year term which is extended to ten years when the party is in government.

Other parties do not set a length for the leadership term. Many of these are parliamentary parties and include Ireland's Fiánna Fail and Fine Gael, all of the principal Canadian parties and New Zealand's National Party. In these parties leaders are chosen for indefinite periods. In most of these cases, as well as in some parties with a fixed leadership term, leaders are subject to removal from their post outside of leadership elections. Again there is significant variance here. In some parties there are regularly scheduled votes of confidence. For example, in the New Zealand National Party the first order of business for the parliamentary party, following each general election, is a vote to determine whether the leader continues to have the confidence of his parliamentary colleagues. If so, he continues in the position and no leadership contest is held until either the incumbent retires or loses such a vote. Other parties hold 'leadership review' votes at each party congress, in effect asking delegates whether they would like a leadership contest to be held.

Some parties allow for spontaneous challenges to be brought against the incumbent leader. Again, these are most common in parties in which parliamentarians have the authority to both select and remove the leader. In these parties, parliamentarians are able to oust the leader from his/her position at virtually any time. In some instances, the mere threat of calling a confidence vote results in the resignation of the incumbent leader in the face of almost certain removal from office. A recent example of this is the 2010 resignation of Australian Prime Minister

Kevin Rudd who acted in the face of near certain removal by his parliamentary colleagues.

The UK Conservatives are an example of a party in which the extra-parliamentary membership plays a central role in leadership selection while MPs maintain the authority to remove leaders. The party's parliamentary caucus used this authority in 2003 to remove Ian Duncan Smith from office two years after he was chosen leader through a vote of the entire party membership. There are parties in which the extra-parliamentary party can act to spontaneously remove a leader, this usually requires support from a large number of local party associations (Cross and Blais 2012a). The hurdles for this sort of removal are typically set very high and extremely rare are the cases where they have succeeded. The result is that while authority to choose the leader has in many parties been expanded to include the party on the ground, the ability to remove him often remains solely with the party in public office.

There are parties in which leaders are chosen for indefinite periods and in which there exists no formal opportunity to remove the leader from his position. The Canadian Liberal and Conservative parties belong to this category during periods when their leader is serving as prime minister. In the wake of the long and bitter dispute between sitting prime minister Jean Chrétien and would-be PM Paul Martin, the Liberals changed their rules to do away with periodic confidence votes for leaders serving in government. The Conservatives adopted similar rules shortly thereafter. The result is that the leaders of these parties, the only parties to have ever governed in Canada, are chosen for indefinite periods and not subject to any formal possibility of removal so long as they win general elections. So while members may play a key role in the selection of these leaders, they have no formal authority to remove them after having done so.

Given the wide variety of circumstances in terms of rules governing leadership selection and removal and the varying degree of electoral success of political parties, it is not surprising that there is significant variance in the length of leadership tenures. In a study of post WWII leaders in Australia, the Netherlands, Sweden, and the United Kingdom, Bynander and t'Hart (2007: 51) report a mean tenure of 75 months with a remarkable standard deviation of 61 months. Cross and Blais (2012a) report similar findings in their study of Westminster systems, with significant inter country variance ranging from a median length of 85 months in the Canadian parties to 48 in New Zealand. Both Andrews and Jackman (2008) and Cross and Blais (2012a) also report significant variance within countries. For example, Cross and Blais find that one-fifth of party leaders last less than two years while one-in-four has a tenure of more than ten years. Both Cross and Blais (2012a) and Ennser and Müller (2011) find that party rules have some relationship with the length of leadership tenure. For example, Ennser and Müller find that Austrian leaders chosen by their party executive, as opposed to a party congress, serve longer terms as do those who are chosen for longer initial terms (four years rather than two). Both of these studies, along with Andrews and Jackman (2008), also suggest that electoral success enhances a leader's likelihood of staying in office.

LEADERSHIP SELECTION AND INTRA-PARTY DEMOCRACY

Consideration of the interplay between party leadership selection and questions of IPD has become more salient as the power and influence of party leaders has increased. If party leaders ever were simply 'first among equals' in their parliamentary caucuses then it may have been fully appropriate for party elites, perhaps in the legislative caucus, to select the leader (see Weller 1985). However, given the rise in importance of leaders in terms of their influence both within the party and in determining public policy direction, this practice is widely under attack. In many countries across the Western world, parties are expanding their leadership selectorates to include rank-and-file members.

The shift is not universal and, while consistently in the same direction, does not lead to a single selection method. Some parties have turned the choice over to conference delegates, some to their long-term grassroots members, others to all partisans in the electorate, and others still have created complex selectorates dividing up the authority among their elected officials, grassroots members and favoured supporters such as trade unions. And even when the leadership franchise is expanded there are many cases of party members or convention delegates being presented with a single candidate by virtue of party elites effectively controlling ballot access and reaching a consensus choice themselves.

Construction of a balance sheet in terms of the advantages and disadvantages of the different methods reflects one's conception of democracy, particularly as it relates to the role of political parties. Broadening the selectorate serves to expand the numbers formally enfranchised in this important decision. At their extreme, however, processes such as primaries risk cheapening the meaning of party membership and removing an important incentive to party activism. At some point these cease to be party events at all.

In making these decisions, parties are faced with determining who their leadership should be accountable to. While every democracy requires their leaders to seek a mandate from voters in a general election, this choice is highly restricted by the prior selection of party leaders. Voters typically choose a prime minister or president from among the two or three leaders presented by the largest parties. How these leaders are chosen is no less important to consider than are the rules governing general elections.

Notwithstanding the importance of these contests, it is appropriate that they are largely left to the parties to self-regulate. State regulation, outside of the United States, is rare and most often limited to questions of campaign financing (see

Scarrow, this volume). The choices made by parties in terms of how their leaders are chosen and removed reflect their democratic ethos. Whether they decide to grant formal influence to trade unions, to count all votes equally or to weight them by region, or to leave the choice to party activists meeting in conference are decisions that reflect their democratic impulses and priorities. What is essential is that parties, and their members, appreciate the importance of these decisions and the democratic trade-offs inherent in them.

8

Policy Development and Intra-Party Democracy

Anika Gauja

This chapter examines the concept of intra-party democracy (IPD), its aspirations and actual practices, in the context of policy development. For advocates of IPD, the participation of citizens in a party's policy formulation process is desirable, not only from the standpoint of providing legitimacy to a party, but in contributing to the citizen-state linkage through interest articulation and aggregation. In this sense, political parties, through their internal policy development processes and the active involvement of their members and supporters, ascertain salient community concerns and combine the views and interests of individuals and groups into coherent policy documents and platforms to present to the electorate. With this in mind, it is arguable that policy development is a natural avenue through which democratic principles and practices could be implemented within a party's organization. Whether in response to perceived public demand or as an attractive marketing tool, in recent years political parties have 'revised their party constitutions in order to give members a greater role in the recruitment of candidates, the election of leaders and in the policymaking process more generally' (Whiteley 2011: 26; see also Young, this volume).

Nevertheless, actual participation within parties' policy processes remains something of a paradox. Notwithstanding the range of formal participatory opportunities on offer, there is continuing evidence of the public's reluctance to engage with these processes and their continuing withdrawal from political parties. The policy development paradox also hints at some uneasy tensions that lie at the heart of IPD: tensions between the normative aspirations of IPD, social expectations, party rhetoric, the actual operation and organization of parties, and the broader design of representative democracy and government. These are tensions that will be explored throughout this chapter, but they can be crystallized into four main questions that will be addressed. First, what basic form(s) does IPD take when it comes to policy development, and what are some of the expectations created on the part of the public, supporters, party members, and leaders? Second, what are the modes of membership participation in policy development? Third, what is the link between the preferences and involvement of the membership and policies developed by the party? Finally, what are the electoral and governance impacts of a democratic intra-party policy process?

WHAT IS INTERNALLY DEMOCRATIC POLICY DEVELOPMENT?

At its most basic, IPD as it relates to policy development within political parties can be conceptualized as simply allowing or enabling party members to 'have their say' when it comes to formulating party policy. Party constitutions and official documents often express this sentiment in terms of policy 'ownership', 'determination', or 'contribution'. For example, in the United Kingdom, the Labour Party claims that 'all members, local parties, affiliates as well as other party stakeholders *have the right to a direct say* in the party's policy development' (UK Labour 2007). In New Zealand, 'Labour Party members have the *opportunity to contribute directly* to party policy, and help implement the commitments made in our manifesto' (NZ Labour 2007), whereas National Party members are 'able to *participate fully in the party's democratic process*' (National 2011; emphasis added). While these examples suggest that within a range of parties policy is 'determined' or 'owned' by the membership, there is significant variation as to how the principles of IPD are expressed in official documents, advertising materials and on party websites. Indeed, thinking about how a party might practically implement the basic proposition that members 'have their say' uncovers an even more complex and contentious set of questions: who are the 'members'? What is 'party policy'? And most importantly, what does it mean to 'have a say'?

Like party scholars, political parties interpret these questions in a variety of different ways. There are significant organizational variations between individual parties as to how members can actually contribute to policy debate. These structures are dynamic: reflecting not only a party's ideology, culture, and its origins, but also its responses to political and organizational challenges such as fluctuating memberships, social norms and legal regulation, electoral competition and the challenges of governance (see, for example, van Biezen, this volume). Comparing policy formulation across a range of political parties across the globe, it is possible to identify four 'types' of membership participation in intra-party policy processes, or perhaps more accurately, four distinct channels of participation through which it can be claimed that members 'own' party policy: direct, representative, delegate, and consultative involvement. Although none of these channels of participation is mutually exclusive within a party, there are several factors that influence the type of membership participation that a party is likely to emphasize, including ideology, history, size, resources (including whether a party is in government or opposition), and technological capabilities.

WHAT IS THE MODE OF MEMBERSHIP PARTICIPATION IN POLICY DEVELOPMENT?

Despite some individual variations, the formal policymaking process of parties (as articulated in documents such as party constitutions) tends to follow a typical model that transcends national differences and is common to political parties of several party types and families. The archetypal model is that policy is developed over a number of months by local branches, working groups or policy commissions with the input of members and interested parties (including party research foundations and 'think tanks') before being voted on by the party membership (whether through a conference, representative body or by direct ballot) for inclusion as 'official' party policy to be adopted by, or to guide, the parliamentary party. Membership participation can therefore occur in two main arenas: during the development process by drafting policy proposals in a local branch, or by being a member of, or consulting with, a working group; and second, by participating in (or being represented in) a vote to adopt, reject, or amend party policy. Viewed in terms of the three faces of the party organization (Katz and Mair 2002), the model process conceptualizes policy development primarily as the preserve of the party on the ground, with varying degrees of input by the party in public office (which may, for example, have official representation in policy working committees and conferences), all coordinated by the party in central office.

Table 8.1 summarizes the four modes of participation involved in a typical policy development process (direct, representative, delegate, and consultative) and provides examples of political parties that use them. To illustrate the range of possibilities, the final row of the table also includes examples of political parties that do not provide for membership participation in policy development.

Direct participation

Direct participation in the policy process is perhaps the most difficult model to practically achieve, as members must be actively involved at the point of decision-making. Under this model, members might represent themselves on policymaking bodies such as working groups and policy commissions, vote as individuals on matters of policy in membership-wide plebiscites, or make autonomous decisions in local groups. Given that this participatory model emphasizes immediate individual involvement in the aggregation of opinions, its success relies primarily on a party's size—favouring those parties that are smaller and well resourced. Despite the practical difficulty of applying this model of participation within political parties, from a normative perspective it offers the most meaningful and effective opportunity for membership involvement in two respects. First, it is a reliable way to aggregate the preferences of those who wish to be involved. Second, as party members are effective participants in this process, direct participation fulfills the

Table 8.1 *Modes of formal membership participation in policy development*

Mode of participation	Examples of party use	Organizational feature	Example of organizational implementation
Direct	Australian Democrats, Green parties, D66 (Netherlands), UK Conservatives	Individuals have the ability to contribute directly to the making of a policy decision	Participation in working groups; policy ballots; autonomous local policy groups
Delegate	Social democratic parties, Green parties	Individual members' interests are represented by delegates who must follow their wishes	Labour party conferences including the PvdA Congress (Netherlands), Sp.a Congress (Belgium); Green party conferences including the Swedish Greens' Congress
Representative	UK Liberal Democrats, UK Labour, Canadian Conservatives	Individual members are represented on policymaking bodies; representatives are not mandated	Canadian Conservatives National Convention; Liberal Democrat Conference; UK Labour National Policy Forum
Consultative	UK Labour, UK Conservatives, Australian Labor Party	Party relies on consultations with the membership and policy submissions from individuals and groups	Policy consultations; forums/ conventions; website posts
No/limited Participation	Populist and radical right parties such as the Party for Freedom (PVV) (Netherlands), One Nation (Australia), British National Party	Party has no members; emphasis on leader to provide policy direction	PVV has no official members—rather supporters, donors and volunteers

goals of education and political self-development as outcomes of policy development (Pateman 1970: 105).

Direct participation in policy development has been implemented in smaller political parties, and typically those in opposition or 'third' parties, such as the Australian Democrats, which polled its entire membership on the adoption of party policies through voluntary postal ballots (Gauja 2005). The D66 in the Netherlands similarly allows all individual party members to vote on the adoption or rejection of party policy through attendance at the party's conference, with important decisions being taken by referendum. Green parties, which typically emphasize grassroots democracy and consensus decision-making in local groups as a key component of their ethos, are a further example of this mode of participation.

Despite the suggestion that effective direct participation is limited by the size of a political party, there is nonetheless evidence to suggest that larger parties are also adopting more direct modes of membership involvement in policy formulation. Beginning with the VLD in 1992, Belgian parties have replaced the traditional system of delegation at party conferences with a model where every individual is entitled to attend and vote (Wauters 2009: 7–8). The Conservatives in the UK conducted a series of membership-wide policy ballots, including on Britain's adoption of the Euro, during William Hague's leadership (1997–2001). However, the adoption and expansion of these initiatives is nevertheless still limited by party resources and cost: Wauters also notes that Belgian parties have used an intra-party referendum to elicit opinions from party members on policy issues on three occasions since 1993, but have refrained from doing so more often due to the expense of the process (Wauters 2009: 9; and see Scarrow, this volume). A further issue of contention concerns the motivations for such reforms; and whether party elites are genuinely seeking to enhance engagement with intra-party policy processes, or shifting to more individualized processes of participation designed to marginalize the voice of party activists (Katz 2001: 293; Blyth and Katz 2005).

Participation through delegation and representation

Both the representative and delegate models of participation create a link between members and policy without their direct involvement in decision-making. As the most common type of participation, members choose one or more of their number to represent their views and interests in policy decisions at a higher level of intra-party decision-making. The important difference between the two models is the degree of agency granted to the member chosen to make the policy decision. Under the representative model, representatives should ideally take the members' interests into account, but ultimately decide according to their own judgment and conscience. On the other hand, delegates exercise no agency—they are chosen to convey the wishes of their members rather than make individual policy decisions.

We most commonly see these types of participation manifest in the larger parties in the operation of party conferences, where conference attendees act either as delegates (social democratic parties) or representatives (for example, in the Liberal Democrats and the Canadian Conservatives) of the wider membership in the decisions affecting the adoption of party policy. Some political parties with a distinct federal structure (for example, the ALP and the Green parties in Australia, and the CDU and FDP in Germany) emphasize the delegate model of membership participation and representation as a means by which to ensure that constituent regional parties are given adequate voice in national decisions.

However, both the delegate and representative relationships obscure some of the tensions inherent in the fundamental question of *who* should be represented and *whose* preferred version of democracy is at play within the party. It is often assumed that delegates represent party members, but these delegates may have a specific constituency to which they feel accountable (for example, unions or local/regional branches), or may not be responsible to any constituency at all. In such a situation, whom might delegates represent: members, supporters of the party, or all voters in general? Might they see themselves as trustees of party policy? A typical example is the conference delegate who supports a policy change that he/she believes is in the best interests of the party and its voters, but against a subset of vocal party activists. These complex representative relationships create tensions in policymaking that reflect different visions of democracy and the role of parties within it.

Consultation

The final model of participation, consultative, involves the participation of members in the policy process through submissions to, and consultations with, party policy working groups. This participation can be distinguished from direct participation as members are not directly making policy decisions; rather they are feeding their views into intermediary groups in the drafting process, such as working groups and policy forums. Although political parties routinely consult with interest groups, think tanks, and other interested parties when developing policies, only relatively recently have policy consultations been used as a strategy to encourage membership and community participation (rather than seeking out expert opinion) in the policy process.

The Swedish Social Democrats set up consultations with party members and affiliated organizations to review the party's official retrenchment policy in the 1990s (Loxbo 2011: 9) and the Spanish Socialists engaged in a large-scale consultative exercise from 1987–90 involving almost one million people to review the party's policy programme (Gillespie 1993: 93–4). Policy consultation initiatives are currently being used by all major political parties in the United Kingdom, led by the Labour Party which has conducted a series of public consultations over the last decade: 'the Big Conversation' (2003), 'Let's Talk' (2006), and most recently, 'Fresh Ideas' (2011). These consultation initiatives are significant in that they typically encourage the involvement of the general public and interested organizations rather than restricting involvement in policy development to the party's financial members.

Apart from consulting with individuals, political parties may also choose to involve interested or affiliated organizations in the policy development process. Such groups may include trade unions (which have traditional links with social democratic parties), party research or policy foundations and party-aligned 'think tanks'. For example, in Germany the social democrats are aligned with the *Friedrich Ebert Stiftung* and the CDU with the *Konrad Adenauer Stiftung*. Typically, these organizations provide policy advice and research for political parties and are often funded from public and party money. Although the extent of their involvement is usually advisory or the provision of expert information, some groups may also command greater influence in the policy process by virtue of their representation at key decision-making venues (for example, as delegates at party conference).

No/limited participation

The final category in Table 8.1 is assigned to political parties that are deliberately structured in order to give their members no, or limited, say over policy development. Parties in this category would range from conservative political parties that have a formal separation between the party in public office and the party in central office and the party on the ground, with the former responsible for the prerogative of policy development and the latter two groupings setting the broader political direction of the party, for example, the Liberal Party of Australia. At the other end of the scale stand political parties such as Geert Wilders' Freedom Party (PVV) in the Netherlands, which is structured and governed without a membership. Citizens may donate or register as volunteers and supporters of the party, but cannot join as members and hence have no say over policy formulation.

THE RELATIONSHIP BETWEEN DIFFERENT TYPES OF PARTICIPATION

Although some parties emphasize a certain type of participation over another, it is entirely possible for different models of participation to coexist within one party at different stages of the policy process. For example, while there is a historical emphasis on delegation in the social democratic parties, many are now combining this process with others that rely on representation (for example, policy commissions) and consultation. The Dutch PvdA amended its constitution and processes in 2009 to accommodate both delegates and the direct participation of individual members in the party's council and congress. Similarly, the decentralized Green parties attempt to combine direct participation in the formulation of local policy with representative/delegate processes for national policymaking.

Nonetheless, whether a particular type of participation is favourable is an inherently normative question that cannot be easily resolved, and reveals potential conflicts between different visions of democracy within the political party, and who advocates for them. While parties' elites might favour a certain model of participation (for example, representative forums such as conferences designed to aggregate the views of the membership or processes such as consultations that leave more scope to the parliamentary party to formulate policy in the name of efficient governance and broader representation), this may potentially diverge from the preferences of the party membership for direct policy involvement that, for example, facilitates political self-development and education. Possible difficulties may arise when considering the relationship between these different types of participation, particularly if they are implemented within one organization and driven by certain actors or groups within the party. Recent reforms to expand policy development beyond the formal membership, such as 'Refounding Labour' in the United Kingdom (see below), have been driven by party leaders, and in this situation, members accustomed to local groups may feel excluded from the political decision-making process by a shift to consultative forums.

ARE TECHNOLOGICAL DEVELOPMENTS AND DECLINING MEMBERSHIPS CHANGING THE NATURE OF POLICY DEVELOPMENT?

There is substantial agreement amongst party scholars that both levels of party membership and activism/engagement within political parties are in decline across nearly all industrialized democracies (Scarrow and Gezgor 2010; Whiteley 2011; van Biezen et al. 2012). At the same time, however, we have witnessed the emergence of new communications technologies that, in the eyes of parties themselves, might fundamentally transform the nature of party organizations by overcoming challenges of interest aggregation traditionally posed by limited human resources and geographic proximity. A recent review of the UK Labour Party's internal organization, 'Refounding Labour', noted that:

> New technology and fresh techniques . . . could help to revive the party's internal democracy by closing the gap between the leaders and the led.

> Genuine two-way communication could assure that the authentic voice of the grassroots is heard and cannot be ignored. (Hain 2011: 15)

Given the low rates of participation in traditional avenues for policy debate (such as branch meetings), political parties have turned to engaging their members through alternate means, for example by using the Internet to create members-only forums and discussion boards (Gibson and Ward 1998; Gibson et al. 2003; Chen et al. 2006; Margetts 2006). However, there has also been a trend to expanding a party's base by establishing supporters' networks and opening up policy consultations to the public, thereby removing (in part) what was once the privilege of party members and which signals a key tension inherent in parties between balancing the views of members with those of party voters and the wider community, and responding to concerns over legitimacy in the face of dwindling memberships. For the most part, this engagement is occurring online.

For example, supporters of political parties in the UK can join either the Labour Supporters' Network or become a friend of the Conservatives or the Liberal Democrats, and contribute to policy formation through consultation initiatives such as 'Fresh Ideas' (Labour), 'Stand Up Speak Up' (Conservatives) or the Liberal Democrats' online policy consultation forum (<http://consult.libdems.org.uk>). 'Fresh Ideas' was launched by the Labour Party in June 2011 (<http://fresh-ideas.org.uk>) and presents a platform through which members of the public have the opportunity to suggest ideas around several Labour policy priorities: 'building a fairer economy', 'helping the next generation get on', 'the cost of living crisis for families', 'strong and safe communities', and a 'secure country in a better world'. The rationale for the consultation was expressed by Labour leader Ed Miliband as follows:

> When I became leader of the Labour Party, I set out to take a new approach to politics. I established a policy review to take a fresh look at Labour's policy in every area; to hear directly from the British people about what matters to you. (UK Labour 2011a)

What is interesting about all three cases of policy consultation and development is the common rationale for their development, expressing a desire to rebrand the party as concerned with establishing a 'new' style of politics, and to expand opportunities for engagement and consultation beyond the traditional party membership, to the public at large, and to utilize new communications technologies.[1]

What is the implication of this for IPD? Moves to outsource policy development through greater community consultation fundamentally alter the chain of policy transmission and the traditional role of party members within it. In the original mass party model of transmission, policies filtered up to the party leadership

[1] For an early Canadian example of attempts to use communication technology to facilitate grassroots participation in party policy development, see Cross (1998).

through the membership and policymaking was formally the preserve of the party on the ground (see, for example, Poguntke 1998: 156; and see Carty, this volume). This partisan connection occurred by virtue of party members consulting with their communities, and belonging to various organizations (such as unions, environmental movements, etc.)—giving members a sense of pertinent policy issues and also serving as a wellspring of ideas. In turn, these ideas were crystallized into party policy through internal party processes such as annual conferences. In the new model of policy development the mediating role of the party membership is downgraded; rather it and the community (or general public) are placed as two alternative sources of policy input. The leadership is able to by-pass the membership by consulting directly with the community and party supporters.

Whether or not this is desirable from a normative perspective can be debated—there are both positive and negative implications. For example, a greater range of interests, or more representative interests, may be accommodated, but this may occur at the expense of a 'bottom-up' stream of policy communication and more active (or high intensity) forms of participation. However, regardless of the normative implications of these developments, they do appear to be changing the nature of the demos with respect to policy development and IPD—from the notion of a party member to a much broader category of potential participants including supporters and the general public.

An even more extreme development of this process of policy participation is captured in the establishment of 'direct democracy' political parties that pledge to communicate all legislative decisions to their members and supporters, who are then asked to vote for their preferred course of action online, which the party's elected representatives will then follow. Although they have not yet achieved electoral success, examples of these types of parties include the Direct Democracy Party in the United States (<http://www.directdemocracyparty.org>) and Senator Online in Australia (<http://senatoronline.org.au>). It may, however, be misleading to label such organizations as political parties, given that the role of an organization as a mediator between citizens and leaders has been completely removed.

WHAT IS THE LINK BETWEEN MEMBERS' PREFERENCES AND ACTUAL POLICIES?

The modes of participation discussed thus far represent the ways through which the policy preferences of the membership are aggregated and turned into 'official' party policy. But what happens then? From one perspective, we might conclude that what parties have to do in order to be internally 'democratic' is to adopt the policies that their members would have adopted if they were fully able to make policies in their own right. From another perspective, however, it is not the quality or outcome of the policies but the direct involvement of the members themselves that defines IPD. These two perspectives highlight a crucial distinction in the analysis of IPD and policy development—the distinction between processes and outcomes.

An outcomes-based analysis: is policy congruent with members' views?

An outcomes-based approach to analysing IPD emphasizes the relationship, or congruence, between party policy and the policy preferences of the membership. While party scholars have undertaken research on the policy positions of political parties relative to one another and across democracies (see, for example, Benoit and Laver 2006) relatively little has been written on the relationship between members' views and the policies adopted by political parties. The difficulty in determining whether a policy process is internally democratic using an outcomes-based approach lies not only in assessing or measuring the policy preferences of the membership (assuming that such preferences exist), but in the task of identifying what *party* policy actually is—given that it could exist in a variety of guises including election manifestos, policy platforms, and speeches by the party leadership and parliamentary party groups.

Rather than looking at specific policy agreements or disagreements, another way of measuring congruence is to assess the relative ideological positions of those involved in intra-party policy processes. Research on the ideological congruence of party voters, members, activists, and leaders has tended to reveal mixed results (see, for example, May 1967; Norris 1995) but usually depicts party leaders as vote-seekers and activists as policy-seekers, committed to purposive goals (Mulé 1997: 503). While such differences do not necessarily preclude a policy development process from being regarded as democratic, they do indicate that there is inherent conflict involved in the formulation of a policy stance. These conflicts may well flow from established patterns of ideological preference between various sub-groups within the party, but in order to establish which voice dominates in the creation of policy it is necessary to examine the interactions between the various actors in the policy process, and the institutions that shape these interactions.

A process-based analysis: do members contribute to policy development?

An alternative approach to evaluating IPD in policy development is to examine the process of policy development rather than the outcomes that are achieved. If IPD is defined by the participation of the membership in policy decisions, in this way, it can be measured or assessed by identifying and evaluating the most common ways in which members can formally participate in the policymaking process of their party.

There are a number of possible ways of evaluating the success of IPD in these particular contexts. For example, one could examine:

- local branch meetings (the number and breadth of policy issues discussed, attendance and levels of participation)
- party conferences and working groups (how representation is divided amongst members of the political party, the official role of party conferences in policy-making, inclusiveness, attitudes towards the task of committee service, conference attendance, travel costs and barriers to participation, the quality of deliberation and debate)
- consultations (number and range of participants involved in consultation exercises, responses and attitudes to consultations and resources deployed by the party to assist in such activities).

IPD is not a one-dimensional concept and therefore it is best measured through a combination of indicators (such as those above), attitudinal surveys, and qualitative studies of the roles of participants who are engaged in these processes. The limited number of existing studies that have sought to examine policy development and IPD (either directly or indirectly) have typically adopted a single case study approach, or small 'n' comparative design (Duverger 1954; Michels 1962; McKenzie 1963; Scarrow 1996; Widfeldt 1999; Gauja 2005; Pettitt 2007; Loxbo 2011). Although a thorough examination of trends in participation in policy development is beyond the scope of this chapter, there are several findings that are useful to highlight as indicators of the current and possible future character of IPD with respect to policy formulation.

In federated democracies such as Australia and Switzerland, and those with distinct territorial divisions marked by numerous layers of government, participation is potentially more vibrant at the local level. This is often obscured in party research focused on national politics, but arises from the functional division of labour between federal, regional, and local party (see Eldersveld 1964; Bolleyer 2011). Parties such as the Liberal Democrats and the Swiss, English, and Australian Greens emphasize the autonomy of their local groups and the potential of members to engage in policymaking that is relevant and more immediate, thereby producing greater perceptions of efficacy and meaning. Nonetheless, the localization of participation has important consequences for the development of national policy as party activists who might otherwise be involved in this process find their time and energy drained by local demands, also creating or emphasizing separate streams of policy expertise. As Burchell (2008: 150) observes,

> While the [Swedish] Greens had placed significant emphasis upon local party autonomy . . . success found them stretched in terms of the number of active members available. In some districts there were simply not enough members to implement office rotation and, in some cases, members had to take on numerous roles within their local party.

One of the most significant factors guiding the patterns of *formal* participation in policy development in parties is the size of the party. In theory, it is far easier to facilitate greater membership participation in parties with fewer members (Barber 1984: 151; Sartori 1987: 113; see also Tan 1998). As an example, the possibilities for individual involvement in policy working groups and conferences are far greater in smaller parties such as the Greens and more remote within the larger social democratic parties. However, if IPD is defined by the direct involvement of party members in the policymaking process, how does the well-documented decline in party membership affect IPD and policy development? On one hand, it may not necessarily be a negative trend—if we accept the claim that membership participation is inversely related to party size, then a reduction in party memberships might facilitate greater opportunities for direct participation.

Nevertheless, empirical evidence indicates that no matter how easy or accessible the participatory opportunities within a political party are, only a fraction of the membership become actively involved. Comparative data on levels of participation in party activities and more specific measures such as attendance at branch meetings and policy forums (for example, Bennie et al. 1996; Seyd and Whiteley 2002; van Schuur 2005: 12; Vromen 2005; Whiteley et al. 2006) suggest that on average, approximately 9 per cent of party members can be regarded as 'active'. As a further example, an internal poll of its membership conducted by the Australian Democrats found that on average only 12 per cent of members participated in policy ballots in the period 1990–2002 (Australian Democrats 2003: 21).

Nevertheless, some variation does exist between parties. In Westminster democracies for example, social democrats tend to suffer from the lowest rates of participation, whereas the Greens exhibit the highest (Gauja forthcoming). On one hand, this could suggest that as parties become more established and professional, rates of active membership participation decline as members are no longer required, or desired, as volunteer labour. However, as the problem of membership disengagement from policy development initiatives extends across party types and democracies, even to those parties with significant participatory opportunities on offer, it might also indicate that the internal organizational structure of political parties is not solely to blame for this trend. Rather, it may provide support for the hypothesis that political participation in society is gradually shifting away from traditional venues such as political parties (see, for example, Mair 2005; and Katz, this volume), or members' preference for a form of democracy by stealth (Hibbing and Theiss-Morse 2002). Owing to the pressures of time, busy lifestyles and a lack of information or interest in particular topic areas, members might be content with more generalized forms of participation—for example, setting the overall political direction of the party through an acquiescence at conference debates rather than voting on specific motions, by 'subcontracting' policy participation through donating to the party, or simply to be led. It also indicates that we cannot necessarily assume that party members desire a greater role in the policy process.

WHAT ARE THE LEGISLATIVE, GOVERNANCE, AND ELECTORAL IMPACTS OF INTERNALLY DEMOCRATIC POLICY DEVELOPMENT?

The legislative dimension

Evaluating the extent to which groups and individuals are able to influence a party's internal policy and decision-making processes is a good indicator of IPD, assuming one crucial factor: that the policy determined by the party is actually translated into legislative actions. Or in other words, what happens after grassroots members' participation in policy development and how does this translate into the actual setting of a party's policy positions or manifesto? It is in this context that the role of the party in public office is paramount.

Even though theories of party organization examine the power of the party in public office in controlling intra-party decision-making (see, for example, Katz and Mair 2002; and Carty, this volume), the activities of the party in public office within the legislative arena are generally under-theorized and remain largely within the realm of legislative studies. For the purpose of assessing IPD, the key element that is relevant here is that a party's elected representatives work to implement the principles and policies of the party. Nonetheless, political parties emerged well after the establishment of representative legislatures and consequently there is a great deal of tension between the design of parliaments that are intended to be comprised of independent/constituency representatives, and the theory and practice of party government. For example, the constitutional design of parliaments in many representative democracies is rooted in Burkean conceptions of the role of the parliamentarian as an independent representative (or trustee) of their electorate rather than a party delegate. Therefore, one of the difficulties encountered by parties and parliamentarians in identifying and enforcing their respective policy responsibilities is the multi-dimensional nature of representation, which involves public, parliamentary, and party duties.

Therefore, how party parliamentarians view their legislative roles and responsibilities will in turn impact upon how members' involvement is translated into party policy, and the operation of IPD. However, ascertaining the extent to which party legislators (either as a group or individually) adhere to the principles of the party and the policies and manifestos it has previously formulated is again problematic. While roll call votes may indicate how cohesive a legislative party grouping is, they cannot of themselves measure the congruence between a legislative position and party policy. Another option is to judge the content of legislation against a party's platform, yet in order to measure IPD it is necessary to show that the platform was *formulated* by democratic means—that is, with the participation of the membership, or at the very least, is congruent with their views or policy preferences.

Another complication might arise in situations where there is no specific party policy on an issue that is being debated in the legislature. How can we measure congruence in these instances? Given these constraints, IPD (in so far as legislators respect the wishes of the party and its members) might be evaluated through the analysis of several complementary factors: the legislative behaviour of party parliamentarians (for example, time spent on party and constituency duties; voting patterns), their attitudes to representation (whether parliamentarians see themselves as trustees or party delegates), and the decision-making processes of parties' elected parliamentarians (the degree of centralization and control vested in the cabinet or key individuals). An analysis of the pervasiveness of these different dimensions can potentially address the broader question of how responsive MPs are to their political parties and the policies on which they were elected—an important aspect of the operation of party government in modern democracies and a crucial element of IPD.

For example, a comparison of studies on parliamentarians' legislative role perceptions suggests that the party to which a parliamentarian belongs will influence his or her attitudes to representation, with left parliamentarians more likely to perceive of themselves as party representatives and conservative parliamentarians as trustees. In Denmark, Damgaard (1997: 84) finds that whilst centre, liberal, and conservative parliamentarians are strongly individualist, the socialists advocate the primacy of party. A similar pattern has been reported between social democratic, liberal, and conservative groupings in the UK (Cowley 2002; Rush and Giddings 2002: 11–13). However, again the evidence is not entirely conclusive: while these findings indicate that socialist parliamentarians might be more responsive to party policy; they can also be contrasted with the general sentiment reported in previous research that a parliamentarian is by and large an independent representative and who spends relatively little time attending party meetings and engaging in party activities when compared with other parliamentary duties (such as committee and constituency service) (see, for example, Burnell 1980: 14).

Internal party democracy and governance

The legislative position of a political party (that is, whether it is in government or in opposition) also influences the distribution of power and influence in terms of IPD and policymaking. Given that engaging the extra-parliamentary party organization in decision-making brings with it the possibility of dissent and difference of opinion, this is easier to achieve in opposition. As political parties increase their legislative importance and move closer to government or a balance-of-power position there is a distinct shift in emphasis to the 'structural requirements of parliamentary politics' (Poguntke 2001: 8), whether this be legislative negotiation in a consensus chamber, considerations of electoral survival, or the associated shift in resource allocation. This changing emphasis has the potential to weaken the parliamentary party's responsiveness to the broader party organization and the policy formulated by it. As in the case of New Labour in the UK (1997–2010), being in government also shifts the rhetoric of policymaking from that of the party's interests, to a broader notion of the public and governance. As Labour parliamentarians Alan Milburn and Charles Clarke argued, the party's shift to a more consultative form of policymaking in government provided an 'opportunity not just of addressing the party—important though that is—but of engaging with the wider public' (*The Guardian* 2007: 2). However, some parties have sought to mediate this trend, to a point, through fostering a culture of engagement (for example, by encouraging parliamentarians to attend party meetings) and establishing processes to integrate both the party in public office and the party on the ground into a joint stream of policymaking (such as policy working groups that include both party members and parliamentarians in the case of the UK Liberal Democrats and the Swedish Social Democrats).

An added tension faced by political parties that must govern in coalition and those that hold balance-of-power positions is the need to negotiate policy and legislative positions with other parties in order to achieve compromise and impact. In these parties, strict adherence to the official policies as developed by the membership may not be possible as parliamentarians are faced with the potential conflict between either staying true to the party's formal position or ideology, or compromising on some issues to achieve effective governance. For example, as Bale and Wilson (2006: 399) reported, in the aftermath of the 2005 general election, NZ Greens' members 'were already questioning whether the support agreement negotiated by party leaders with the Labour government was worth it, and why the agreement was not subjected to a vote by party members'. More recently, since the 2010 general election in the UK, the Liberal Democrats have faced a number of policy challenges in their coalition experience with the Conservatives. One of the most contentious of these has been the issue of tuition fees for university students, over which the Liberal Democrats' leadership backed down from the party's official policy to abolish university tuition fees in order to honour the coalition agreement.

Furthermore, the organizational development of Green parties throughout Europe appears to indicate that an internally democratic policy process may not be conducive to effective and responsive governance. As Green parties have gained legislative significance, organizational reforms and evolutions in working practices tend to privilege a typically pragmatic parliamentary party at the expense of the broader membership (see Poguntke 2001; Rihoux and Rüdig 2006: 17–19; Frankland 2008: 36). This experience is consistent with recent findings that the distribution of power within a political party affects its decision-making efficiency, especially in coalition negotiations. In her study of Danish political parties, Pedersen showed that 'parties close to the government in policy terms whose parliamentary party group is powerful participate more often in legislative accommodation than do parties where power is located in the national party organization' (2010: 738). Hence a political party with internally democratic policy development processes, in which decision-making power is located within the party's membership, will find it more difficult to participate in governing coalitions. In this sense, while members may be adopting the policies they would like the government to adopt if their party won a majority, in doing so they might make it more likely that the other side will actually govern.

The electoral impact of an internally democratic policy process

This chapter has sought to highlight the complexity and challenges of assessing the relationship between an internally democratic policy process and a political party's ability to govern and transfer the policy preferences of its membership to the legislative arena. The final question that remains to be considered is whether a political party—by producing policies more to the liking of the members, or by adopting policies produced by the members—will be advantaged or disadvantaged at the polls. That is, does IPD have an electoral benefit?

It is perhaps not a surprise to learn that no systematic empirical studies have been undertaken of the specific effect of internally democratic policymaking processes on the electoral fortunes of a political party. At face value, there does not appear to be much of a link. Political parties that portray themselves as being internally democratic, such as Green parties, the Australian Democrats, D66 (the Netherlands) and the New Democrats (Canada), have experienced electoral fluctuations throughout their histories. Nevertheless, there are quite a few theoretical expectations that again suggest mixed results. For example, Alan Ware advocates IPD as a remedy to ameliorate the deficiencies of a competitive system. By making the party leadership more accountable to its members, parties would be kept more closely aligned to shifts in the electorate and hence this policy responsiveness should produce electoral benefits (Ware 1979: 78). However, Ware's argument has been criticized because it assumes members are representative of the electorate, which may not be the case empirically (Teorell 1999: 367).

As discussed previously, several attempts have been made to analyse the relationship between party voters, members, activists, and leaders in ideological terms. The law of curvilinear disparity postulates that voters will take the most moderate line on issues, while active party members, driven by ideological principles, are the most ideologically extreme. Legislators, dependent on the electorate for re-election, must be aware of and cater to voter opinions and consequently fall between the two groups (May 1973: 148–9). In contrast to Ware's argument, 'if party sub-leaders are more extreme than most party voters, and they influence the platform and elected representatives, this may produce a radically polarized party system out of tune with public opinion. If party leaders try to move towards the 'catch-all' centre ground, sub-leaders may act as a drag on change' (Norris 1995: 31–2). Yet, assessing the law of curvilinear disparity with respect to British parties, Norris found that party activists were not consistently the radical stratum within the party, and that the distinction between parliamentarians and activists is much fuzzier than suggested by May's law (1995: 42). Ideological diversity (see Kitschelt 1989: 403) within a party therefore complicates the notion of a coherent party membership, and its effect on policy popularity and electoral outcomes. Furthermore, the electoral impact of the ideological positions of party members will only come into play *if they influence the platform and elected representatives*, that is, ideological difference matters only so far as these groupings actually have a say.

Irrespective of the policy link produced by internally democratic procedures, they are often used by political parties as an advertising mechanism to highlight the legitimacy and strength of their organizations. For example, in Belgium, Wauters (2009: 13) notes that parties have done this with respect to leadership elections and internal referenda: 'After the SP referendum, the party described it as a 'dialogue without predecessor' and 'an immense success.' Similarly, the PSC called their 2002 referendum 'a brilliant proof of the members' interest in their party'. In Germany, the Greens stressed the 'grassroots' nature of their party organization during their early electoral success (Frankland 2008: 28). Such 'democratic' initiatives are also undertaken by political parties that have suffered electoral setbacks, for example the UK Conservatives' use of policy ballots after the party's defeat in the 1997 general election, and the Labour Party's 'unprecedented' public consultation exercise 'Fresh Ideas', undertaken as a way of reconnecting with supporters after it returned to opposition in 2010 (UK Labour 2011b: 5). Yet the extent to which the voters are actually aware of the internal organizational arrangements of political parties is another matter altogether: a survey of Belgian voters showed that they generally tended to overestimate the degree of IPD within parties (Wauters 2009: 14–15), suggesting that there may only be limited additional benefit for parties seeking to advertise, or indeed genuinely implement internally democratic policy processes within their organizations.

The trend for political parties to advertise for greater community and supporter input in policymaking (as discussed previously) and the shift to more consultative forums for policy development appears to be consistent with a longer-term political marketing strategy. As Lees-Marshment and Quayle (writing within the sub-discipline of political communication) argue, 'attention to [membership] demands can be incorporated within a marketing strategy designed to achieve electoral success' (2001: 211–12). However,

> electoral imperatives dictate (and political marketing advises) that the party should formulate a policy programme on the basis of input from the wider electorate, not just the membership, and that the leadership should have a firm

> grip on policymaking. Within a market-oriented party there is little room for the excessive ideology of the activists. (Lees-Marshment and Quayle 2001: 208)

Notwithstanding the assumption regarding the 'excessive ideology' of party activists, the notion of the 'market-oriented party' raises some very interesting questions regarding the future of policy development and IPD. By extending the policy process to the general public, we might be witnessing the emergence of a more expansive and arguably inclusive form of IPD. By the same token, however, at what stage does expanding policy consultation effectively remove the notions of 'intra' and the 'party' as a mediating organization from our understandings of IPD?

CONCLUSION

Political parties commonly attempt to implement principles associated with IPD into the processes by which they formulate official party policies, manifest in the common mantra that members can 'have their say'. However, what actually constitutes having a say is far more difficult to determine and hence one of the major difficulties in implementing and measuring IPD in terms of policy development is the fact that it is conceptualized and evaluated differently by different groups and individuals—depending on who is asking the questions. This is not to say, however, that internally democratic policy development cannot be analysed, but that the benchmarks used to evaluate its effectiveness need to be made explicit. Furthermore, as a multi-dimensional concept, a diverse range of indicators (of processes, outcomes, attitudes, etc.) is required to assess the extent to which policymaking within parties can be described as democratic. This chapter highlighted some of the complexities and challenges involved in attempting to analyse the relationship between IPD and effective governance, its impact upon legislative dynamics and actual policy adoption, and finally the electoral advantages and disadvantages of IPD—all of which reveal mixed results.

The chapter also articulated some of the ways in which IPD is implemented through different types of participation in the policy process, and in particular the shift towards more consultative forms of participation and the engagement of party supporters and the wider community at the expense of traditional channels of communication that privileged the party membership. This trend illustrates one of the key tensions inherent in IPD and its application to policy development: who should be represented in this process? IPD, by its very nature, is conceived of as privileging party members in the making of internal policy decisions. But is this desirable if party memberships are unrepresentative of the general electorate, and is it viable for political parties in government? With these questions in mind, there are two ways of interpreting the opening up of policy development: either as a potential breakdown of IPD, or as an indicator of what is now becoming accepted and usual practice. If we accept the latter interpretation, we need to think through what this might mean for the nature of party membership, and whether there is any real meaning to the prefix 'intra' in intra-party democracy.

9

What Is Democratic Candidate Selection?

Gideon Rahat

Candidate selection takes place prior to general elections. It is the process by which parties decide whom to present as their candidates in elections. These may be candidates on a list or in single member districts. Because some candidacies are worth much more than others—for example, in a safe district or at the top of a list—candidate selection is as important to individual politicians as are general elections.

As this chapter will demonstrate, if we adhere to the notion that democracy has the same meaning within parties as it does at the state level, then we have to admit that such democracy is a rare phenomenon. To illustrate this, imagine a country (we cannot call it a democracy) in which general elections look like candidate selection. There is limited suffrage, and not all citizens have the right to stand for election. Freedom and fairness of elections are not strictly upheld because of a lack of resources and will, and thus the results may not be seen as legitimate. Moreover in many cases, incumbents face no subsequent competition and thus lack an incentive to be responsive to their voters and accountable for their actions and misdoings.

Following this exercise, we may end up thinking that primaries in the US are the most democratic, as they most closely resemble general elections. Yet scholars are not at all unequivocal on this point. When proposing a recipe for democracy, they tend to be cautious, to expose the reader to possible risks of inclusiveness and openness (Norris 2004; Scarrow 2005; Ashiagbor 2008; Williams and Paun 2011). In doing so, they highlight some of the different democratic norms that may be at tension among varying forms of candidate selection.

Methods of candidate selection vary over time, from party to party and even within the same party in different districts. This, in itself, does not mean that it is impossible to find a common denominator that defines democratic candidate selection. After all, electoral systems also vary, yet we know what democratic election is and what it is not. The goal of this chapter is both to determine whether candidate selection—as the possible 'twin sister' of elections—adheres to the standards of democratic elections and to assess what the expectations from it are in terms of democracy.

The chapter starts with an examination of the implementation of the basic shared standards of democratic elections for candidate selection. These two institutions—elections and selections—are functionally similar in the sense that they are supposed to regulate democratic choice. They are also seen as sequential elements in the chain of the recruitment process (Norris 1997). Yet I could find no comparison in the literature between candidate selection and election—they are addressed only separately (except for studies analysing the impact of one on the other, e.g. divisive primaries and their influence on elections results). Take, for example, the Inter Parliamentary Union's expanded edition of 'Free and Fair Elections' (Goodwin-Gill 2006): in all its 214 pages, it makes almost no mention of candidate selection. Meanwhile, three impressive NGO reports that promote candidate selection as a means to enhance democracy do not compare selections to elections (Norris 2004; Scarrow 2005; Ashiagbor 2008). Having said that, a closer look suggests that the comparison is there, if embedded in the background. Even scholars who are critical of primaries call their adoption 'democratization', admitting that inclusiveness in candidate selection, which approaches the idea of universal suffrage, is 'more' democratic (Rahat and Hazan 2001). Not surprisingly, the comparison that will be conducted here ultimately concludes that, rather than being its twin sister, candidate selection is at best the (democratically) impoverished cousin of elections.

The second part of the chapter reviews the democratic expectations that parties have of candidate selection. Parties usually set limited expectations of candidate selection, and these tend to pertain to inclusiveness and representation. They may present reforms that increase the inclusiveness of their selectorates and/or that oblige them to ensure certain kinds and levels of representation (adoption of representation correction mechanisms, such as quotas) as enhancements of IPD. In short, IPD in candidate selection is perceived in terms of an inclusive participatory process and a representative outcome.

SELECTION AS THE TWIN SISTER OF ELECTIONS

Our starting point is the notion that, in general, democracy has the same meaning both at the state level and within parties. That is, we should look for the same traits and impose the same standards at both levels. In particular, candidate selection is to the party what elections are to the democratic state: parties and (sometimes) individual candidates compete in democratic legislative elections while individuals and, rarely, party factions (e.g. Argentina; see De Luca, Jones, and Tula 2002) compete for a realistic candidacy in internal party selection.

When we define national elections as democratic, we expect them to be inclusive, free, fair, and (periodically) competitive. Can we expect the same from candidate selection? Let us see whether candidate selection in democratic states fulfils the real-world expectations that are set for elections.

Inclusive

Democratic elections need to be inclusive in terms of the electorate (universal suffrage) and in terms of candidacy (the right to run for office and/or be elected).[1] When it comes to candidate selection, only the US primaries uphold such a high standard of inclusiveness in terms of both candidacy and the selectorate (which is similar to the electorate). This is clearly the case for the most open methods—(nonpartisan, blanket, and also open primaries). But even American closed primaries are highly inclusive in comparative terms. This cannot be understood to directly result from the fact that United States' legislation regulates candidate selection. In other countries where the law requires parties to adopt relatively inclusive selectorates—such as Germany, New Zealand, and Finland—the standard is direct and even indirect involvement of party members, not of all voters. The depth of regulation and the actual 'nationalization' of US parties, however, are of a different kind and, as we shall see, do constitute a case in which democratic election and selection are highly similar, if not identical, institutions.

In general, levels of inclusiveness of candidate selection methods vary across democratic countries, within them, and even within parties at different times and in different districts and regions. In some cases selection is restricted to party members, in others to delegates who were selected by party members, and in still others to non-selected party elites or even to a single leader. For example, variance is found among the Nordic countries that usually hold common high democratic standards (Narud, Pedersen, and Valen 2002). In Iceland, parties often conduct open primaries in which all voters in the relevant district can participate. In Finland (by law) and Denmark (without a law), party primaries—which are restricted to membership participation—are the norm. In Norway, in most cases, the selectorate is composed of selected delegates who ratify or change a list that a small nomination committee prepared before the selection meeting. Meanwhile, in Israel, high variance is found in the level of inclusiveness of the selectorate: in some Israeli parties members are the selectorate, in others delegates are, and still in others the selectorate is a small party elite or even a single leader. In Belgium (with no law) and in Germany (by law), within the same party, in some districts party members are involved in candidate selection, in others delegates select the candidates.

Parties also often include several selectorates with varying levels of inclusiveness. This is the case for the British parties that use a multi-stage selection process that starts, many times, with a small screening committee, continues with a delegate-nominated shortlist and ends with membership selection. In the

[1] Opening selection to the whole electorate does not imply that it is, as a whole, the relevant demos, but that we allow all of those that support the party to be part of its demos. We cannot, of course, be sure that all those who take part in candidate selection are supporters of the party, even in the weak sense that they will vote for it or for its candidates in the general elections.

Conservative Party, before the 2010 elections, the process even ended with a selection meeting open to all voters in about 100 districts (selection was still subject to members' approval) and open primaries through postal ballot in two districts (McIlveen 2009; McSweeney 2010).

Adopting more inclusive selectorates may seem to be democratic in the sense that it indicates a narrowing of the gap between the size of the selectorate and the electorate. Yet, it remains unclear whether opening up the selectorates makes them more representative of the electorate. In fact, it may actually provide disproportional power to those individuals and groups that have the ability to mobilize people to join parties (in case of party primaries) and/or to take part in selection (in case of open primaries). Israel, for example, has seen several attempts by groups to recruit members to parties in order to use the opening up of the selection process to promote their own interests and ideologies. There are several extreme right groups and—recently—also a left-wing group publicly calling on the people—especially voters of other parties—to take on membership in the Likud, the right-wing governing party, in order to influence candidate selection. To encourage the trend, the recruiters stress that selecting Likud candidates and then in the general election voting for other parties will double voters' political influence.

As long as only a small minority of the electorate takes part in the opened-up selection events, it may actually distort responsiveness. On the other hand, this claim also applies to many second-order elections, so it can be argued that parties should be (democratically) praised for opening up; it is the people who are to be blamed for not taking advantage of the opportunity given to them to enhance their influence. Whatever the case, the discussion above brings to the fore the question: who is the party demos? Is it the party's voters or all voters? If it is one of them, but it is practically smaller—because only a small minority join parties and take part in candidate selection—should it be representative of them?

Candidacy requirements also vary. Parties use a mix of formal and informal mechanisms to tailor their pool of candidates. Some parties might let anyone (anyone, that is, eligible to do so according to the national law) compete for candidacy, while others might require party membership for a certain period of time prior to selection and some even add additional restrictions. Candidacy in many of the US Democratic and Republican primaries is, in principle, open to all citizens, and this in itself is seen as a way to assure the implementation of the democratic right to stand for elections. In Ireland, as in most democracies, the parties effectively control who can and cannot seek candidacy under their party label. Some parties chose not to limit candidacy to people who were members for a fixed period before selection, while others restricted it to those who were members for six months, a year, and even two years (Gallagher 1988).

Additional restrictions include age restrictions: Austrian and Belgian parties, for example, limited the maximum age of their candidates (De Winter 1988; Müller 1992). Such a limitation, we can reasonably assume, would not be adopted through a national law because—unlike the requirements for minimal age—it would be seen as an unfair restriction of the right to stand for election. What country would dare block the election of its seniors? A party or parties may do it, and still the golden-agers will have the chance to get elected, through other parties or by establishing a party of their own (possibly a pensioners' party). This may underscore why state-level democracy should abide by stricter standards than parties. After all, parties are sub-units within a democratic whole. Yet, on the other hand, especially in cases where parties monopolize elections, achieving democracy at the state level might require that parties too abide by certain rules, such as allowing ethnic minorities or women to join them and take part in their candidate selections.

Unlike democracy at the state level, at the party level there is no norm or standard for inclusiveness—for either the selectorate or for candidacy—that serves as a threshold that a party must pass to be considered a democratic party. In short, most democracies fail the inclusiveness test. This might lead us to conclude, already at this early stage, that most democracies are deficient in this sense. This would be the case even for those relatively inclusive cases in which parties allow all citizens to join them as members and take part in candidate selection if they are ready to pay a membership fee. No country that would ask a citizen to pay a fee in order to participate in elections would be considered democratic these days. This leaves us with the US as the only case that comes close to meeting the standard.

Or it might indicate that elections and selections are not twin sisters.

Free

> Freedom entails the right and the opportunity to choose one thing over another. (Elklit and Svensson 1997: 35)

In mass democratic elections, free individual choice is the norm. Citizens make their own choices and are not coerced into choosing a specific party or candidate. Candidate selection in a democracy is as free as elections when it comes to those traits that define the polity as a democracy and its elections as democratic: freedom of movement, speech, assembly, association, press, and so on.

However, in the intra-party environment we might face phenomena that we would not tolerate at the national level. The secret ballot is an important feature of democratic elections as it is meant to ensure that those who can potentially pressure the voter do not know whether he/she ultimately complied or not. In parties in which selection is a result of elite bargaining secrecy is not kept in the sense that the few who engage in the bargaining make their preferences explicit, at least to each other. In those cases, coercion is unlikely when the few selectors are powerful enough to expose their preferences and negotiate them with others who have different preferences. Coercion is likely when a single leader is much more powerful than other members of the selectorate. We may thus say that in parties in which selection is typically under the guidance of a single leader, it is not free. Such intra-party realities seem to be typical for the extreme right in Europe (for example, the French National Front), for parties that were established and dominated by a single leader, such as Silvio Berlusconi's Forza Italia and Winston Peters' New Zealand First, and for religious parties. But even in parties in which the norm is using inclusive selectorates—such as the Liberal and Conservative parties in Canada, that use party members to select many of its candidates—we witness instances in which party leaders make the choice.

It seems that in wider selectorates (those composed of party delegates, members or supporters), secrecy is also the norm. Yet we encounter accounts and allegations of patron-client and other corrupt practices that defy the principle of free elections. We cannot quantitatively determine that these cases are more frequent or that they are more decisive in their influence on selection results. Yet, on the basis of what we hear and what is occasionally exposed, we can reasonably assume that at least in some parties and districts there is a Pandora's box concerning this element of the freedom of selection (Back and Solomos 1994; Baum and Robinson 1995; Criddle 1997; Rahat and Sher-Hadar 1999; Combes 2003; Navot 2006; Scherlis 2008).

Another aspect of free elections has to do with the opportunity to participate in the election (Elklit and Svensson 1997). Parties do not have resources at the scale that states have, and thus when we deal with mass selection within parties—membership ballots or primaries that are open to all citizens—the decision over where to hold the selection meeting or where to locate the polling booths (or whether—or not—to use postal ballot or online voting) might become critical in its influence on selection results. That is, a decision that implies that a selection meeting will take place in the hometown of one of the candidates may enhance her/his chances to win candidacy.

A final aspect of the freedom of elections is the legal possibility of complaint (Elklit and Svensson 1997). Parties in democracies can have judicial or semi-judicial organs that deal with complaints concerning breaches of the freedom (and fairness) of their internal elections. Yet, these organs are suspected (often with reason) of being partial. Sometimes state-level judicial organs are called in to decide and it is their policy towards parties (how autonomous they are) that will strongly affect their willingness to make decisions that may contradict those of the intra-party organs.

It is only when the democratic state gets involved, to regulate and administrate, that selection can be seen as upholding the standards of freedom of elections. Yet, this also requires parties to relinquish their autonomy.

Fair

> *Fairness* means impartiality. The opposite of fairness is unequal treatment of equals, whereby some people (or groups) are given unreasonable advantages.

> Thus, fairness involves both *regularity* (the unbiased application of rules) and *reasonableness* (the not-too-unequal distribution of relevant resources among competitors). (Elklit and Svensson 1997: 35)

Fairness of elections refers to many things relating to their administration and regulation.[2] These range from certain rules regarding the conduct and financing of campaigns to vote counts that do not distort the voters' verdict. They also include a requirement for transparency that will help demonstrate that the elections were indeed fair. Over the years democracies developed rules and mechanisms that by and large have succeeded in regulating elections according to the norms set by the legislators in each country. What about fairness in candidate selection?

From different accounts concerning candidate selection in established democracies we learn that parties do not have the ability (or sometimes the will) to ensure fair selection (Duverger 1954; Malloy 2003; Rahat 2008). Their abilities are limited because parties do not possess, as states do, the resources and apparatuses needed for administrating and regulating elections. Their motivation to investigate and punish candidates for breaking the rules is also low because candidate selection takes place on the eve of general elections, and the last thing they need then are allegations of intra-party corruption. Thus it is not surprising that democracies in which parties are formally and legally the basic units of electoral competition (democracies with proportional and mixed electoral systems) often choose to ignore this problem altogether (Hofnung 2008). Put differently, the 'solution' is not to take care of potential problems in advance but rather to keep selection a private matter and to find ad hoc solutions in case those problems arise.

A solution to the problem of unfair candidate selection is to involve the state in its regulation and even its administration (Hofnung 2008). As the American experience teaches us, this move implies that the notion of the party as a voluntary association is abandoned. That is, assuring fairness by harnessing the power and ability of the state is not cost-free. It can reduce the autonomy of the party up to the point that it would not be able to decide who can stand for candidacy and who can join as members. Nevertheless, it seems that the trend of increased regulation of parties by states is a reality (van Biezen 2004 and this volume). The real challenge is to see whether the American way is the only way, or perhaps there is another path that allows regulated parties some autonomy from the state. In short, and returning to our main concern here, it is safe to say that the little we know about unfairness in candidate selection—and perhaps even more the fact that we cannot know too much (which breaches the norm for transparency)—teaches us that selection is not likely to be as fair as are elections (save, maybe, for the US case).

[2] For a list of conditions that have to be fulfilled to make elections fair, see table 1 in Elklit and Svensson (1997).

(Periodically) competitive

Democratic elections should be competitive because they are supposed to allow different people and worldviews to compete for public posts. Periodic competition is important because it is supposed to keep elected representatives responsive and accountable to their voters. Democratic elections, then, are periodic so the elected representatives will know that they have to face the public from time to time and thus be accountable for their failures and successes.

We know that in practice, some elections are more competitive than others. If we take, for example, the success rate of incumbents to be re-elected as a sign of competition, we encounter high variance (Somit et al. 1994). When we look at the intra-party level, we also encounter high variance. In some cases—such as parties in the US, Canada, New Zealand, and the UK—incumbents are rarely removed and are even virtually irremovable. Once they are elected they stay in parliament either until they are defeated in national elections or until they decide to retire. In other cases—Israel (Hadar 2008), and Spain and Portugal (Montabes and Ortega 1999), for instance—selection seems to be a significant source for turnover.

We can reasonably expect candidate selection to be synchronized with elections. That is, prior to each election candidates have to be selected in order to compete (at least on a party ticket, which is the common phenomenon) in the general election. However, we know of many cases in which incumbents are automatically re-nominated. Sometimes it is a *de facto* phenomenon—there is a formal opportunity for competition but nobody contests. Sometimes it is the explicit decision of the party; this phenomenon is especially common in countries with elections in single member districts and small multi-member ones (Hazan and Rahat 2010).

Unlike the cases of inclusiveness, freedom, and fairness, it is here that candidate selection is not necessarily democratically 'inferior', or rather, as this chapter will argue, of a different kind. In other words, in democracies with large multi-member districts—and (relatively) centralized candidate selection—candidate selection may be an important arena for competition. Moreover, it is claimed that competition is actually higher in the less-inclusive case of selection by delegates rather than by party members (Rahat, Hazan, and Katz 2008). That is, wider inclusiveness does not breed more competition. While state regulation may ensure *de jure* competition in candidate selection, *de facto* competition seems to result from other features of the candidate selection method such as candidacy requirements, inclusiveness, and centralization (Hazan and Rahat 2010).

Summary: elections versus selections

American primaries are closer to elections than other candidate selection methods. They are highly inclusive, and because they are run by the state they can be as fair and free as general elections are. True, American primaries are not highly competitive, but we cannot definitively blame inclusiveness for that (Rahat, Hazan, and Katz 2008) because low competitiveness is found in most cases where a small district-magnitude electoral system results in a highly decentralized candidate selection method (Hazan and Rahat 2010). Yet, in following the participatory ethos, making candidate selection more inclusive, and in highly regulating it, to make selection free, fair and formally competitive, 'America's politicians helped to propel [the parties] down a path in which they became arguably less important political intermediaries than parties in other democracies' (Ware 2002: 264). In short, highly inclusive, regulated candidate selection is not without a price, maybe because it becomes too similar to elections.

It is clear that selection is democratically inferior to general elections when we compare them using the terms we expect the latter to fulfil. Elections at most times are more inclusive, fair, and free. In terms of periodic competition we cannot make the same claim, but neither can we argue that selection is democratically superior here, except perhaps in some cases of candidate selection in large multi-member districts. This should lead us to reformulate our expectations. A growing number of countries do achieve the standards of democratic elections. Yet, these same standards are not fulfilled when it comes to candidate selection. This reflects a democratic reality in which candidate selection is not judged by the same standards as elections (except for the exceptional American case). If so, what is democratic candidate selection? The next section looks at how parties (and, in a few cases, countries) deal with this quandary.

THE PERCEPTION OF DEMOCRATIC CANDIDATE SELECTION

In the last decades, parties reformed their candidate selection methods in the name of enhancing IPD. They did so in two central ways. One was to democratize the selection process: in the last fifty years, more and more parties have given their members a central (and some even an exclusive) role in the selection of their candidates (Scarrow et al. 2000; Bille 2001; Caul-Kittilson and Scarrow 2003).[3] In the UK, for example, the Labour and Conservative parties increasingly involve their members—and the latter, even non-members—in the final stage of the selection of their candidates. The same trends—the adoption of increasingly

[3] Another development in candidate selection that could also reflect democratization, and could have been—but was not—presented as such was the easing of candidacy requirements. There is no systematic study that maps this trend. Yet more electorally oriented parties seem to prefer to open their ranks to potentially popular outsiders, rather than limiting candidacy to those who served within the party for long periods before being eligible to present for candidacy.

inclusive selectorates—are reported from all over the democratic world, including second-wave democracies such as Israel and third-wave democracies such as Taiwan, Argentina, and Botswana.

Yet, it should be noted that in many cases, parties open their selection in an incremental way, and even then with caution—that is, they involve their members in selection but do not give them the sole authority to select candidates, In other words, party members are one selectorate out of a few that participate in selection. They may be selecting from a shortlist that was designed by small exclusive selectorates (the UK parties fall into this category), or they might have a voice that is then combined with that of other selectorates (as with New Zealand's Labour Party). Or they may be the only selectors, yet their decision can be vetoed by another party actor; this is the case for Canadian parties, where party members select the candidates but the party leader can veto their decision (Cross 2006). In other cases, such as the Labor party in Israel (since 1992), members are the single exclusive selectorate that select the party candidates.

The second kind of reform has to do with outcomes of the selection process. Since the 1970s, we have seen an evident trend, at the intra-party level, of adopting measures—such as quotas—to enhance women's representation (Krook 2009). Such measures are also sometimes adopted to enhance the representation of other groups, such as minorities and youth.

Parties present the adoption of these measures in public as an attempt to reform and to become more democratic. Such reforms are spotlighted as ensuring widening participation (when adopting more inclusive selectorates) and enhancing representation (when adopting representation correction mechanisms such as quotas). The following words of UK prime minister David Cameron reflect the way parties present their reforms:

> One of the reforms I'm most proud of is the widespread introduction of open primaries for the selection of Conservative parliamentary candidates in recent years. I want to see that continue, with much greater use of open primaries for the selection of parliamentary candidates—and not just in the Conservative Party, but every party. In time, this will have a transformative effect on our politics, taking power from the party elites and the old boy networks and giving it to the people. (PoliticsHome 26 May 2009)

It can be argued, of course, that parties adopt these measures not because they are really interested in democracy. They might 'democratize' because doing so could help the party in the competitive electoral market or because it serves specific actors within the party. Yet, this does not mean that they do not adhere to specific democratic norms (or at least are limited by them) when they try to serve their interests. The trend of democratization points to the direction of reform in candidate selection methods and sets its boundaries (Barnea and Rahat 2007). Party leaders might democratize to weaken the influence of party activists and increase their autonomy in policymaking, as the cartel party approach claims (Katz and

Mair 1995; Katz 2001; Carty, this volume). But the choice of democratizing points to the limited space for manoeuver of the leaders that is dictated by what is widely perceived as democratic. That is, leaders would be better off if they were the selectors; democratization is not their ideal strategy for increasing their autonomy but their second best. Only a few, however, adopt this ideal option (e.g. Italy's former prime minister Berlusconi). Thus, even if IPD is promoted out of instrumental and self-serving motivations (as happens, often, with national-level democratization), it can and should be seen, at least, as also adhering to established democratic norms.

A few established democracies have legislation that concerns the process of candidate selection, specifically the required inclusiveness of candidate selection. The legal definition varies, from the most inclusive American nonpartisan and blanket primaries through American open, semi-open, and closed primaries, to direct (e.g. Finland) and indirect (Norway 1920–2002) selection by party members. Germany allows parties to choose between direct and indirect selection by party members while New Zealand adds a third alternative, a combination of these two. The more inclusive candidate selection methods are seen as the norm, but the inclusiveness level varies widely. In short, while few countries set inclusiveness as the main standard for democratic selection, even among them there is no shared norm and the selectorate is stretched from party delegates to all voters. It can be argued that they make exclusive selection by a single leader or a small party elite illegal. Yet in terms of inclusiveness of selection, even in these countries, party elites and leaders play a central role in candidate selection, for example, in pre-designing an agreed list of candidates for the delegates to ratify. If we can generalize something from these cases, it is that the involvement of wider selectorates in candidate selection is perceived to be more democratic.

The second kind of legislation that has to do with candidate selection concerns its products rather than the process *per se*. Many countries these days define by law a minimum quota of female (and male) candidacies (and sometimes minority groups) that each party must put forward in elections (Htun 2004; Krook 2009). These include veteran democracies such as Belgium and France and younger democracies in Latin America and Southern Europe. This legislation has to do with notions of proper and just representation, usually in terms of gender. In this case, parties are told what they should produce, rather than what method they should use. In other words, it does not matter whether a single leader or hundreds of thousands of party members or supporters select women as party candidates—as long as there are 'enough' female candidates. In fact, it would be easier for parties with more exclusive selectorates to uphold these laws, while parties with large selectorates often need to use rules to restrict selection.

An interesting case is when requirements for both inclusiveness and representation are set. And here we witness, in fact, a real intra-democratic dilemma between inclusiveness and representation. That is, parties cannot observe internal regulations or national laws that require them to present a minimal number of candidates from a certain gender unless they have some control over their selectorates' choices. This seems to have led the Mexican legislature to determine that gender quotas would not be required in cases of selection through primaries (Baldez 2007). This need not be an either/or case. There are mechanisms that allow for primaries and ensure women's representation at the same time. Still, such a combination does require that the selectors' choices are guided or limited.

To summarize, inclusiveness is seen as enhancing democracy in the candidate selection process while representation is seen as the main issue when it comes to the outcomes of candidate selection. Other potential democratic considerations might arise from time to time but they do not take center stage. Candidacy seems to have become more inclusive over the years, yet this development was not presented as democratization. Decentralization of candidate selection could have been perceived and presented as democratization in candidate selection. But in this case, there was no clear trend of decentralization but rather of centralization, which was used, among other things, to enable the leadership to control candidacies in a way that would ensure more representative outcomes.

DISCUSSION

It is only now that we are beginning to ask and answer the question of what exactly democratic selection is. Unlike the case of elections, we hardly have the comparative tools to answer it—there are no Freedom House or Polity indices. What we can claim on the basis of Cross (2008), Rahat (2009), and Hazan and Rahat (2010) is that the assessment of candidate selection should be different from elections, but relate to them—that is, it should add to democracy. But here we already have discord between the relatively positive view of inclusiveness of Cross (2008) and the much-less-enthusiastic view of Hazan and Rahat (2010).

According to Cross (2008), candidate selection is a possible compensatory tool that helps to counter flaws of the democratic order at the national level. There are no general standard norms that a candidate selection method need abide by. Rather, selection is a flexible mechanism that should be adapted to each democracy according to its specific needs. These result from the specific features of its electoral system, party system and the role of the members of parliament as policymakers. Cross puts inclusiveness as the democratic norm, yet claims that its significance for democracy is a function of the national level polity—the kind and level of democratic enhancement that it needs—not a must in every case. He argues, for example, that inclusive candidate selection is more important in cases where a closed-list system is used because it compensates for the lack of a personal element in the general elections.

While Cross stresses the process, Rahat (2009) and Hazan and Rahat (2010) put more emphasis on outcomes. Hazan and Rahat claim that inclusiveness of candidate selection might breed low-quality participation (Rahat and Hazan 2007), low levels of representation, and medium-level competition (Rahat, Hazan, and Katz 2008). It may also expose the party to the influences of non-party actors in a way that might distort the chain of delegation and harm its ability to be responsive to its voters (Rahat 2008). Furthermore, inclusiveness might hurt the ability of a party to sustain itself as an organization that is based, at least partly, on voluntarism and volunteer work. That is because it takes away its ability to use the right to select candidates as an important part of its arsenal of selective incentives (Rahat 2009). Thus, if a party is indeed a part of the whole—a democratic whole in which inclusiveness is strictly kept at the state level—it may trade inclusiveness for other elements that can enhance democracy.

Hazan and Rahat also see candidate selection as a possible compensatory tool, but one that is less sensitive to the characteristics of the national level democratic order. Their approach is based on two notions. First, that parties, in any democracy, should help to compensate for some common deficiencies at the national level that result from the undeniable need for inclusiveness in democratic elections. They can do this by enhancing representation and competition and creating balanced responsiveness in candidate selections.[4] Inclusiveness should not be seen as a must, as it is at the national level, if the involvement of less inclusive selectorates can help strengthen these other democratic dimensions. Second, parties are important institutions in themselves. As such, they should be able to sustain themselves by allocating selective incentives—that is, a privileged position to activists—in candidate selection. They should also be internally democratic by having a system of checks and balances. This trait is expressed, when it comes to candidate selection, in spreading selection among several selectorates.

The difference between Cross's approach and Hazan and Rahat's is illuminated in the examination of the American case—the one that was found to be the closest to the democratic election ideal in the first section. The US has all five justifications that Cross outlines—at the level of the electoral and party system and regarding the role of deputies—to use primaries as a compensatory tool for national-level elections. For Hazan and Rahat, however, the US case is an example of the trade-off that highly inclusive primaries create: while wide participation and high levels of candidate-centered responsiveness are achieved, inclusiveness breeds relatively low levels of representation, competition, and party cohesion.

[4] That is, responsiveness in which the party actors still play a central role vis-à-vis non-party actors.

CONCLUSIONS

When it comes to candidate selection, the differences in the perception of IPD—like those differences in the general debate on democracy—stem from a different perception on the importance of the various elements of democracy: Should we emphasize the process or the outcomes? What is the optimal balance between participation, representation, competition, and responsiveness? These days, the definition of IPD is clearly less strict than that of national-level democracy, both in the political world and among experts.

There are uneasy relationships between the two prominent elements in the perception of IPD in the real world, participation and representation (Rahat, Hazan, and Katz 2008; McIlveen, 2009). To illustrate this point, think of two poles: at one end, we have candidate selection that is conducted by millions of citizens who happen to select men and only men as candidates. At the other end, we have a single leader, an enlightened dictator, who ensures that half of the candidacies would be awarded to women. In short, to ensure a representative outcome, parties are required to regulate the decisions of the selectors. In between the two poles we can locate the current perception of IPD; the dilemma and the debate concentrate—as a result of the uneasy relationships between these two—on preferring one or the other, or on the optimal balance between them.

10

Intra-Party Democracy and Party Finance

Susan E. Scarrow

This chapter turns a financial lens on the impact of intra-party democracy, examining how the financing of intra-party contests affects power relations within parties. The expansion of inclusive IPD, understood here as procedures which give party members and/or supporters a direct say in party affairs, creates new costs for parties and for aspiring candidates and leaders. The ways that they meet these costs can shape the distribution of power within a party, and can help determine whether decisions made by party-wide votes actually make a difference.

This account begins by examining factors that affect the costs of implementing IPD, using examples from recent intra-party contests to show how procedural choices influence both the magnitude and the distribution of the costs. The chapter then broadens its financial focus to consider how the potential impact of IPD may be affected by various models of political funding. As this examination will show, from a democratic standpoint the role of money in politics can be as problematic for intra-party competition as it is for competition between parties.

THE COSTS OF INTRA-PARTY DEMOCRACY

Implementing inclusive types of IPD can be an expensive proposition, because there are costs to run the selection procedures and campaign costs for those competing in this added layer of elections. In contemporary democracies the state usually pays for the administration of all public elections, be they referenda or contests to fill public offices. In contrast, political parties and would-be candidates usually have to pay to administer their internal polls (though as will be explained below, there are some exceptions to this). These costs are potentially quite high, particularly when selectorates are large and geographically dispersed. Costs can also vary due to political circumstances and procedural rules, including regulations imposed by the party and/or the state. Power relations within parties generally dictate the ways that these costs are distributed among different levels of the party, and between would-be candidates and the party organization.

Procedural costs

The size of the potential selectorate may be the most important determinant of the procedural costs of IPD. When contests are held at the local level, or when national decisions are made by aggregating local decisions, IPD can be implemented by holding meetings and giving a vote to each member who shows up. That vote may be conducted by show of hands or by secret ballot, but either way, it does not require sophisticated technology, and procedures can be run by local volunteers. Thus, when selectorates are small and geographically compact, the financial costs of expanding IPD may be only slightly higher than the costs of holding elite-dominated local meetings—the main difference being the need to rent a bigger room.

Procedures can become more costly for party-wide decisions, such as selecting a party leader or a referendum on a party policy. Parties wishing to poll their entire membership in a single stage may use a postal ballot (for instance, the British Labour and Conservative parties in recent leadership contests), they may set up their own local polling stations (the German SPD leadership contest in 1993, the Greek New Democracy leadership contest in 2009), they may use home-based Internet voting and/or phone voting (Ontario, Canada, NDP 2009 leadership contest), or they may use some combination of all these methods. An example of the latter is the French UMP in its 2007 leadership contest, which had an Internet ballot that party members could either access at home, or at party-run local polling stations.

Of these various methods, postal balloting is potentially the most expensive, with costs varying directly according to the size of the electorate. For instance, the price of the postal ballots for the Labour Party's deputy leadership contest in 2007 was an estimated £2 million.[1] In fact, some leading Labour Party members (unsuccessfully) called for the abolition of the deputy leader election on cost grounds alone, arguing that it was a luxury that the heavily indebted party could not afford (Morris and Brown 2006). One reason for the high cost of this contest was that members of affiliated trade unions were eligible to participate (as was true with the Labour Party's leadership ballot in 2010). Because of this, many more ballots were mailed than if the election had been restricted to individual party members.

The link between the size of the party electorate and ballot costs is less direct if parties opt for Internet voting or set up local polling stations, since these costs are relatively inelastic (and probably smaller, though no parties have provided figures on what it costs to run an Internet election). However, running a smooth electronic election is not costless: it requires good web servers to handle the maximum

[1] In comparison, total party spending to reach the entire British electorate in the 2009 European Parliament election was legally capped at £3.1 million.

possible traffic, and parties must pay for the software and the expertise to ensure (and to reassure participants) that the ballots are secret and the results are counted accurately. Parties may hire firms to conduct the elections on their behalf, as insurance against appearances of factional bias if there are technical difficulties. These are mostly fixed costs, but prices may rise as the size of the potential electorate increases (more computer terminals will be needed in local polling stations, more local officials will need to be trained, servers will have to be capable of handling more traffic, and in some cases parties may incur postage costs to mail security codes, not ballots, to all eligible members).

Another procedural cost of IPD arises if parties do not already maintain an accurate and up-to-date register of paid-up members. With any election it is important to publish and adhere to clear standards of eligibility if the outcome is to be perceived as legitimate and decisive. In the case of intra-party elections, eligibility is often confined to paid-up party members who have joined a certain number of days or months in advance of the poll. If the ballot is administered by the central party, then the central party needs information about who these members are and when they joined. The easiest way for party headquarters to obtain this information is by having a centralized membership database. Creating and maintaining these central records is not a huge cost, but it does require a certain level of professionalism in the national party organization. In addition, if the central party does not already have such records, creating and maintaining a national party membership database for the purposes of intra-party ballots can have political implications, potentially shifting internal power balances. Such a database gives national party leaders (and often, those campaigning for the leadership) direct access to the membership base, unmediated by local or regional party leaders. It also deprives local or regional parties of a practice that was once common in some parties, the opportunity to sponsor spurious memberships in order to obtain extra representation at party conferences (see for instance Müller 1994 on such practices in the Austrian People's Party).

Parties can avoid these record-keeping costs by opening 'intra-party' procedures to a wider circle of supporters, using a very broad definition of who is actually inside the party. Parties that are newly created or newly merged, or that are weakly organized for some other reason, may choose to use very inclusive procedures because they do not have a well-defined membership. Thus, in Italy in 2005 the newly formed Union Party became the first Italian party to hold an open primary to select its leader, a procedure repeated in 2007 by its center-left successor, the Democratic Party. In both cases, these were umbrella parties created out of electoral mergers, and they were too new to have well-defined memberships. The open procedures sidestepped the question of membership eligibility, and also served as a good way to identify and rally support for the new parties.[2]

[2] In 2009, after the Democratic Party was better-established, it held another leadership election, but this time as a two-stage vote: the first stage was for members only; the second stage was an open primary contest between the top two vote-getters in the first round.

In the open primaries used in many US states and in Argentina, all registered voters are eligible to participate in parties' candidate-selection pre-elections—indeed, in Argentina, voting in primaries is obligatory. Even in 'closed' primaries in the United States it is public offices which maintain the records of whether voters have signed up to participate in one party's primaries. Using open participation rules may eliminate the parties' costs of record keeping and of checking eligibility, but it greatly increases the size of the *potential* electorate, and hence greatly increases other costs, especially campaign costs (see below).

Who pays the costs associated with these procedures? To some extent, this depends on which procedures are used. Central organizations tend to assume the costs when postal ballots are used, or when members can vote directly using telephone or Internet voting sites. Local parties have to provide personnel and equipment for Internet voting when ballots are cast at local polling stations, though in these cases the central parties probably pays for computer capacity and technical expertise. If parties do not want to cover these expenses out of existing revenues, they generally employ one of two options to defray the costs.

The first is to charge a participation fee to those who take part in the ballot. For instance, the Italian Union Party charged a very modest one Euro fee for supporters who voted in its 2005 leadership ballot. Though that charge was small, the revenue it generated was significant because over three million people participated in this vote (Pasquino 2009). Some Canadian parties have also charged participation fees in addition to membership dues, monies which are supposed to offset the costs of the voting technology; these costs have sometimes been high enough to potentially deter participation (Cross 2004: 87). In 2011 the French Socialist Party (PS) charged a participation fee of 'at least' one Euro in its open primary to select a presidential candidate; even paid-up party members were required to pay this fee. Parties which do not charge this type of 'poll tax' may still benefit from extra membership dues generated by those who join a party just to participate in the vote—though such surges happen only in parties which allow last-minute recruits to participate.

Another way that parties may defray the costs of internal votes is by taxing the contestants, effectively and sometimes even explicitly requiring them to fundraise on behalf of the party. For instance, under the original rules of its 2005 leadership contest, the Canadian Liberal Party required contestants to pay a $50,000 deposit to the party; it also required candidates to pay to the party 20 per cent of all funds raised in excess of $500,000 (Cross and Crysler 2011: 162). Such an arrangement affects the relationship between party leaders and the party's central organizational structures, emphasizing that the organization depends on the leader to be a good fundraiser, but also suggesting that good fundraisers may have some autonomy from these organizational structures. Perhaps for this reason, this method has not been widely adopted in other parliamentary democracies.

Some parties have defrayed the costs of internal elections by passing some of them onto the state. For instance, parties can hold open primaries that require no registration other than eligibility to participate in a national election (as in the Italian cases cited above). In this case parties do not have to maintain their own separate voter rolls. This reduces parties' expenses, and it provides an outside guarantor of fairness, but it does so at the cost of opening the ballot to non-supporters, including to those who may be actively opposed to the party's goals. This may be a risk worth taking where parties have an ill-defined and potentially large selectorate, but organizationally strong parties are unlikely to welcome the concomitant loss of control.

In short, while the costs of running a fair and glitch-free internal contest can be significant, parties have not settled on uniform funding strategies to offset these costs. If leadership contests and intra-party referendums are relatively rare events, most parties can absorb these in their general operating budgets. However, were they to become more frequent occurrences, parties would need to carefully consider the financial implications when selecting the voting method.

Intra-party campaign costs

A variety of factors affect the costs of running an effective intra-party campaign. Foremost among these are the extent of competition, and the size and geographic dispersion of the potential electorate. Party norms and public regulations also can affect fundraising and spending in these campaigns.

The competitiveness of the race is a big determinant of the time and resources that candidates spend on securing a leadership position or candidate nomination. Many internal ballots involve little or no actual competition (see Rahat and Cross, this volume), particularly when elections are held because party statutes require a vote even when the incumbent leader wishes to continue in the post (for instance, in the Portuguese Socialist Party or the Irish Green Party), or there is a popular incumbent in constituency-level candidate nomination contests. Yet even in races that are basically uncontested, candidates still need to campaign: an internal election only provides legitimacy and publicity if the candidates attend party meetings and use the occasion to connect with party supporters.

The size of the potentially eligible electorate dictates what kind of campaigning will be effective: if it is large enough that a would-be leader or candidate cannot meet all eligible participants in regional or local meetings, contestants will need to supplement personal contact with more costly communication approaches, such as mailings, telephone calls and even paid advertisements. But even if candidates cannot hope to meet every party member, they are likely to appear at party meetings throughout the district or country, and that can be an expensive proposition in a large country. Leadership campaigns in Canada first became expensive—to the tune of hundreds of thousands of dollars—in the 1960s, when it became expected that leadership candidates would tour the country to meet with party members ahead of the leadership conference (Courtney 1973: 91). Other kinds of communications strategies can become costly as well. For instance, the costs of Portuguese leadership campaigns grew over the past decade as candidates began hiring staff to help them run media-oriented campaigns (Lisi 2010: 144).[3]

Campaign costs may be even higher in parties that permit participation by last-minute registrants, or which allow unregistered supporters to participate in ballots. In these cases, successful candidates must mobilize those who are not yet members in addition to those who already are. This is by definition a much bigger and more diffuse target audience. Contestants cannot rely on party-supplied lists of members' addresses or e-mail contacts, but instead may need to get attention in non-partisan news outlets to reach supporters who lack prior organizational ties to a party. This is a much bigger, and more expensive, task.

As with elections to public offices, the cost can be affected by the length of the campaign, both the formal contest and the more informal lead-up to it. Shorter contests tend to be cheaper. Campaigns are likely to be longest and most expensive when it is apparent long in advance that there will be a vacancy. For instance, would-be candidates for the opposition French Socialist Party began their internal campaigns well ahead of the party's presidential primaries in 2005 and 2011. In these contests the PS gave plenty of notice that it would use internal ballots to select the party candidate, and there was no clear frontrunner for the job. In many other cases, vacancies cannot be as easily anticipated, for instance when a leader of a parliamentary party resigns after an electoral defeat. When unexpected vacancies occur, opposition parties vary in how long they take to fill the slot: a party which has just lost an election may choose to have a long intra-party campaign as a component of a party-renewal strategy, especially if there are several strong contenders for the leadership job. A party that will soon be facing a general election may fill the leadership post as quickly as possible. These circumstances will affect the costs of campaigns, dictating how many meetings the candidates are able to attend, and whether they have time to contact potential voters with mailings.

Last but not least, campaign costs can be affected by rules and norms about fundraising and spending for these contests. Political parties may make their own rules about how much candidates are permitted to spend on a contest, or they may implicitly cap spending by prohibiting candidates from employing more expensive campaign activities. For instance, in 2005 the national executive of the Dutch Labor Party decreed that candidates should 'hold back' in using personal funds for the contest, and that they should not purchase paid advertising for the campaign (Koole 2006: 258). Both the British Conservative and Labour parties have set formal spending limits for candidates in their leadership elections. The Conservatives capped this at £100,000 per candidate in 2001; two candidates came very close to spending the allowable amount (Alderman and Carter 2002: 582). For its

[3] This strategy has had political as well as financial implications because it helps candidates to side-step local party leaders and to reach members directly.

2010 leadership contest the British Labour Party limited spending to £156,000 per candidate, equivalent to £1 per member who was registered at the start of the campaign (although this cap did not include the potentially large expense of staff costs) (Mulholland 2010). Such party rules seem to be the exception. Even where they exist, they are probably hard to enforce without the force of law behind them (see below). In any case, after internal contests finish, party leaders are more likely to seek to rebuild party unity than to further erode it by pursuing investigations about campaign spending malfeasance.

With so many variables, it is impossible to generalize about campaign costs in intra-party elections: these vary widely according to the circumstances. It is difficult even to give answers about the costs of specific campaigns, because there are only a few countries where candidates for party-internal offices have been required to issue any kind of financial report. The United Kingdom and Canada are two exceptions to this rule, and for these countries we can say something about the costs of recent party leadership selection contests.

Tables 10.1 and 10.2 show candidate fundraising for four British and one Canadian leadership contests, reporting all the races for which information was available as of mid-2011. In accordance with the different reporting requirements, the British table shows totals for all donations above £1,000; the Canadian table shows totals for all donations. For the British contests these are calculated on a per

TABLE 10.1 *Campaign spending in intra-party elections: Liberal Party (Canada) leadership contest, 2006*

Name of contestant	Number of contributors	Total number of contributions through mid-2007($)*	Total expenses ($)
Carolyn Bennett	230	177,200.21	254,863.57
Maurizio Bevilacqua	133	149,036.50	700,775.79
Scott Brison	569	401,452.59	593,637.24
Stéphane Dion	***1,925***	***953,396.12***	***1,882,367.92***
Ken Dryden	530	212,247.16	650,266.46
Martha Hall Findlay	483	163,334.39	422,958.08
Hedy Fry	71	29,313.68	194,779.05
Michael Ignatieff	2,483	1,500,469.08	2,316,027.85
Gerard Kennedy	1,121	689,338.19	1,425,086.09
Robert Keith Rae	1,730	2,149,868.57	2,989,822.42
Joseph Volpe	295	396,775.00	768,110.13
TOTAL	9,570	6,822,431.49	12,198,694.60

Winning candidate in bold italics.

* exact filing dates varied among candidates.

Source: Elections Canada, 'Financial Reports', <http://www.elections.ca> accessed 7 July 2011.

TABLE 10.2 *Campaign fundraising in British party leadership elections: large donations*

Year	Party	Votes cast	Candidate	Large donations*	£ per vote
2001	*Conservative*	*155,993*	David Davis	£18,250	£0.12
			Kenneth Clarke	£93,000	£0.60
			Iain Duncan Smith	£100,008	£0.64
			Michael Portillo	£94,967	£0.61
			TOTAL	£306,225	£1.96
2005	*Conservative*	*134,446*	Kenneth Clarke	£94,500	£0.70
			David Davis	£291,300	£2.17
			David Cameron	£509,985	£3.79
			TOTAL	£895,785	£6.66
2006	*Liberal Democrat*	*52,036*	Chris Huhne	£30,900	£0.59
			Sir Menzies Campbell	£44,735	£0.86
			TOTAL	£75,635	£1.45
2007	*Liberal Democrat*	*41,465*	***Nick Clegg***	£73,500	£1.77
			Chris Huhne	£57,000	£1.37
			TOTAL	£130,500	£3.14
2010	*Labour*	*126,874*	Ed Balls	£158,110	£1.25
			Andy Burnham	£48,400	£0.38
			Harriet Harman	£0	£0.00
			David Miliband	£623,809	£4.92
			Edward Miliband	£336,776	£2.65
			TOTAL	£1,167,095	£9.20

* Only donations above £1,500 needed to be reported. Winning candidates in bold italics.

Source: UK Electoral Commission Donation Database (accessed 7 June 2011).

capita basis, using actual votes cast as the denominator.[4] Winning candidates are indicated in bold italics. A little background is useful to help interpret the differences shown in this table.

As of the beginning of 2012, the Canadian Liberal Party's 2006 leadership election contest was the only contested race in a large Canadian party that had occurred since disclosure legislation went into effect for party's leadership contests. When this race took place, the rules limited individual contributions to leadership campaigns to $5,000 per contest, and limited corporate donations to $1,000.[5] Costs in this contest were boosted by the $50,000 non-refundable deposit which the party required from candidates to help defray the costs of the procedure, but even without this they would have been high, since most candidates spent many times that amount. This election was a two-stage process: pledged convention delegates were elected in a member-only vote at the local level, with the final

[4] Votes cast is the denominator rather than total membership, because in several of the contests supporters who joined after the start of the contest were eligible to vote, meaning that the potential electorate was much bigger than the membership at the start of the campaign.

[5] The current rules limit individual donations to $1,100 per contest.

vote occurring several weeks later at a national party convention. The campaign effectively lasted over ten months, from the party's January defeat in federal elections to the leadership convention in early December. It was a crowded field, with eleven candidates (only eight of whom stayed through the convention ballot); it took four ballots to decide the outcome. The Liberal Party set spending limits, but at $3.4 million per candidate, these limits exceeded most candidates' fundraising capacity (Cross and Crysler 2011). The result was a very expensive contest, and one that was not fully financed before it ended.[6] Six months after the election candidates had almost $4 million in outstanding loans and unpaid expenses; five years later, four of the candidates still owed a combined half million dollars (Beange 2009; Naumetz 2011). Subsequent Canadian leadership elections will be even more difficult to finance at these levels because legislation that came into effect in 2007 lowered individual contribution limits for these races and banned corporate and trade union donations.

In comparison, the British leadership contests have been more modest affairs, though fundraising has still been important. Table 10.2 shows the amounts that candidates in various contests collected from the largest contributions (over £1,000). It shows that whereas the 2001 Conservative candidates raised only slightly more than the party-imposed spending limit for this contest, in the 2010 Labour Party election two of the five candidates raised significantly more than the £156,000 spending limit their party set for the contest. Some of these 'excess' funds may have been spent on staff costs, not covered by the cap. In addition, David Miliband pledged to turn over much of the funds he raised to the party's central coffers. In other words, he used some of the fundraising as a competitive marker, not as a direct campaign resource.

One thing that is clear from examining both the British and the Canadian leadership contests is that successful fundraising does not guarantee success. In the five leadership elections in the UK reported in Table 10.2, the biggest fundraisers won only three of the five elections. Similarly, in 2007 Harriet Harman won the Labour Party's 2007 deputy leadership election even though she raised less than two of her three competitors (Wintour and Hencke 2008). In the Canadian Liberal contest, the winning candidate came in third as both fundraiser and campaign spender. These were well-publicized contests with a great deal of free media coverage, which may help explain the absence of a relationship between electoral success and fundraising capacity.

We do not have enough information from other countries to know whether they are in any way typical of leadership races elsewhere. However, these episodes give some idea of the large amounts that can be spent in this type of contest, and they suggest that the introduction of open leadership contests is likely to create strong

[6] There is no available estimate of the number of participants in the first stage ballots, so the *per capita* cost cannot be estimated.

pressures for fundraising unless candidate spending is strictly limited or subsidized by the parties themselves, or by public sources.

Who pays the costs of the internal campaigns? Parties differ in how they distribute campaign costs between the contestants and the central party offices. In some parties, many of the costs of campaigning are paid for by the party. For instance, parties may sponsor public meetings around the country, they may provide candidates with web pages, they may print a limited amount of material for them, and they may let candidates use party distribution lists to send e-mail communications to members. Thus, in the UK Conservative and Liberal Democratic leadership contests in 2005, and in the Labour Party contest of 2010, it was the central parties that organized and paid for regional party meetings so that members could see the candidates debate the issues. In 2002 the Dutch Labor Party, and in 2006 the Dutch VVD and D66 all provided leadership candidates with some campaign and communications resources, including organizing meetings, though candidates were expected to pay their own travel costs for party-organized campaign events (Koole 2006: 6).

However, in all these cases contestants needed to find at least some funds to campaign in intra-party elections. When candidates need to find large sums to finance personal campaigns, they are likely to develop their own formal or informal support organizations. These networks of personal loyalty operate outside the orbit of central party structures. Such networks are most familiar from presidential democracies, but they can arise in parliamentary democracies as well, particularly if contestants need to be independent fundraisers in order to compete within their parties.

Personal campaign networks can undercut the central party's power over its legislators, diminishing its ability to enforce party policy decisions. Moreover, candidates' reliance on their own backers is likely to create new privileges for the members of the community who have the deepest pockets, providing some of them with special access to the successful candidate. If so, the need to fundraise to compete within the party may undercut some of the promised virtues of IPD. Such procedures are premised on the equality of all members (or of all party supporters), with decisions no longer delegated to party notables or party conferences, but instead authenticated by the collective wisdom of the entire party community. This equality disappears if competitors become beholden to those who finance their campaigns.

Dampening the influence of money in state-level election campaigns is the main reason that many countries have introduced extensive political finance regulations. In contrast, states have moved much more cautiously to regulate the influence of money in parties' internal contests.

Regulating finance for intra-party campaigns

Canada, France, the United Kingdom, and the United States are among the few countries in which political finance laws cover some aspects of the funding of intra-party election campaigns. Canada has directly regulated donations to leadership candidates since 2004, initially limiting donations to such campaigns to $5,000, later lowered to what became (an inflation-indexed) $1,100 per donor by the year 2011. Leadership candidates must report extensively on who is making these contributions, and how it is being spent. Unspent funds must be turned over to either the federal party or to a single constituency association (Elections Canada 2011). Since 2002 Canadian laws have also limited how much prospective parliamentary candidates can spend on their internal campaigns, setting the limit at 20 per cent of the official limit for general election campaigns in that constituency.

Britain does not directly regulate spending in party leadership contests. However, donations to the candidates in these contests are indirectly affected by other regulations. Members of Parliament must report personal donations and gifts-in-kind to the register of Members' Interests, and these in turn have been reported to the Electoral Commission, with the same reporting thresholds and restrictions that apply for contributions to candidates for public office (£1,500 as of 2011).[7] There are no public regulations regarding expenditures in British intra-party elections, in contrast to strict spending limits for parties and candidates in general elections. However, as noted above, the British parties have imposed their own spending caps.

France has adopted a middle ground in regards to the regulation of spending in presidential primaries. The body in charge of political finance regulation has declared that only some spending in these elections counts as part of the (regulated) official campaign expenditures, namely, some of the spending by the candidate who wins the party primary—and who thus becomes the party's official candidate. Of particular interest to the regulators is spending conducted once a candidate has *de facto* or *de jure* secured the nomination (for instance, spending between the party ballot and the party congress which gives the official nomination, or spending by a candidate in an uncontested nomination race). Spending by losing 'pre-candidates' is not regulated by the legislation (CNCCFP 2008: 31–2).[8]

Such public regulation of parties' private contests is more the exception than the rule, even in countries with otherwise extensive regulation of campaign and party finance. There are several explanations for this legal neglect. One is that in many countries intra-party contests are a relative novelty, not yet used by all parties, and often introduced after the initial adoption of political finance regulations. Yet novelty is certainly not the whole explanation, because political finance frameworks could easily be revised to include money raised and spent for internal

[7] Given that British parties have required their leadership candidates to be sitting legislators, all of the candidates have been covered by these dual Parliamentary and Electoral Commission rules, but under the Political Parties and Elections Act of 2000 candidates for party office who are not MPs would also be required to report donations to the Electoral Commission (UK Electoral Commission 2011).

[8] Thanks to Eric Phelippeau for this reference.

campaigns (as happened in Canada once party leadership ballots became common). Moreover, financial regulation of internal campaigns was omitted in at least one country that adopted its major political finance laws after intra-party leadership elections had become the norm (Belgium). A more important factor may be a reluctance to regulate parties' internal affairs because of their quasi-private status, though as van Biezen (this volume) shows, many countries do regulate parties' internal affairs, and such regulation tends to expand to cover new areas. More importantly, there may be pragmatic reasons to minimize financial regulation of parties' internal contests: it is difficult to write appropriate rules when parties can and do change their internal selection practices from election to election. Yet as long as the financing of internal contests remains outside the law, donations to intra-party candidates can become a backdoor route for the corruption (and perceived corruption) which other political finance laws seek to combat (Hofnung 2008).

In countries such as Argentina and the United States some of these questions are obviated because candidate selection in open or almost-open primaries has become a public affair, with most aspects of the elections governed by the state. This makes it easier to justify and to structure state regulation of the financial side of these contests. Thus, in the United States donations to candidates in primary elections at the state and federal level are governed by rules that are similar or identical rules to those that apply to candidates in general elections, although there are separate donation caps for each phase of the election cycle. As of 2011 US donors could give no more than $2,500 per federal candidate per contest (primary or general election), and candidates had to report names, addresses, and amounts of all who give a total of $200 or more per election cycle (FEC 2011). Meanwhile, in Argentina the 2009 law that made primary elections mandatory for all parties and electoral groups also included provisions for state subsidies for these contests. The law introduced caps on candidate spending in primaries, set at half of what was permissible for general election contests. Under this law the state also prints the ballots and it operates the polling stations, the same ones used for the general elections (Argentina 2009).

Regulation of campaign finance for intra-party elections may be easier to justify and to structure when public laws govern other aspects of these elections. However, the Canadian and British examples show that it is possible to expand such regulation even when the contests themselves are otherwise treated as private affairs.

The preceding discussion of procedural and campaign costs has shown the wide variations in the financial implication of implementing IPD. Costs are affected by political circumstances, party finance norms, and the size of the selectorate. IPD can be very expensive, though it is important to note that even high-priced procedures such as party-wide postal ballots are not necessarily more expensive than possible alternatives. For instance, mounting a party conference to select a party leader can also be a very pricey undertaking. Nevertheless, the costs of internal contests are often high, and because of this the ways that they are financed can have political consequences. Indeed, in some cases how these costs are distributed among candidates and party organizations may have as many long-term consequences as the decisions themselves. This brings us to a more general conundrum for those considering the possibilities and limits of IPD: that whatever procedures for party governances are employed, the sources and structures of party finance may in practice limit the actual impact of grassroots decision-making The next section examines this possibility in greater depth, showing how some party funding models diminish the impact of IPD either by undermining the authority of party decisions, and/or by giving big donors unequal influence in party affairs.

FUNDING SOURCES AS CONSTRAINTS ON INTRA-PARTY DEMOCRACY

Political finance systems have been extensively examined to understand their effects on relations between citizens and their representatives (for a recent comprehensive discussion, see Nassmacher 2009). The focus in this section is on the much narrower question of how political finance structures shape political dynamics *within* a party, and especially how they can enhance or limit the possibilities for internal democracy. There are two basic ways in which party funding patterns can constrain the potential for IPD. The first relates to the sources of funds, and to the possibility that donors' money will speak more loudly than formal decision procedures. The second relates to the distribution of funds among different actors within the party, and how this distribution enhances or shrinks the ability of central party leaderships to enforce formal party decisions, however these are reached.

Contemporary political parties have four main revenue sources: public funds, organizations and individuals who give large contributions, individuals who give small donations (including party members), and party members who are public officials. As Table 10.3 summarizes, each of these sources has different implications for the distribution of influence within the party.

Public funding

In the past forty years public funding has become a—or, in many cases, *the*—major source of income for political parties in parliamentary democracies. In some countries public subsidies were initially introduced to support the work of legislative parties, but beginning in the 1960s and 1970s many countries added public support to extra-parliamentary parties to cover campaign costs and even routine

TABLE 10.3 *Party funding sources and intra-party democracy*

Funding sources	Potential impact on party governance
Public funding	Diminishes central party reliance on grassroots and other funding sources. Strengthens independence of recipients (regional vs. national party layers; party bureaucracy vs. party candidates; extra-parliamentary party vs. legislative party).
Plutocratic	Big donors may get access and possible influence, even if formal rules empower grassroots.
Grassroots	Tensions may arise between cultivating members as funders and expanding the party base.
Officeholder	High mandatory contributions from officeholders to party suggest that party is in a position to enforce policy decisions.

organizational work. These subsidies were generally justified as tools to help maintain a healthy democracy, funds which gave parties the means to create an informed electorate while at the same time reducing financial disparities between the major competitors. According to International IDEA's Political Funding Database, 56 per cent of the 144 democracies which it tracked offered some form of direct public funding for political parties in the year 2010 (International IDEA 2010). However, the extent and details of such payments vary widely and in ways that affect the distribution of power within political parties, including in the relative levels of public subsidies, and in the beneficiaries of these funds.

Public funding for parties in established parliamentary democracies ranges from relatively small campaign subsidies to substantial annual payments for parties' routine political work. High levels of public funding may have contributed to the professionalization and centralization of party organizations, fostering what Panebianco dubbed the 'electoral professional' party (1988). The expansion of parties' bureaucratic offices can affect the distribution of power within parties, because as Max Weber pointed out almost a century ago, the interests of those who 'live from politics' differ from the interests of those who 'live for politics' (1919/90). Yet professionalized central party organizations are not inevitably at odds with the premises of IPD, just as large public bureaucracies do not necessarily conflict with the operation of representative government. Efficient organizations have the capacity to help implement the decisions reached by those who govern; they do not necessarily (or at least, exclusively) pursue their own interests. Even to the extent that they do, it may well be in the interests of a professionalized party organization to bolster popular participation within a party, because the popular side of a party can serve as a counterweight to the influence of the parliamentary party. Furthermore, if parties are to conduct internal contests that are regarded as fair and definitive, they need organizational capacity to maintain membership registries of eligible participants, to mail ballots, and to adjudicate results. In other words, while professionalized party organizations have often been equated with a loss of power for political 'amateurs', some level of professionalization may be a necessity for the smooth operation of IPD.

Generous public subsidies, especially when coupled with campaign spending limits, may free parties from the need to conduct extensive fundraising. As Table 10.3 suggests, from a democratic standpoint such freedom may be a double-edged sword. On the one hand, it may reduce a party's dependence on plutocratic funding (discussed below), thus reducing the influence of major donors. On the other hand, it may reduce parties' attentiveness to *all* supporters, freeing them from pressures to recruit members and other grassroots support, and possibly making party leaders less attentive to the links that can be provided by IPD. The latter effect is the primary consequence of public subsidies envisaged in the cartel party literature (Katz and Mair 1995), though others have questioned whether parties actually neglect membership recruitment as a result of subsidies being introduced (for a good overview, see Nassmacher 2009: ch. 10). In practice, whether a big increase in public subsidies makes leaders of a particular party more or less attentive to grassroots opinion may depend on how the party was previously funded: does the increase in public funds move the party away from grassroots or from plutocratic funding?

Table 10.3 also suggests that public funds affect intra-party power balances in another way, by favouring some parts of the party over others in the distribution of these funds. Such distribution can potentially privilege the parliamentary over the extra-parliamentary party, can favour candidates rather than a central party campaign fund, and can reinforce the independence or dependence of regional party organizations. Such considerations were taken into account in Germany, for instance, after a 1992 Constitutional Court ruling on party finance legislation forced a consolidation of state and federal party subsidy regimes. In order to preserve the political balance between state and federal parties, the new German legislation mandated that a certain portion of the new subsidies should be paid to the state party organizations as a matter of law, not at the discretion of the federal party. If public funds are paid primarily to candidates and not to parties, legislators may feel less bound by parties' official policy documents, however democratically these are adopted. If the threshold for creating subsidy-eligible parties and candidacies is low, as in France, public payments may exacerbate party factionalism and foster party splits.

Plutocratic funding

For many parties, the primary alternative (or supplement) to public funding has been plutocratic funding—large donations from individuals or organizations. Large donations to political parties may be motivated by quid-pro-quo expectations, whether donors are prompted by general policy orientations or are looking for more specific favours (McMenamin 2008). Even if these expectations are never spelled out, big donors are likely to reduce their giving if they are disappointed with the direction of party policies.

Plutocratic funding models create obvious conflicts with procedures which aim to disperse decision-making authority, as Table 10.3 suggests. At the least, plutocratic funding fosters unequal political access: those who may or do give richly are likely to find an attentive audience for their concerns. The extent of this effect may depend on the size of the donor base: the fewer the big contributors, the more likely it is that recipients will be attentive to their requests. Thus, one donor who gives £1 million is likely to have better access to party leaders than a hundred people who give £10,000—even though gifts of both sizes are well beyond the reach of most of the population. If plutocratic giving follows the latter model, consisting of many large gifts of roughly the same size, it may be difficult for donors to claim individual favours, but recipients are likely to keep in mind issues that are generally of concern to wealthy donors.

At the state level plutocratic funding models are often criticized for being in conflict with electoral democracy: parties compete for support of all voters, but they have financial reasons to pay more attention to their financial supporters rather than their electoral supporters—even when these financial supporters are associations or corporations without voting rights. At the party level such funding models have similar implications for IPD. Party conventions may vote on detailed party platforms, and parties may develop other elaborate procedures to give party members a say in the development of party policies (as detailed by Gauja, this volume), but such consultative processes may have little meaning if generous donors get an extra hearing when it comes time to implement party pledges.

Parties funded by trade unions are a special case of plutocratic funding. In some cases, labour and socialist parties were founded with the explicit aim of representing the interests of union members, and trade union representation and trade union funding may have been built into the parties' original organizational structures. As a result, changes in one may lead to changes in the other. For instance, originally the biggest trade union contributions to the British Labour Party were in the form of annual fees to affiliate their members with the political party. Unions received voting rights in the party in proportion to the number of members they affiliated (paid for). In the past three decades this funding model has changed along with the decline of the trade unions' formal power and the increased voting rights of individual members. Starting in the 1980s, the Labour Party began experimenting with new formats for selecting party leaders and party candidates, ones that capped the weight of the union vote and gave more weight to the votes of individual members. The specific rules have changed over time, but the net effect has been to diminish the direct power of the union organizations. Under these circumstances, and with some trade unions increasingly unhappy with the policies implemented by the Blair and Brown governments, it was no surprise that British trade unions threatened to cut their funding for the Labour Party (Oliver 2009). These tensions illustrate the conflicts that can arise between plutocratic funding and IPD, because big givers may well expect to have a larger say than the member who pays only a small fee to join.

Grassroots funding

Grassroots funding would seem to be the funding arrangement most in harmony with IPD, yet even here there are some possible tensions. The idea of a party funded largely from the small contributions of its large membership is one that goes back to the nineteenth-century social democratic parties. The ideal was embodied in neighbourhood dues collectors making their weekly rounds to collect pennies from the party faithful. That picture is long obsolete, and dues collection has largely moved to the impersonal medium of automatic bank deductions. Along the way, campaign costs have grown, party bureaucracies have professionalized, and many countries have introduced public subsidies for political parties as a way of satisfying parties' seemingly insatiable appetite for funds. As a result, grassroots funding has become a minor source of funds for most parties in established democracies. As long as public funds are generously available it is unlikely to regain a leading position. Even so, such funds can make a high marginal contribution to overall fundraising, and parties can reap political benefits from a publicized ability to attract support from small donors. In addition, in some cases, public subsidies are directly or indirectly linked to parties' ability to raise such donations. For instance, the current German formula for distributing public subsidies factors in parties' ability to attract dues and other relatively small donations from individuals. In Germany, Canada, and other countries with tax subsidies for partisan donations, one part of the public subsidy for political parties is the favourable tax treatment for small donations, including dues payments.

The goal of reaping a financial benefit from party members' dues may be at odds with some of the goals associated with the expansion of IPD. Most basically, higher membership dues may result in lower enrolments. Parties seeking to build legitimacy and popular support by holding high-participation primaries have an incentive to set membership dues very low in order to encourage supporters to take part in the ballot. But if they reduce dues to make membership more attractive, they may also reduce revenues. The actual effect depends on the slope of the demand curve for the party membership 'product', and the size of the potential customer base—if the opportunity to participate in the ballot attracts enough new members, this increase will offset the foregone revenues.

One way that many parties resolve the tension between openness (low dues rates) and membership-based financing (higher dues rates) is by setting income-related membership levels. For instance, in 2011 the British Conservatives set the normal minimum dues at a relatively high £41, but higher earners were expected to pay more, and those who were 'unwaged' were expected to pay half this rate. Most parties similarly offer reduced rates for older members, youth, and those who are unemployed, allowing them to charge other supporters a fee that is more than nominal. The Canadian Conservatives, Liberals and Bloc Québécois were some of the few parties in established parliamentary democracies that were not offering such reduced rate memberships in 2011—but these parties also had some of the lowest minimum dues rates ($5 for the Bloc, $10 for the other two.)

In parties with differentiated dues levels, the party membership 'product' has variable pricing. Under such rules, the relationship between party dues and voting rights resembles that enjoyed by taxpayers in modern polities—the weight of the vote is not dictated by the amount of taxes an individual voter pays. The equal distribution of voting rights within political parties seems unproblematic when justified in this way. However, it is worth noting that this equal distribution differs from the rules used by another type of public association, public corporations, in which voting rights are distributed proportionally to the amount invested.

Funding by party office holders

For some political parties, contributions from party members in public office constitute a fourth income pillar. This type of revenue, sometimes known as a party tax, is only available to parties which capture a significant number of public offices. Originally such payments were a feature of socialist parties, justified in part as a way to ensure that the party's salaried public officials did not earn much more than those whom they represented. More recently, parties of all political stripes have come to rely on such payments as a kind of indirect public subsidy from their well-compensated representatives. Some parties even formalize these payment expectations. One of the most matter-of-fact examples was Silvio Berlusconi's People of Liberty party, which in 2011 published a sliding dues scale for office holders that varied according to the level of office and whether the positions were elected in single- or double-round elections (Il Popolo della Liberta 2011).

Elected officials have often been expected to support the organizations that help get them elected and re-elected. In terms of the impact of such support on IPD, the most important question is: who receives these funds? If office holders contribute a large portion of their public salaries to the central party, it suggests that the parties are cohesive enough to enforce such policies. If so, they probably can enforce other policies as well. If, instead, office holders contribute to provincial or state-level parties, this may suggest that parties are divided into regional strongholds, and possibly less cohesive (Bolleyer and Gauja 2011). Finally, if office holders' political contributions flow not to a party but to their personal electoral organizations, the political 'taxes' they pay from their public salaries or their own purses may well strengthen their autonomy from all party levels. The more independent the office holders are from the party, the smaller the scope for IPD to shape actual party policies. At the extreme, self-funded candidates may have the resources to leave one party for another, or to start their own parties.

Self-funding candidacies are not common in today's established parliamentary democracies, but it was not so long ago that some parties regularly recruited candidates based on their personal wealth and ability to defray their own campaign costs (a practice that was common in the British Conservative Party at least through the 1930s, and one which is still found in the high-priced election environment in the non-parliamentary United States). More generally, whenever financial arrangements reinforce factionalism or weaken the central party organization, decisions adopted by the party as a whole will hold less sway, however democratic the internal mechanism by which these policies are adopted.

CONCLUSION: INTRA-PARTY DEMOCRACY AND POLITICAL FINANCE

The preceding discussion of party financing models shows that the limits and challenges of IPD are closely connected to the question of who pays the piper. It may not be strictly true that 'he who pays the piper calls the tune'; indeed, as many street musicians know, it is often the other way around—people listen to the tune first and then decide whether to pay. Yet either way, the piper is likely to be attentive to the tastes of potential donors. In political terms, the challenge for implementing effective and credible IPD is that party leaders and would-be party candidates are likely to be attentive to major donors, regardless of what the party constitution says about one-member-one-vote decision procedures.

This effect has been most studied for state-level party financing, but this chapter has argued that the effect exists at the intra-party level in two ways. To begin with party finance models may limit the potential impact of decisions reached by intra-party democracy by strengthening the autonomy of individual legislators, and/or by making parties and legislators particularly attentive to a limited number of wealthy donors, however internally democratic the selection procedures. Additionally, the costs of intra-party campaigning can themselves become an opportunity for plutocratic interference. When selectorates expand and campaigning becomes more expensive, candidates with wealthy backers are likely to have an advantage unless spending or donations are limited by the parties themselves, or by the state.

So far most states have been reluctant to intervene in these internal contests to the same extent as in general elections, and therefore have not imposed the types of regulation that are supposed to curb plutocratic influence in general elections (donation and spending caps and disclosure rules). In the absence of effective state or party regulation of contributions to intra-party campaigns, and in the absence of public subsidies for parties' internal contests, one of the biggest effects of more inclusive party decision procedures could be to increase the influence of big donors–something that would surely be an unintended effect of the supposed democratization of party life. Yet if states do intervene, the cost of such regulation is a reduction in party autonomy, and an expansion of state intervention into areas which were previously regarded as parties' private and internal matters.

Thus, those seeking to expand inclusive procedures within political parties would do well to pay attention to the many financial questions raised by such an expansion. If they do not, some seemingly democratic arrangements could have the unintended result of weakening party unity and strengthening party plutocrats, producing parties that are less representative of the grassroots supporters who are supposed to be empowered by the new procedures.

11

Problematizing Intra-Party Democracy

Richard S. Katz and William P. Cross

At the beginning of 1968, it was widely assumed that Lyndon Johnson would have no trouble securing the Democratic nomination for re-election as president of the United States, notwithstanding deep division within the party over the war in Vietnam. On 12 March, however, Senator Eugene McCarthy won 42 per cent of the vote in the New Hampshire primary (to Johnson's 49 per cent), and four days later Robert Kennedy declared his candidacy was well, leading Johnson to announce at the end of the month that he would not be a candidate after all.

Although the pivotal role of the New Hampshire primary in leading to Johnson's withdrawal might look like an example of intra-party democracy, two important qualifications must be borne in mind. First, although Johnson withdrew from the presidential contest, he was actually the winner in New Hampshire. Second, although New Hampshire represented an important opportunity for a limited segment of the Democratic (plus independent) electorate to make their views known, the vast majority of the delegates to the 1968 Democratic Convention were not selected in primary elections, but rather in state conventions and caucuses that were largely under the control of local elites. Despite the fact that he did not enter any of the primaries, Vice President Hubert Humphrey, who was the choice of the party leadership, easily won the nomination in a highly divisive convention, and went on to a narrow defeat by Richard Nixon in the general election. The party's response to discord and defeat was to democratize, going from roughly one-third of the states holding primaries to roughly two-thirds. Moreover, more of the primaries selected delegates who were pledged to particular presidential candidates, rather than merely being 'beauty contests' that might inform party leaders of popular sentiment while actually deciding nothing. In the new environment, in 1972 the party's anti-war activists were able to impose their choice of George McGovern on the party leadership, leaving many large donors feeling marginalized and alienated. McGovern then went on to electoral disaster, winning only 37.5 per cent of the popular vote to Richard Nixon's 60.7 per cent.

The American direct primary system is an unusual form of IPD. Nonetheless, the Democrats' experiences in 1968 and 1972 illustrate some of the strengths and weaknesses of IPD. The oligarchic nature of the 1968 decision certainly alienated many young and committed activists, who in taking to the streets in Chicago both seriously tarnished the party's image and gave the Democratic establishment the opportunity to divide the party even more. The party had the complementary problem in 1972. By allowing the groundswell of anti-war sentiment to prevail in the party's choice of nominee, the newly 'democratized' structure led to the alienation, and in some cases defection to the Republicans, of core supporters without whom the party could not compete effectively in the general election. One explanation is simply that when a party is deeply divided, neither the presence nor the absence of IPD is adequate to prevent defeat.

Even without deep internal division, however, IPD can be a two-edged sword for a political party. On one side, IPD may help to convert passive supporters into actively invested participants in the party's competition with other parties both to hold governmental office and to shape public discourse whether in government or in opposition. It may help to inform political leaders of the desires of their supporters, and of the public more broadly. It may further the image of the party as one committed to democratic principles more generally, and as a firmly rooted movement in society.

On the other side, however, the principle that a ruling party or coalition is supposed to act in the national interest rather than in the sectional interest of its own supporters may be undermined by IPD. Although parties may influence policy from outside of government, there can be little doubt that a party's influence is greater when in government than when outside. In this sense, the common suggestion that parties may have to make a choice between office and policy is misleadingly simple; generally, office is a means to policy influence rather than an alternative. The real choice is between maintaining ideological purity at the possible expense of office, on the one hand, and bowing to electoral expediency or accepting compromise, on the other hand: between standing on principle and accepting half-a-loaf (or even a quarter-of-a-loaf) rather than none. For a variety of reasons, party leaders are likely to give relatively higher priority to winning elections and achieving office, while members are likely to give relatively higher priority to what they think is right, whether or not it will 'sell' at the polls. The price of being responsive to the party's members may be limited capacity to be responsive to the broader electorate.

This, in turn, addresses a contrast between two conceptions of democracy, and of the place of parties, and of IPD, within it. On one side, there is the family of models represented by the mass party conception of democracy (see Carty's chapter, this volume). Democracy involves competition between collectives of citizens who share common interests and ideologies. Parties are the organized political expression of these collectivities, and party leaders are their agents. Hence, members are the real heart and proper voice of the party; the possibility of active participation in politics, which is to say in parties, is an essential element of full democratic citizenship; parties will express real differences of policy; electoral politics is primarily about the mobilization of the party's natural supporters. On the other side, there are models that derive from the rational or social choice school. Democracy involves competition between teams of politicians seeking public office. To the extent that parties are more than labels for those teams, they are organizations of their supporters. Hence, while members may always exercise the option of exit, the real rulers of the party are and should be its leaders; system-level democracy does not require active popular participation within parties, but only free choice among parties; the policy proposals of parties (or coalitions of parties) should converge toward the median voter; because, electoral competition is primarily about appeal to moderate and unattached voters. IPD is central to the mass party conception of democracy, but potentially inimical to the second.

The chapters in this book have problematized the concept of intra-party democracy. In the book's introductory chapter we noted that many who are concerned with democratic promotion champion IPD as a necessary part of a vibrant democratic state. This perspective is premised on the long established belief that political parties are an essential part of contemporary democracy. This sentiment is captured best in Schattschneider's (1942) often quoted observation that there can be no democracy without parties. In most modern democracies parties organize both the electoral and the legislative spheres, dominating policymaking processes, and occupying the central roles in election campaigns. The conclusion many draw from this is that if parties are so central to democracy then they themselves should be democratically organized. Additionally, reflecting their central role, parties increasingly receive significant resources from the state, which, as van Biezen notes, leads some to view them as public utilities rightfully subject to significant state regulation of their affairs.

However, as Sartori (1965) has warned, state-wide democracy need not be the sum of many smaller democracies. And, as argued at times in this volume, it is possible that internal party democracy may even partially detract from state-wide democracy. For example, as suggested by Rahat, highly participatory party decision-making, in areas such as candidate selection, may lead to less inclusive legislatures. To some extent this may reflect a clash of competing democratic values—not all best manifested through internally democratic parties.

Even when there is agreement that IPD is a good thing, this does not get us particularly far in assessing how parties conduct their internal affairs. As illustrated in the preceding chapters there are many forms of IPD and parties are faced with a multitude of decisions when deciding whether and how to democratize their operations. The decisions parties reach reflect many different factors and these are often not as simple as whether or not a party wishes to be 'democratic'. A party with democratic impulses may find that different relative priorities given to the values of accountability, participation, inclusiveness, or responsiveness lead to different preferred outcomes in terms of IPD.

Scarrow, in this volume, shows how internally democratic practices can be very expensive both for parties and participants. For example, internally organized membership votes for candidate and leadership selection can cost parties many thousands of dollars that often need to be raised from private sources. Similarly these contests can be very expensive for would-be candidates, both raising the threshold for candidacy and making it impossible for some to compete while forcing those who do enter the contests to raise significant amounts from donors. The question then is whether these costs allow private donors to gain undue influence in party decision-making—as Scarrow asks, does he who pays the piper call the tune? Thus while these contests may be seen to increase participation in terms of a broader selectorate, they may be more exclusive in terms of candidacy and raise other issues concerning to whom a party is responsive.

When considering IPD, one is faced not only with normative questions relating to the definition, or perhaps preferred form, of democracy but also with questions relating to the scope and form of a political party. At their core, questions relating to IPD revolve around consideration of *who* has authority over *what*. In terms of who, most attention in IPD debates revolves around the role of a party's rank-and-file membership. As Young and Katz note in their contributions to this volume, the vast majority of parties are membership organizations and at least give lip service to the desire to have large numbers of members. As party membership numbers in many Western democracies are in decline, parties are increasingly engaged in discussions, and sometimes real efforts, aimed at increasing the size of their membership. A larger membership is seen as increasing a party's legitimacy and as a potentially useful instrument in waging electoral campaigns.

Support for increased IPD is frequently stimulated by this decline in party membership and activism. The argument is often made that few join political parties because voters increasingly do not see party membership as an effective form of political participation. In this view, parties are overly hierarchical and grassroots members have little say in determining their direction. The result is that those interested in politics, and in influencing public policy, increasingly choose alternative methods of participation, such as activism in advocacy groups, over party membership. In turn, some parties have taken steps to become more plebiscitarian in their decision-making, for example adopting membership votes for candidate and leadership selection, as part of an effort to increase the value of party activism and thus attract more members to their organizations. Katz, however, suggests that the decline in party activism may have little to do with the form of party organization and degree of IPD but rather may reflect broader societal changes. In this view, forces largely exogenous to the internal arrangements of the parties have made partisan involvement less attractive to citizens, and so should have been expected to result in declining party membership. This observation raises the question of whether there is anything parties themselves can do to reverse the trends of declining membership numbers.

Among parties desiring to increase the role of their members there are alternative views regarding the definition of membership. Some take a very expansive position resulting from their belief that an empowering of members may lead a desired growth in membership numbers by attracting new supporters. This view is manifested in events such as party leadership contests allowing anyone who joins up to the day of the vote to participate. These contests often result in the recruitment of many new members and in that narrow sense can be viewed as successful. Research, however, suggests that many of these recruits have little commitment to the party and few remain as party members once the contest is over. Others, for IPD purposes, restrict member involvement to those with a longer commitment to the party. As Cross notes in his discussion of leadership selection, some parties restrict the franchise to those who have belonged to the party for a year or more while others require attendance at party meetings or some other evidence of active membership.

While parties taking either approach can argue they are practicing IPD by means of empowering their members, they are engaged in very different exercises and are granting influence to very different categories of party supporters. The first are more casual partisans who come to party membership for the sole purpose of participating in an important party event, and indeed their commitment may be limited to support of a particular candidate rather than generalized to the party as a whole; the latter are more likely to be committed party activists. The arguments for inclusion of the first group are both to grow the party membership and to benefit from the collective wisdom of a large group of party supporters. The alternative position is that participation in key party events should be limited to those with an ongoing interest in the party as a way of rewarding them for their commitment, and to encourage others who would like a voice in these decisions to first illustrate an ongoing participation in party affairs.

Young also warns that party memberships are typically unrepresentative of the general electorate. Older, from high socio-economic classes and often male-dominated, party memberships are often not able to represent all of a party's voters effectively. This then raises several questions for a party, including whether it is both illegitimate and electorally dangerous to allow such an unrepresentative body to make key decisions that may not reflect the views of supporters generally. As is apparent in Gauja's discussion of party policymaking, the supposedly democratic impulse to empower grassroots members in the setting of policy direction raises concerns relating to other democratic norms given the unrepresentativeness of the party membership.

Often under the cover of IPD, some parties have addressed the under-representation of particular societal groups in their organizations. This has been most common with regard to gender as parties have formalized women's organizations within their decision-making structures, adopted affirmative action programmes (including in some cases quotas) to increase the number of female candidates for public office and mandated gender equity in internal decision-making bodies. Childs' contribution to this volume considers the intersection of IPD and issues of gender and politics. The primacy in much of the IPD debate of concerns with increasing the number of those participating, which results in adoption of procedures such as one-member-one-vote decision-making, may run counter to efforts to ensure equitable representation of groups such as women, youth, and ethnic minorities who may be under-represented in the general membership. More exclusive decision-making bodies may be more easily engineered to ensure fair group representation.

This example also illustrates another of the classic tensions that arises among different democratic norms that parties struggle with in adopting IPD, a theme that recurs throughout this volume. This is whether IPD concerns should be primarily directed towards decision-making processes or outcomes. In other words is it more important that decisions are made in an inclusive and participatory manner or that the outcomes reflect these democratic norms? This may be most apparent in terms of candidate selection. Is the primary concern with producing candidate pools that are inclusive and generally representative of the electorate or with decentralized and participatory selection processes regardless of the outcomes they produce?

Declining and unrepresentative memberships, coupled with what Katz identifies as a general disinterest among voters in joining parties, has resulted in what seems to be a growing phenomenon among parties to include their 'supporters' rather than solely their members in their internal decision-making. Sometimes this is accomplished through adoption of a very liberal definition of membership, but in some recent cases parties are not even 'pretending' to require membership but rather are explicitly inviting 'supporters' to participate in their internal decision-making. Parties in Australia, Canada, and the United Kingdom, for example, have experimented in recent years with candidate and leadership selection mechanisms that grant a share of the vote to self-proclaimed party supporters who decline to join the party formally. These are similar to the primary processes long used by the US parties. While these are potentially highly participatory and inclusive insofar as they are open to virtually all voters, they largely eliminate the privileged place of party members.

While parties hope these processes will eventually attract supporters to membership, by extending one of the central benefits of membership to non-members, they run the risk of further cheapening the value of party membership and actually making it less attractive. As raised by several authors in this collection, at some point efforts to be inclusive of all voters remove the basic 'partyness' from these supposedly intra-party affairs. When membership is not required, and increasingly when these processes are governed by state regulation, can they continue be viewed as intra-party events?

When we deconstruct and problematize IPD it is obvious that there are no easy answers to the multitude of questions that result. It has not been our objective in this volume to argue that IPD is necessarily a good thing nor that any one form of internal party organization is preferable to all others. If pushed, we suspect that the contributors to this volume, while all committed democrats, would not agree on many of these issues. At their core, these are often highly normative questions that require the balancing, and prioritizing, of many important democratic values. In our view, there is no universally correct answer to many of these questions. Rather, parties, and their voters, need to reflect on the various issues and compromises at play and make judgments reflecting their values and priorities. Our task has been to set out these challenges and to identify the potential pitfalls and compromises inherent in a comprehensive consideration of intra-party democracy. In doing so, our objective has been to help inform consideration of the possibilities of intra-party democracy and to highlight the implications of decisions parties and their supporters make.

Bibliography

Alderman, K. and N. Carter 2002. 'The Conservative Party Leadership Election of 2001', *Parliamentary Affairs* 55 (3), pp. 569–85.

Allern, E. H. and K. Pedersen 2007. 'The Impact of Party Organisational Changes on Democracy', *West European Politics* 30 (1), pp. 68–92.

Almond, G. A. and G. B. Powell 1978 [1966]. *Comparative Politics: System, Process, and Policy*. Boston: Little, Brown.

Andrews, J. and R. Jackman 2008. 'If Winning Isn't Everything, Why Do They Keep Score? Consequences of Electoral Performance for Party Leaders', *British Journal of Political Science* 38 (4), pp. 657–75.

Appleton, A. and A. Mazur 1993. 'Transformation or Modernization'. In: J. Lovenduski and P. Norris (eds.), *Gender and Party Politics*. London: Sage.

Argentina 2009. *Ley 26.571* <http://www.mininterior.gov.ar/asuntos_politicos_y_alectorales/dine/infogral/archivos_legislacion/Ley_26571_.pdf> [accessed 3 August 2011].

Ashe, J., R. Campbell, S. Childs et al. 2010. 'Stand By Your Man,' *British Politics* 5, pp. 455–80.

Ashiagbor, S. 2008. *Political Parties and Democracy in Theoretical and Practical Perspectives: Selecting Candidates for Legislative Office*. Washington, DC: National Democratic Institute <http://www.ndi.org/files/2406_polpart_report_engpdf_100708.pdf> [accessed 24 February 2010].

Australian Democrats 2003. *Freedom, Fairness and the Future: Report of the Australian Democrats National Review*. ACT: Kingston.

Avnon, D. 1995. 'Parties' Laws in Democratic Systems of Government', *Journal of Legislative Studies* 1 (2), pp. 283–300.

Bacchi, C. 2006. 'Arguing For and Against Quotas.' In: Dahlerup, D. (ed.), *Women, Quotas and Politics*. London: Routledge.

Back, H. 2008. 'Intra-Party Politics and Coalition Formation,' *Party Politics* 1 (1), pp. 71–89.

Back, L. and J. Solomos 1994. 'Labour and Racism: Trade Unions and the Selection of Parliamentary Candidates,' *Sociological Review* 42 (2), pp. 165–201.

Baer, D. L. 2003. 'Women, Women's Organizations, and Political Parties.' In: S. J. Caroll (ed.), *Women and American Politics*. Oxford: Oxford University Press.

Baldez, L. 2004. 'Elected Bodies,' *Legislative Studies Quarterly* 29 (2), pp. 231–58.

——2007. 'Primaries vs. Quotas: Gender and Candidate Nominations in Mexico, 2003,' *Latin American Politics and Society* 49 (3), pp. 69–96.

Bale, T. and J. Wilson 2006. 'The Greens.' In: R. Miller (ed.), *New Zealand Government and Politics*, 4th ed. South Melbourne: Oxford University Press.

Ballington, J. 2004. 'Strengthening Internal Political Party Democracy: Candidate Recruitment from a Gender Perspective.' Paper presented at EISA/NIMD workshop on How to Strengthen Internal Party Democracy? February 2004.

Barber, B. 1984. *Strong Democracy: Participatory Politics for a New Age*. Berkeley, CA: University of California Press.

Barbera, A. 2008. 'La democrazia "dei" e "nei" partiti, tra rappresentanza e governabilita'. Relazione al Convegno organizzato dal Cesfin 'Alberto Predieri' e dal Centro di studi politici e costituzionali Piero Calamandrei—Paolo Barile, Rettorato Universita' di Firenze, 19 October 2007.

Barbera, O., A. B. J. Rodriguez, and Montserrat Baras 2011. 'The Stability of the Leadership Selection Methods in Spain: Exploring its Causes and Consequences'. Paper presented at the ECPR Joint Sessions, St. Gallen.

Barnea, S. and G. Rahat 2007. 'Reforming Candidate Selection Methods: A Three-Level Approach', *Party Politics* 13 (3), pp. 375–94.

Bartolini, S. and P. Mair 2001. 'Challenges to Contemporary Political Parties'. In: L. Diamond and R. Gunther (eds.), *Political Parties and Democracy*. Baltimore, MD: Johns Hopkins University Press.

Basso, L. 1966. 'Il partito nell'ordinamento democratico moderno'. In: *ISLE, Indagine sul partito politico. La regolazione legislative*. Vol. I. Milan: Giuffré, pp. 5–127.

Bauer, G. and M. Tremblay 2011. *Women in Executive Power*. London: Routledge.

Baum, J. and J. A. Robinson 1995. 'Party Primaries in Taiwan: A Reappraisal', *Asian Affairs: An American Review* 22 (2), pp. 3–14.

Beange, P. 2009. 'Canadian Campaign Finance Reform since 2000: Path Dependent or Dynamic?' Paper prepared for Canadian Political Science Association Meetings, Ottawa, Canada, 27–30 May.

Beer, S. 1965. *Modern British Politics*. London: Faber.

——1969. *British Politics in the Collectivist Age*. New York: Random House.

Bennie, L., J. Curtice, and W. Rüdig 1996. 'Party Members'. In: Don MacIver (ed.), *The Liberal Democrats*. London: Prentice-Hall.

Benoit, K. and M. Laver 2006. *Party Policy in Modern Democracies*. London: Routledge.

Bértoa, F. C., D. R. Piccio and E. Rashkova Forthcoming. 'Party Laws in Comparative Perspective: Evidence and Implication'. In I. C. van Biezen and H. M. ten Napel (eds.), *Political Parties and Public Law: The Netherlands in Comparative Perspective*. Leiden: Leiden University Press.

Biezen, I. van 2000. 'On the Internal Balance of Party Power,' *Party Politics* 6 (4), pp. 395–417.

——2003. *Political Parties in New Democracies: Party Organization in Southern and East-Central Europe*. Basingstoke: Palgrave Macmillan.

——2004. 'Political Parties as Public Utilities', *Party Politics* 10 (6), pp. 701–22.

——2012. 'Constitutionalizing Party Democracy: The Constitutive Codification of Political Parties in Post-war Europe', *British Journal of Political Science* 42 (1), pp. 187–212.

——and G. Borz 2012. 'Models of Party Democracy: Patterns of Party Regulation in Post-war European Constitutions', *European Political Science Review*. First View Online.

——P. Mair, and T. Poguntke 2012. 'Going, Going,... Gone? The Decline of Party Membership in Contemporary Europe', *European Journal of Political Research* 51 (1), pp. 24–56.

Bille, L. 2001. 'Democratizing a Democratic Procedure: Myth or Reality? Candidate Selection in Western European Parties 1960–1990', *Party Politics* 7 (3), pp. 363–80.

Blyth, M. and R. S. Katz 2005. 'From Catch-All Politics to Cartelization', *West European Politics* 28 (1), pp. 33–60.

Bolleyer, N. 2009. 'Inside the Cartel Party', *Political Studies* 57 (3), pp. 559–79.

——2011. 'New Party Organization in Western Europe: Of Party Hierarchies, Stratarchies and Federations', *Party Politics*. First View Online.

——and A. Gauja 2011. 'Parliamentary Salaries as a Power Resource: Party Organizational Power in Westminster Democracies', *Party Politics*. First View Online.

Boucek, F. 2009. 'Rethinking Factionalism', *Party Politics* 15 (4), pp. 455–85.

Bratton, K. A. and L. P. Ray 2002. 'Descriptive Representation, Policy Outcomes, and Municipal Day-Care Coverage in Norway', *American Journal of Political Science* 46 (2), pp. 428–37.

Bruter, W. and S. Harrison 2009a. *The Future of Our Democracies: Young Party Members in Europe*. Basingstoke: Palgrave Macmillan.

—— —— 2009b. 'Tomorrow's Leaders? Understanding the Involvement of Young Party Members in Six European Democracies', *Comparative Political Studies* 42 (10), pp. 1259–91.

Burchell, J. 2002. *The Evolution of Green Politics: Development and Change within European Green Parties*. London: Earthscan Publications.

——2008. 'Sweden: Miljopartiet de Grona'. In: E. G. Frankland, P. Lucardie, and B. Rihoux (eds.), *Green Parties in Transition: The End of Grassroots Democracy?* Farnham: Ashgate.

Burnell, J. 1980. *Democracy and Accountability in the Labour Party*. Nottingham: Spokesman.

Butler, D. 1960. 'The Paradox of Party Difference', *American Behavioral Scientist* 4, pp. 3–5.

——and D. Stokes 1969. *Political Changes in Britain: Forces Shaping Electoral Choice*. New York: St. Martin's Press.

Bynander, F. and P. t'Hart 2007. 'The Politics of Party Leader Survival and Succession: Australia in Comparative Perspective', *Australian Journal of Political Science* 42 (1), pp. 47–72.

Calamandrei, P. 1970. *La Costituzione della Repubblica nei lavori preparatori dell'Assemblea Costituente*. Vol. I. Rome, pp. 154–7.

Campbell, B. 1987. *Iron Ladies*. London: Virago.

Campbell, R. and S. Childs 2010. 'Wives, Wags and Mothers. . . . But What about Women MPs, Sex and Gender at the 2010 General Election'. In: A. Geddes and J. Tonge (ed.), *Britain Votes: The 2010 General Election,* Special Edition of *Parliamentary Affairs*. Oxford: Oxford University Press.

Carroll, S. J. 2001. *The Impact of Women in Public Office*. Bloomington, IN: Indiana University Press.

Carty, R. K. 1991. *Canadian Political Parties in the Constituencies*. Toronto: Dundurn.

——1997. 'For the Third Asking: Is There a Future for National Political Parties?' In: T. Kent (ed.) *In Pursuit of the Public Good: Essays in Honour of Allan J. MacEachen*. Montreal: McGill-Queens University Press.

——2002. 'The Politics of Tecumseh Corners: Canadian Political Parties as Franchise Organizations', *Canadian Journal of Political Science* 35 (4), pp. 723–45.

Carty, R. K. 2004. 'Parties as Franchise Systems: The Stratarchical Organizational Imperative', *Party Politics* 10 (1), pp. 5–24.

——2008. 'Brokerage Politics, Stratarchical Organization and Party Members: The Liberal Party of Canada'. In: K. Kosiara-Pedersen and P. Kurrilo-Klitgaard (eds.), *Partier Og Partisystemer i Forandring: Festkrift til Lars Bille*. Odense: Syddansk Universitetsforlag.

——and W. Cross 2006. 'Can Stratarchically Organized Parties be Democratic? The Canadian Case', *Journal of Elections, Public Opinion and Parties* 16 (2), pp. 93–114.

————and L. Young 2000. *Rebuilding Canadian Party Politics*. Vancouver: UBC Press.

——————2012. 'The Lortie Commission and the Place of Political Parties as Agents of Responsible Government'. In: H. Bakvis and M. Jarvis (eds.), *From 'New Public Management' to 'New Political Governance': Essays in Honour of Peter C. Aucoin*. Montreal: McGill-Queens University Press.

Caul-Kittilson, M. and S. E. Scarrow 2003. 'Political Parties and the Rhetoric and Realities of Democratization'. In: B. E. Cain, R. J. Dalton, and S. E. Scarrow (eds.), *Democracy Transformed? Expanding Political Opportunities in Advanced Industrial Democracies*. Oxford: Oxford University Press.

Celis, K. 2008. 'Gendering Representation'. In: G. Goertz and A. Mazur (eds.), *Politics, Gender, and Concepts*. Cambridge: Cambridge University Press.

——and S. Childs 2012. 'The Substantive Representation of Women: What to Do with Conservative Claims', *Political Studies* 60 (1), pp. 213–25.

————J. Kantola et al. 2008. 'Rethinking Women's Substantive Representation', *Representation* 44 (2), pp. 99–110.

——————et al. 2010. 'Women's Interests,' unpublished paper.

——M. L. Krook, and P. Meier 2011. 'The Rise of Gender Quota Laws', *West European Politics* 34 (3), pp. 514–30.

Chaney, P. 2006. 'Critical Mass, Deliberation, and the Substantive Representation of Women: Evidence from the UK's Devolution Programme', *Political Studies* 54 (4), pp. 671–91.

Chen, P., R. Gibson, and K. Geiselhart 2006. *Electronic Democracy? The Impact of New Communications Technologies on Australian Democracy*, Democratic Audit of Australia Report No. 6. Canberra: Australian National University.

Childs, S. 2004. *New Labour's Women MPs*. London: Routledge.

——2006. 'Political Parties'. In: Dunleavy et al. (eds.), *Developments in British Politics*. Basingstoke: Macmillan.

——2008. *Women and British Party Politics*. London: Routledge.

——and M. L. Krook 2006. 'Should Feminists Give Up on Critical Mass? A Contingent Yes,' *Politics and Gender* 2 (4), pp. 522–30.

————2008. 'Critical Mass Theory and Women's Political Representation,' *Political Studies* 56 (3), pp. 725–36.

——and J. Lovenduski 2012. 'Representation'. In: *Oxford Handbook on Gender and Politics*. Oxford: Oxford University Press.

——and P. Webb 2012. *Sex, Gender and the Conservative Party*. Basingstoke: Palgrave.

——and J. Withey 2006. 'The Substantive Representation of Women: The Case of the Reduction of VAT on Sanitary Products', *Parliamentary Affairs* 59 (1), pp. 10–23.

CNCCFP (Commission nationale des comptes de campagne et des financements politiques) 2008. *Dixième Rapport d'Activité 2007*. Paris: CNCCFP.

Combes, H. 2003. 'Internal Elections and Democratic Transition: The Case of the Democratic Revolution Party in Mexico (1989–2001)'. Paper presented at the European Consortium for Political Research Joint Sessions of Workshops, Edinburgh.

Courtney, J. 1973. *The Selection of National Party Leaders in Canada*. Toronto: Macmillan of Canada

Cowley, P. 2002. *Revolts and Rebellions: Parliamentary Voting Under Blair*. London: Politico's.

Criddle, B. 1997. 'MPs and Candidates'. In: D. E. Butler and D. Kavanagh (eds.), *The British General Election of 1997*. London: Macmillan.

Cross, W. 1998. 'Teledemocracy: Canadian Political Parties Listening to their Constituents'. In: C. Alexander and L. Pal (eds.), *Digital Democracy: Policy and Politics in the Wired World*. Toronto: Oxford University Press.

——2004. *Political Parties*. Vancouver: UBC Press.

——2008. 'Democratic Norms and Party Candidate Selection: Taking Contextual Factors into Account', *Party Politics* 14 (5), pp. 596–619.

——and A. Blais 2012a. *Politics at the Centre: The Selection and Removal of Party Leaders in the Anglo Parliamentary Democracies*. Oxford: Oxford University Press.

—— —— 2012b. 'Who Selects the Party Leader?' *Party Politics*. First View Online.

——and J. Crysler. 2011. 'Financing Party Leadership Campaigns'. In: L. Young and H. Jansen (eds.), *Money, Politics and Democracy*. Vancouver: UBC Press.

——and L. Young 2004. 'The Contours of Political Party Membership in Canada', *Party Politics* 10 (4), pp. 427–44.

————2008. 'Factors Influencing the Decision of the Young Politically Engaged to Join a Political Party', *Party Politics* 14 (3), pp. 345–69.

————Forthcoming. 'Personalization of Campaigns in an SMP System: The Canadian Case'.

Cular, G. 2004. 'Organisational Development of Parties and Internal Party Democracy in Croatia', *Politicka misao* 41 (5), pp. 28–51.

Curtin, J. 2008. 'Women, Political Leadership and Substantive Representation: The Case of New Zealand', *Parliamentary Affairs* 61 (3), pp. 490–504.

Dahlerup, D. 2011. 'Engendering Representative Democracy'. In: S. Alonso, J. Keane, and W. Merkel (eds.), *The Future of Representative Democracy*. Cambridge: Cambridge University Press.

——and L. Freidenvall 2005. 'Quotas as a Fast Track to Equal Political Representation for Women: Why Scandinavia Is No Longer the Model', *International Feminist Journal of Politics* 7 (1), pp. 26–48.

————2010. 'Judging Gender Quotas: Predictions and Results', *Policy & Politics* 38 (3), pp. 40725.

————2011. *Electoral Gender Quota Systems and Their Implementation in Europe*. Report for the European Parliament <http://www.europeanpwn.net/files/euquotaonderzoek.pdf> [accessed 28 August 2012].

——and B. Gulli 1985. 'Women's Organizations in the Nordic Countries'. In: E Haavio-Mannila (ed.), *Unfinished Democracy: Women in Nordic Politics*. Oxford: Pergamon Press.

Dalton, R. J. 1985. 'Political Parties and Political Representation: Party Supporters and Party Elites in Nine Nations', *Comparative Political Studies*, 18, pp. 267–99.

——and M. P. Wattenberg 2000. *Parties without Partisans: Political Change in Advanced Industrial Societies*. Oxford: Oxford University Press.

Damgaard, E. 1997. 'The Political Roles of Danish MPs', *The Journal of Legislative Studies* 3 (1), pp. 79–90.

De Luca, M., M. P. Jones, and M. I. Tula 2002. 'Back Rooms or Ballot Boxes? Candidate Nomination in Argentina', *Comparative Political Studies* 35 (4), pp. 413–36.

De Winter, L. 1988. 'Belgium: Democracy or Oligarchy?' In: M. Gallagher and M. Marsh (eds.), *Candidate Selection in Comparative Perspective: The Secret Garden of Politics*. London: Sage.

Detterbeck, K. 2011. 'The Rare Event of Choice: Party Primaries in German Land Parties'. Paper presented at the ECPR Joint Sessions, St. Gallen.

Dodson, D. 2006. *The Impact of Women in Congress*. Oxford: Oxford University Press.

Dogan, M. 2001. 'Class, Religion, Party: Triple Decline of Electoral Cleavages in Western Europe'. In: L. Karvonen and S. Kuhnle (eds.), *Party Systems and Voter Alignments Revisited*. London: Routledge.

—— 2002. 'Accelerated Decline of Religious Beliefs in Europe.' *Comparative Sociology* 1 (2), pp. 127–49.

Dovi, S. 2007. *The Good Representative*. Malden, MA: Blackwell.

Downs, A. 1957. *An Economic Theory of Democracy*. New York: Harper & Row.

Duverger, M. 1954. *Political Parties*. New York: Johns Wiley and Sons.

Eldersveld, S. 1964. *Political Parties: A Behavioural Analysis*, Chicago, IL: Rand McNally.

Elections Canada 2011. *Registration and Political Financing of Leadership Contestants* <http://www.elections.ca/content.aspx?section=vot&dir=bkg&document=ec90531&lang=e&textonly=false> [accessed 7 June 2011].

Elia, L. 2009. 'A quando una legge sui partiti?' In: S. Merlini (ed.), *La democrazia dei partiti e la democrazia nei partiti*. Florence: Passigli Editore.

Elklit, J. and P. Svensson 1997. 'What Makes Elections Free And Fair?' *Journal of Democracy* 8 (3), pp. 32–46.

Ennser, L. and W. Müller 2011. 'Intra-Party Democracy, Political Performance, and the Survival of Party Leaders: Austria, 1945–2010'. Paper presented at the ECPR Joint Sessions, St. Gallen.

Epstein, L. 1967. *Political Parties in Western Democracies*. London: Pall Mall.

——1988. *Political Parties in the American Mold*. Madison, WI: University of Wisconsin Press.

European Commission for Democracy through Law 2008. *Code of Good Practice in the Field of Political Parties* Venice: European Commission for Democracy through Law.

Federal Election Commission 2011. *The FEC and the Federal Campaign Finance Law* <http://www.fec.gov/pages/brochures/fecfeca/shtml#Disclosure> [accessed 21 July 2011].

Festinger, L. 1962. *A Theory of Cognitive Dissonance*. Stanford, CA: Stanford University Press.

Fisher, J., E. Fieldhouse, and D. Cutts 2011. 'Members Are Not the Only Fruit: Volunteer Activity in Political Parties'. Paper presented at the Annual Conference of the PSA Elections, Public Opinion and Parties Specialist Group (EPOP), September.

Flanagan, T. 2007. *Harper's Team: Behind the Scenes in the Conservative Rise to Power.* Montreal: McGill-Queen's University Press.

Florida, A. 2009. 'Partiti e partecipazione politica: modelli alternativi di "democrazia interna", tra ricerca empirica e riflessione normativa'. Paper presented at the XXIII annual meeting of the Società Italiana di Scienza Politica, Rome, 17–19 September.

Franceshet, S. and J. Piscopo 2008. 'Gender Quotas and Women's Substantive Representation: Lessons from Argentina', *Politics and Gender* 4 (3), pp. 393–425.

Frankland, E. G. 2008. 'The Evolution of the Greens in Germany: From Amateurism to Professionalism'. In: E. G. Frankland, P. Lucardie, and B. Rihoux (eds.), *Green Parties in Transition: The End of Grass-roots Democracy?* Farnham: Ashgate.

Freidenvall, L., D. Dahlerup, and H. Skjeie 2006. 'The Nordic Countries: An Incremental Model.' In: D. Dahlerup (ed.), *Women, Quotas and Politics*. London: Routledge.

Gallagher, M. 1988. 'Introduction'. In: M. Gallagher and M. Marsh (eds.), *Candidate Selection in Comparative Perspective: The Secret Garden of Politics*. London: Sage.

——1988. 'Ireland: The Increasing Role of the Centre'. In: M. Gallagher and M. Marsh (eds), *Candidate Selection in Comparative Perspective: The Secret Garden of Politics*. London: Sage.

——and M. Marsh 2004. 'Party Membership in Ireland,' *Party Politics* 10 (4), pp. 407–25.

Gardner, J. A. 2000. 'Can Party Politics be Virtuous?' *Columbia Law Review* 100 (3), pp. 667–701.

Gauja, A. 2005. 'The Pitfalls of Participatory Democracy: A Study of the Australian Democrats' GST', *Australian Journal of Political Science* 40 (1), pp. 71–85.

——Forthcoming. *The Party Versus Parliament in Representative Democracy.* Basingstoke: Palgrave Macmillan.

Ghergina, S. and M. Chiru 2011. 'Keeping the Doors Closed: Leadership Selection in Post-Communist Romania'. Paper presented at the ECPR Joint Sessions, St. Gallen.

Gibson, R. and S. Ward 1998. 'UK Political Parties and the Internet', *The Harvard International Journal of Press/Politics* 3 (3), pp. 14–38.

——P. Nixon, and S. Ward 2003 (eds.) *Political Parties and the Internet. Net Gain?* New York: Routledge.

Gillespie, R. 1993. 'Programa 2000: The Appearance and Reality of Socialist Renewal in Spain', *West European Politics* 16 (1), pp. 78–96.

Ginsberg, B. and M. Shefter 2002. *Politics by Other Means*. New York: W. W. Norton.

Goodwin-Gill, G. S. 2006. *Free and Fair Elections*. New expanded edition. Inter-Parliamentary Union <http://www.ipu.org/PDF/publications/Free&Fair06-e.pdf> [accessed 18 July 2010].

Gotell, L. and J. Brodie 1991. 'Women and Parties: More Than an Issue of Numbers'. In: H. G. Thorburn (ed.), *Party Politics in Canada*. Scarborough: Prentice-Hall Canada.

Haavio-Mannila, E. et al. 1985. *Unfinished Democracy: Women in Nordic Politics*. Oxford: Pergamon Press.

Hadar, Y. 2008. 'Turnover of Knesset Members in Israel 1949–2006'. MA dissertation, The Hebrew University of Jerusalem.

Hain, P. 2011. *Refounding Labour: A Party for the New Generation*. London: Labour Party <http://www.campaignengineroom.org.uk/refounding-labour/news/refounding-labour-launched> [accessed 12 September 2011].

Halman, L., R. Inglehart, J. Díez-Medrano et al. 2008. *Changing Values and Beliefs in 85 Countries: Trends from the Values Surveys from 1981 to 2004*. Leiden: Brill.

——and O. Riis 2003. 'Contemporary European Discourses on Religion and Morality'. In: L. Halman and O. Riis (eds.), *Religion in Secularizing Society: The Europeans' Religion at the End of the 20th Century*. Leiden: Brill.

Hawkesworth, M. 2003. 'Congressional Enactments of Race-Gender: Toward a Theory of Raced-Gendered Institutions', *American Political Science Review* 97 (4), pp. 529–50.

Hazan, R. Y. and G. Rahat 2010. *Democracy within Parties: Candidate Selection Methods and their Political Consequences*. Oxford: Oxford University Press.

Heffernan, R. 2007. 'Tony Blair as Labour Party Leader'. In: A. Seldon (ed.), *Blair's Britain*. Cambridge: Cambridge University Press.

——2009. 'British Political Parties'. In: C. Hay (ed.) *The Oxford Handbook of British Politics*. Oxford: Oxford University Press.

Heidar, K. 1994. 'The Polymorphic Nature of Party Membership', *European Journal of Political Research* 25 (1), pp. 61–86.

Hibbing, J. and E. Theiss-Morse 2002. *Stealth Democracy: American's Beliefs about How Government Should Work*. Cambridge: Cambridge University Press.

Hoffman, D. 1961. 'Intra-Party Democracy: A Case Study,' *Canadian Journal of Economics and Political Science* 27 (2), pp. 223–35.

Hofnung, M. 2008. 'Unaccounted Competition: The Finance of Intra-Party Elections', *Party Politics* 14 (6), pp. 726–44.

Hopkin, J. and C. Paolucci 1999. 'The Business Firm Model of Party Organization: Cases from Spain and Italy', *European Journal of Political Research* 35 (3) pp. 307–39.

——2001. 'Bringing the Members Back in? Democratizing Candidate Selection in Britain and Spain', *Party Politics* 7 (3), pp. 343–61.

——2006. 'Conceptualizing Political Clientelism: Political Exchange and Democratic Theory'. Paper presented at the annual meeting of the American Political Science Association, Philadelphia.

Htun, M. 2004. 'Is Gender Like Ethnicity? The Political Representation of Identity Groups', *Perspectives on Politics* 2 (3), pp. 439–58.

Hughes, M. and P. Paxton 2008. 'Continuous Change, Episodes and Critical Periods,' *Politics and Gender* 4 (2), pp. 233–64.

Il Popolo della Liberta 2011. *Quote* (dues) <http://www.pdl.it/adesioni/quote.htm> [accessed 21 July 2011].

Inglehart, R. 1977. *The Silent Revolution*. Princeton, NJ: Princeton University Press.

International IDEA 2007. *Internal Democracy of Parties Canvassed in The Hague* <http://www.idea.int/parties/internal_democracy07.cfm> [accessed 6 June 2012].

——2010. *Political Finance Database* <http://www.idea.int/parties/finance/db/index.cfm> [accessed July 2010].

Issacharoff, S. 2007. 'Fragile Democracies', *Harvard Law Review* 120, pp. 1407–67.

Janda, K. 2005. 'Adopting Party Law'. Working paper series on 'Political Parties and Democracy in Theoretical and Practical Perspectives'. Washington, DC: National Democratic Institute for International Affairs.

Jeffrey, B. 2010. *Divided Loyalties: The Liberal Party of Canada, 1984–2008*. Toronto: University of Toronto Press.

Jun, U. 2011. 'Volksparteien under Pressure: Challenges and Adaptation', *German Politics* 20 (1), pp. 200–22.

Karvonen, L. 2007. 'Legislation on Political Parties: A Global Comparison', *Party Politics* 13 (4), pp. 437–55.

Kasapovic, M. 2001. 'Nominating Procedures in Democratic Polities', *Politička misao*, 38 (5), pp. 3–17.

Kathlene, L. 1995. 'Position Power Versus Gender Power.' In: G. Duerst-Lahti and R. M. Kelly (eds.), *Gender Power, Leadership and Governance*. Ann Arbor, MI: University of Michigan Press.

Katz, R. S. 1986. 'Party Government: A Rationalistic Conception.' In: F. Castles and R. Wildenmann (eds.), *Visions and Realities of Party Government*. Berlin: de Gruyter.

——1987. 'Party Government and Its Alternatives.' In: R. S. Katz (ed.), *Party Governments: European and American Experiences*. Berlin: de Gruyter.

——1990. 'Party as Linkage: A Vestigial Function?' *European Journal of Political Research* 18 (1), pp. 143–61.

——1997. *Democracy and Elections*. New York: Oxford University Press.

——2001. 'The Problem of Candidate Selection and Models of Party Democracy', *Party Politics* 7 (3), pp. 277–96.

——2002. 'The Internal Life of Parties'. In: K. R. Luther and F. Müller-Rommel (eds.), *Political Challenges in the New Europe: Political and Analytical Challenges*. Oxford: Oxford University Press.

——2004. 'Democracy and the Legal Regulation of Political Parties'. Paper presented at the USAID conference on 'Change in Political Parties', Washington DC, 1 October.

——and P. Mair 1993. 'The Evolution of Party Organization in Europe: The Three Faces of Party Organization', *The American Review of Politics* 14 (Winter), pp. 593–617.

————1995. 'Changing Models of Party Organization and Party Democracy: The Emergence of the Cartel Party', *Party Politics* 1 (1), pp. 5–28.

————2002. 'The Ascendancy of the Party in Public Office: Party Organizational Change in Twentieth-Century Democracies'. In: R. Gunther, J. Ramon-Montero, and J. Linz (eds.), *Political Parties: Old Concepts and New Challenges*. Oxford: Oxford University Press.

————2009. 'The Cartel Party Thesis: A Restatement', *Perspectives on Politics* 7, pp. 753–66.

————L. Bardi et al. 1992. 'The Membership of Political Parties in European Democracies, 1960–1990', *European Journal of Political Research* 22 (3), 329–45.

Kenig, O. 2009a. 'Classifying Party Leaders' Selection Methods in Parliamentary Democracies', *Journal of Elections, Public Opinion and Parties* 19 (4), pp. 433–47.

——2009b. 'Democratization of Party Leadership Selection: Do Wider Selectorates Produce More Competitive Contests?' *Electoral Studies* 28 (2), pp. 240–47.

Kirchheimer, O. 1966. 'The Transformation of the Western European Party Systems'. In: J. LaPalombara and M. Weiner (eds.), *Political Parties and Political Development*. Princeton, NJ: Princeton University Press.

Kitschelt, H. 1989. 'The Internal Politics of Parties: The Law of Curvilinear Disparity Revisited', *Political Studies* 37 (3), pp. 400–21.

Kittilson, M. C. 2006. *Challenging Parties, Changing Parliaments*. Columbus, OH: Ohio State University Press.

——2011a. 'Women, Gender, and Party Politics.' In: *Oxford Handbook on Gender and Politics*. Oxford: Oxford University Press.

——2011b. 'Women, Parties and Platforms in Post-Industrial Democracies,' *Party Politics* 17 (1), pp. 66–99.

Kommers, D. P. 1997. *The Constitutional Jurisprudence of the Federal Republic of Germany*. Durham, NC: Duke University Press.

Koole, R. 1996. 'Cadre, Catch-all or Cartel? A Comment on the Notion of the Cartel Party', *Party Politics* 2 (4), pp. 507–23.

——2006. 'Lijsttrekkersverkiezingen in Nederlandse politieke partijen', *Beleid en Maatschappij* 33, pp. 253–65.

Krook, M. L. 2009. *Quotas for Women in Politics: Gender and Candidate Selection Reform Worldwide*. Oxford: Oxford University Press.

——2010. 'Women's Representation in Parliament: A Qualitative Comparative Analysis', *Political Studies* 58 (5), pp. 886–908.

Lees-Marshment, J. and S. Quayle 2001. 'Empowering the Members or Marketing the Party? The Conservative Reforms of 1998', *Political Quarterly* 72 (2), pp. 204–12.

Leyenaar, M. 2004. *Political Empowerment of Women*. Amsterdam: Martinus Nijhoff.

Lijphart, A. 1984. *Democracies: Patterns of Majoritarian and Consensus Government in Twenty-One Countries*. New Haven, CT: Yale University Press.

——1999. *Patterns of Democracy: Government Forms and Performance in Thirty-Six Countries*. New Haven, CT: Yale University Press.

Linde, J. Forthcoming. 'Why Feed the Hand that Bites You? Perceptions of Procedural Fairness and System Support in Post-communist Democracies', *European Journal of Political Research*.

Lisi, M. 2010. 'The Democratisation of Party Leadership Selection: The Portuguese Experience', *Portuguese Journal of Social Science* 9 (2), pp. 127–48.

Lovenduski, J. 2005a. *Feminizing Politics*. Cambridge: Polity.

——2005b. *State Feminism and Political Representation*. Cambridge: Cambridge University Press.

——and M. Guadagnini 2010. 'Political Representation'. In: D. McBridge and A. Mazur (eds.), *The Politics of State Feminism*. Philadelphia, PA: Temple University Press.

——and P. Norris 1993. *Gender and Party Politics*. London: Sage.

Loxbo, K. 2011. 'The Fate of Intra-Party Democracy: Leadership Autonomy and Activist Influence in the Mass and the Cartel Party', *Party Politics*. First View Online.

Magolowondo, A. n.d. 'Internal Party Democracy: The State of Affairs and the Road Ahead'. Report commissioned for the Netherlands Institute for Multiparty Democracy Knowledge Centre <http://www.nimd.org/documents/I/internal_party_democracy_state_of_affairs_and_the_road_ahead.pdf> [accessed 6 June 2012].

Maguire, G. E. 1998. *Conservative Woman*. Oxford: Macmillan and St Anthony's.

Mair, P. 1994. 'Party Organizations: From Civil Society to the State.' In: R. S. Katz and P. Mair (eds.), *How Parties Organize: Change and Adaptation in Party Organizations in Western Democracies*. London: Sage.

——1998. 'Representation and Participation in the Changing World of Party Politics', *European Review* 6 (2), pp. 161–74.

——2005. 'Democracy Beyond Parties'. Discussion Paper, Centre for the Study of Democracy, University of California, Irvine.

——and I. van Biezen 2001. 'Party Membership in 20 European Democracies 1980–2000', *Party Politics* 7 (1), pp. 5–21.

Malloy, J. 2003. 'High Discipline, Low Cohesion? The Uncertain Patterns of Canadian Parliamentary Party Groups', *Journal of Legislative Studies* 9 (4), pp. 116–29.

Mansbridge, J. 1999. 'Should Blacks Represent Blacks and Women Represent Women? A Contingent Yes', *The Journal of Politics* 61 (3), pp. 628–57.

Margetts, H. 2006. 'Cyber Parties'. In: R. S. Katz and W. Crotty (eds.), *Handbook of Party Politics*. London: Sage.

Marsh, M. 1993. 'Introduction: Selecting the Party Leader', *European Journal of Political Research* 24 (3), pp. 229–31.

Massicotte, L. and A. Blais 2000. In R. Rose (ed.), *International Encyclopedia of Elections*. Washington, DC: Congressional Quarterly Books.

Mateo Diaz, M. 2005. *Representing Women: Female Legislators in West European Parliaments*. Essex: ECPR.

May, J. D. 1973. 'Opinion Structure of Political Parties: The Special Law of Curvilinear Disparity,' *Political Studies* XXI (2), pp.135–51.

Mazur, A. G. 2002. *Theorizing Feminist Policy*. Oxford: Oxford University Press.

McIlveen, R. 2009. 'Ladies of the Right: An Interim Analysis of the A-List', *Journal of Elections, Public Opinion and Parties* 19 (2), pp. 147–57.

McKenzie, R. T. 1963. *British Political Parties*. London: Mercury Books.

——1964. *British Political Parties: The Distribution of Power within the Conservative and Labour Parties*. London: Heinemann.

McMenamin, I. 2008. 'Business, Politics and Money in Australia: Testing Economic, Political and Ideological Explanations', *Australian Journal of Political Science* 43 (3), pp. 377–93.

McSweeney, D. 2010. 'Primary Elections for Britain', *The Political Quarterly* 81 (4), pp. 537–44.

Merkl, P. 1980. 'Attitudes, Ideology and Politics of Party Members'. In: P. Merkl (ed.), *Western European Party Systems*. New York: Free Press.

Mersel, Y. 2006. 'The Dissolution of Political Parties: The Problem of Internal Democracy', *International Journal of Constitutional Law* 4 (1), pp. 84–113.

Michels, R. 1962. *Political Parties: A Sociological Study of the Oligarchical Tendencies of Modern Democracy*. New York: Collier Books.

Mikulska, A. and S. Scarrow 2011. 'Assessing the Impact of Candidate Selection Rules: Britain in the 1990s', *Journal of Elections, Public Opinion, and Parties* 20 (3), pp. 311–33.

Miller, W. 1988. *Without Consent: Mass-Elite Linkages in Presidential Politics*. Lexington, KY: University of Kentucky Press.

——M. K. Jennings, and B. G. Farah 1986. *Parties in Transition: A Longitudinal Study of Party Elites and Party Supporters*. New York: Russell Sage Foundation.

Montabes, J. and C. Ortega 1999. 'Candidate Selection in Two Rigid List Systems: Spain and Portugal'. Paper presented at the European Consortium for Political Research Joint Sessions of Workshops, Mannheim, Germany.

Morris, N. and C. Brown 2006. 'Labour May Call Off Deputy Leader Race', *The Independent* [online 9 December 2006] <http://www.independent.co.uk>.

Mulé, R. 1997. 'Explaining the Party-Policy Link: Established Approaches and Theoretical Developments', *Party Politics* 3 (4), pp. 493–512.

Mulholland, H. 2010. 'Diane Abbott accuses David Miliband of 'Buying' Labour Leadership Contest' [online 2 August 2010] <http://www.guardian.co.uk/2010/aug/02/diane-abbott-david-miliband-buying-labour-leadership>.

Müller, W. 1989. 'Party Patronage in Austria: Theoretical Considerations and Empirical Findings'. In: Anton Pelinka and Fritz Plasser (eds.) *The Austrian Party System*. Boulder, CO: Westview.

——1992. 'Austria'. In: R. S. Katz and P. Mair (eds.) *Party Organizations: A Data Handbook on Party Organizations in Western Democracies*. London: Sage.

——1994. 'The Development of Austrian Party Organizations in the Post-war Period'. In: R. S. Katz and P. Mair (eds.), *How Parties Organize*. London: Sage.

——and U. Sieberer 2006. 'Party Law'. In: R. S. Katz and W. Crotty (eds.), *Handbook of Party Politics*. London: Sage.

Murray, R. 2008. 'The Power of Sex and Incumbency', *Party Politics* 14 (5), pp. 539–54.

——2010a. *Cracking the Highest Glass Ceiling*. London: Praeger.

——2010b. *Parties, Gender Quotas and Candidate Selection in France*. Basingstoke: Palgrave.

Narud, H. M., M. N. Pedersen, and H. Valem 2002. 'Parliamentary Nominations in Western Democracies'. In: H. M. Narud, M. N. Pedersen, and Henry Valen (eds.), *Party Sovereignty and Citizen Control: Selecting Candidates for Parliamentary Elections in Denmark, Finland, Iceland and Norway*. Odense: University Press of Southern Denmark.

Nassmacher, K.-H. 2009. *The Funding of Party Competition: Party Finance in 25 Democracies*. Baden-Baden: Nomos Verlagsgesellschaft.

National 2011. *Building a Brighter Future* <http://www.national.org.nz> [accessed 1 September 2011].

Naumetz, T. 2011. 'Four Former Liberal Leadership Contenders Still Owe $576,000 in Bank Loans', *The Hill Times online* <http://www.thehillties.ca/page/view/loans-05-16-2011> [accessed 16 May 2011].

Navot, D. 2006. 'Party Primary Elections and Corruption'. In: G. Rahat (ed.), *Candidate Selection in Israel: Reality and Ideal*. Tel Aviv: Society Research Institute.

New Zealand Green Party n.d. 'Memorandum from Central Party Office to Local Electorates'.

Noble, T. 2000. 'The Mobility Transition: Social Mobility Trends in the First Half of the Twenty-first Century', *Sociology* 34 (1): 35–51.

Norris, P. 1995. 'May's Law of Curvilinear Disparity Revisited: Leaders, Officers, Members and Voters in British Political Parties', *Party Politics* 1 (1), pp. 29–47.

——1997. 'Introduction: Theories of Recruitment.' In: P. Norris (ed.), *Passages to Power: Legislative Recruitment in Advanced Democracies*. Cambridge: Cambridge University Press.

——2000. *A Virtuous Circle? Political Communications in Post-Industrial Democracies*. Cambridge: Cambridge University Press.

——2004. *Building Political Parties: Reforming Legal Regulations and Internal Rules*. Report commissioned by the International IDEA <http://www.idea.int/parties/upload/pippa%20norris%20ready%20for%20wev%20_3_.pdf> [accessed 24 February 2010].

——and J. Lovenduski 1993. *Gender and Party Politics*. London: Sage.

————1995. *Political Recruitment*. Cambridge: Cambridge University Press.

NZ Labour [New Zealand Labour Party] 2007. *Party Groups*, Available online: <http://www.labour.org.nz/labour_team/party_groups/index.html> [accessed 14 September 2007].

Oliver, J. 2009. 'Left-wing Union Coup May Rob Labour of Donations', *The Sunday Times online* <http://www.timesonline.co.uk> [accessed 6 September 2011].

Olson, M. 1965, *The Logic of Collective Action: Public Goods and the Theory of Groups*. Cambridge: Harvard University Press.

Panebianco, A. 1988. *Political Parties: Organization and Power*. Cambridge: Cambridge University Press.

Paolucci, C. 2006. 'The Nature of Forza Italia and the Italian Transition', *Journal of Southern Europe and the Balkans* 8 (2), pp. 163–78.

Parisi, A. and G. Pasquino 1979. 'Changes in Italian Electoral Behaviour: The Relationships Between Parties and Voters.' In: P. Lange and S. Tarrow (eds.), *Italy in Transition*. London: Frank Cass.

Parliamentary Assembly Council of Europe 2010 <http://assembly.coe.int/Main.asp?link%20=/Documents/WorkingDocs/Doc10/EDOC12107.htm> [accessed 6 June 2012].

Pasquino, G. 2009. 'The Democratic Party and the Restructuring of the Italian Party System', *Journal of Modern Italian Studies* 14 (1), pp. 21–30.

Pateman, C. 1970. *Participation and Democratic Theory*. Cambridge: Cambridge University Press.

Pedersen, H. 2010. 'How Intra-Party Power Relations Affect the Coalition Behaviour of Political Parties', *Party Politics* 16 (6), pp. 737–54.

Pedersen, K., L. Bille, R. Buch et al. 2004. 'Sleeping or Active Partners? Danish Party Members at the Turn of the Millennium', *Party Politics* 10 (4), pp. 367–83.

Pennings, P. and R. Y. Hazan 2001. 'Democratizing Candidate Selection: Causes and Consequences', *Party Politics* 7 (3), pp. 267–75.

Perrigo, S. 1995. 'Gender Struggles in the British Labour Party from 1979 to 1995', *Party Politics* 1 (3), pp. 407–17.

Pettitt, R. 2007. 'Challenging the Leadership: The Party Conference as a Platform for Dissenting Membership Voice in British and Danish Parties of the Left', *Scandinavian Political Studies* 30 (2), pp. 229–48.

——2011. 'Exploring Variations in Intra-Party Democracy: A Comparative Study of the British Labour Party and the Danish Centre-Left', *The British Journal of Politics and International Relations*. First View Online.

Phillips, A. 1995. *The Politics of Presence*. Oxford: Clarendon Press.

Piccio, D. R. 2012. 'Party Regulation in Europe: Country Reports'. The Legal Regulation of Political Parties, Working Paper 18 <http://www.partylaw.leidenuniv.nl/uploads/wp1812.pdf> [accessed 8 June 2012].

——and M. C. Pacini 2012. 'Party Regulation in Italy and Its Effects.' Paper prepared for the VI Annual Congress of the Portuguese Political Science Association, Lisbon, 1–3 March 2012.

Pilet, J.-B., W. Cross, and A. Blais 2011. 'Does Consociationalism Matter? Leadership Selection in Belgium in a Comparative Perspective'. Paper presented at the ECPR Joint Sessions, St. Gallen.

Poguntke, T. 1998. 'Party Organisations'. In: J. W. van Deth (ed.), *Comparative Politics: The Problem of Equivalence*. London: Routledge.

——2001. 'From Nuclear Building Sites to Cabinet: The Career of the German Green Party', Keele European Parties Research Unit (KEPRU) Working Paper 6, Keele University, UK.

——and Paul Webb (eds.) 2005. *The Presidentialization of Politics: A Comparative Study of Modern Democracies*. Oxford: Oxford University Press.

Politics Home 2009 <http://www.epolitix.com/latestnews/article-detail/newsarticle/david-cameron-fixing-broken-politics-speech-in-full/> [accessed 8 January 2012].

Polsby, N. W. and A. Wildavsky 1991. *Presidential Elections: Contemporary Strategies of American Electoral Politics*, 8th edn. New York: Free Press.

Powell, G. B. 1982. *Contemporary Democracies: Participation, Stability and Violence.* Cambridge, MA: Harvard University Press.

Punnett, R. M. 1992. *Selecting the Party Leader: Britain in Comparative Perspective.* Hertfordshire: Harvester Wheatsheaf.

Putnam, R. 1995. 'Bowling Alone: America's Declining Social Capital,' *Journal of Democracy* 6 (1), pp. 65–78.

Rahat, G. 2008. 'Entering Through the Back Door: Non-party Actors in Intra-Party (S)electoral Politics'. In: D. M. Farrell and R. Schmitt-Beck (eds.), *Non-Party Actors in Electoral Politics: The Role of Interest Groups and Independent Citizens in Contemporary Election Campaigns*. Baden-Baden: Nomos Verlagsgesellschaft.

——2009. 'Which Candidate Selection Method Is the Most Democratic?' *Government and Opposition* 44 (1), pp. 68–90.

——and R. Y. Hazan 2001. 'Candidate Selection Methods', *Party Politics* 7 (3), pp. 297–322.

————2007. 'Political Participation in Party Primaries: Increase in Quantity, Decrease in Quality'. In: T. Zittel and D. Fuchs (eds.), *Participatory Democracy and Political Participation: Can Participatory Engineering Bring Citizens Back In?* London: Routledge.

————and R. S. Katz 2008. 'Democracy and Political Parties: On the Uneasy Relationships Between Participation, Competition and Representation', *Party Politics* 14 (6), pp. 663–83.

——and N. Sher-Hadar 1999. *Intra-Party Selection of Candidates for the Knesset List and for Prime-Ministerial Candidacy 1995–1997*. Jerusalem: Israel Democracy Institute.

Raniolo, F. 2006. 'Forza Italia: A Leader with a Party', *South European Society and Politics* 11 (4), pp. 439–55.

Reingold, B. 2000. *Representing Women*. Chapel Hill, NC: University of North Carolina Press.

——2008. *Legislative Women, Getting Elected, Getting Ahead*. Boulder, CO: Riener.

Rihoux, B. and W. Rüdig 2006. 'Analyzing Greens in Power: Setting the Agenda', *European Journal of Political Research* 45, pp. 1–33.

Rose, R. 1974. *The Problem of Party Government*. New York: Free Press.

——and P. Davies 1994. *Inheritance in Public Policy: Change without Choice in Britain.* New Haven, CT: Yale University Press.

Rush, M. and P. Giddings 2002. 'Parliamentary Socialisation: The UK Experience'. Paper presented at the ECPR Workshops, Turin.

Russell, M. 2005. *Building New Labour.* Basingstoke: Palgrave.

Sandri, G. and T. Pauwels 2010. 'Party Membership Role and Party Cartelization in Belgium and Italy: Two Faces of the Same Medal?' *Politics and Policy* 38 (6), pp. 1237–66.

Sartori, G. 1965. *Democratic Theory.* New York: Praeger.

——1976. *Parties and Party Systems: A Framework for Analysis*. London: Cambridge University Press.

——1987. *The Theory of Democracy Revisited*. Chatham, NJ: Chatham House.

Savoie, D. 1999. *Governing from the Centre: The Concentration of Power in Canadian Politics*. Toronto: University of Toronto Press.

Scarrow, S. 1996. *Parties and Their Members: Organizing for Victory in Britain and Germany.* Oxford: Oxford University Press.

——1999a. 'Democracy within—and without—Parties', *Party Politics* 5 (3), pp. 275–82.

——1999b. 'Parties and the Expansion of Direct Democracy: Who Benefits?', *Party Politics* 5 (3), pp. 341–62.

——2000. 'Parties without Members? Party Organization in a Changing Electoral Environment'. In: R. J. Dalton and M. P. Wattenberg (eds.), *Parties without Partisans: Political Change in Advanced Industrial Democracies*. Oxford: Oxford University Press.

——2005. *Political Parties and Democracy in Theoretical and Practical Perspectives: Implementing Intra-Party Democracy.* Washington, DC: NDI.

——and B. Gezgor 2010. 'Declining Memberships, Changing Members? European Political Party Members in a New Era', *Party Politics* 16 (6), pp. 823–43.

——P. Webb, and D. Farrell 2000. 'From Social Integration to Electoral Contestation: The Changing Distribution of Power within Political Parties'. In: R. J. Dalton and M. P. Wattenberg (eds.), *Parties without Partisans: Political Change in Advanced Industrial Democracies*. Oxford: Oxford University Press.

Schattschneider, E. E. 1942. *Party Government*. New York: Rinehart.

Scherlis, G. 2008. 'Machine Politics and Democracy: The Deinstitutionalization of the Argentine Party System', *Government and Opposition* 43 (4), pp. 579–98.

Schneider, C. J. 1957. 'Political Parties and the German Basic Law of 1949', *Western Political Quarterly* 10 (3), pp. 527–40.

Schumpeter, J. 1962 (1942), *Capitalism, Socialism and Democracy.* New York: Harper Books.

Schuur, W. van 2005. 'Green Activism: What Party Members Do.' Paper presented at the 3rd ECPR Conference, Budapest, 7–11 September 2005.

Seddone, A. and F. Venturino 2011. 'Choosing the Leader: The Italian Democratic Party at the Polls, 2007 and 2009'. Paper presented at the ECPR Joint Sessions, St. Gallen.

Seisselberg, J. 1996. 'Conditions of Success and Political Problems of a 'Media-mediated Personality-party': The Case of Forza Italia', *West European Politics* 19 (4), pp. 715–43.

Seyd, P. and P. Whiteley 1992. *Labour's Grass Roots: The Politics of Party Membership*. Oxford: Clarendon Press.

————1999. 'New Parties, New Politics? A Case Study of the British Labour Party', *Party Politics* 5 (3), pp. 383–405.

————2002. *New Labour's Grassroots: The Transformation of the Labour Party Membership*. London: Palgrave.

————2004. 'British Party Members: An Overview', *Party Politics* 10 (4), pp. 355–66.

Shaw, E. 1988. *Discipline and Discord in the Labour Party: The Politics of Managerial Control in the Labour Party, 1957–1987*. Manchester: Manchester University Press.

Somit, A., R. Wildenmann, B. Boll et al. (eds.) 1994. *The Victorious Incumbent: A Threat to Democracy?* Aldershot: Dartmouth.

Speaker's Conference 2010. *Speaker's Conference (on Parliamentary Representation) Final Report* (HC 239–1, The Stationery Office: London) <http://www.publications.parliament.uk/pa/spconf/239/239i.pdf>.

St. Leger, M. 2009. 'German Court Upholds Tax Challenge', *National Catholic Reporter*, 28 August <http://ncronline.org/news/global/german-court-upholds-church-tax-challenge> [accessed 11 May 2011].

Stewart, D. and R. K. Carty 2002. 'Leadership Politics as Party Building: The Conservatives in 1998'. In: W. Cross (ed.), *Political Parties, Representation and Electoral Democracy in Canada*. Toronto: Oxford University Press.

Stokes, S. C. 1999. 'Political Parties and Democracy', *Annual Review of Political Science* 2, pp. 243–67.

Strøm, K., W. C. Müller, and T. Bergman 2003. *Delegation and Accountability in Parliamentary Democracies*. Oxford: Oxford University Press.

Sundberg, J. 1986. 'The Failure of Maintaining Party Membership in Denmark'. Paper presented at the ECPR Workshop on Internal Party Arenas, Gothenburg, 1–6 April.

Susser, L. 2008. 'The Kadima Vote: How the Election Could Play Out', *Jewish Telegraphic Agency*, 8 September.

Swers, M. L. 2002. *The Difference Women Make: The Policy Impact of Women in Congress*. Chicago, IL: University of Chicago Press.

Tan, A. 1998. 'The Impacts of Party Membership Size: A Cross National Analysis,' *The Journal of Politics* 60 (1), pp.188–98.

Teorell, J. 1999. 'A Deliberative Defence of Intra-Party Democracy', *Party Politics* 5 (3), pp. 363–82.

Thomas, S. 1994. *How Women Legislate*. New York: Oxford University Press.

Trimble, L. and J. Arscott 2003. *Still Counting: Women in Politics Across Canada*. Canada: Broadview.

Trollope, A. 1874. *Phineas Redux*. London.

Tsatsos, D. T. and Z. Kedzia (eds.) 1994. *Parteienrecht in mittel- und osteuropäischen Staaten*. Baden-Baden: Nomos Verlagsgesellschaft.

——D. Schefold and H.-P. Schneider (eds.) 1990. *Parteienrecht im europäischen Vergleich. Die Parteien in der demokratischen Ordnungen der Staaten der Europäischen Gemeinschaft*. Baden-Baden: Nomos Verlagsgesellschaft.

UK Electoral Commission 2011. *Legislation on Regulated Donees* <http://www.electoralcommission.org.uk/party-finance/legislation/legislation-on-regulated-donees> [accessed 21 July 2011].

UK Labour 2007. *Partnership in Power Institutions* <http://www.labour.org.uk/Partnership_in_power_institutions> [accessed 17 September 2007].

——2011a. *New Politics, Fresh Ideas Consultation Document* <http://fresh-ideas.org.uk/uploads/a338d4bd-2c84-f474-75d7-01ded170e516.pdf> [accessed 29 August 2012].

—— 2011b. *A Better Future for Britain*, National Policy Forum, 25 June. London: The Labour Party.

Varnagy, R. and G. Ilonszi 2011. 'The Function of Party Leader Selection, Consolidation and Destabilization: The Hungarian Case.' Paper presented at the ECPR Joint Sessions, St. Gallen.

Verba, S. 1961. *Small Groups and Political Behavior.* Princeton, NJ: Princeton University Press.

Vossen, K. 2010. 'Populism in the Netherlands after Fortuyn: Rita Verdonk and Geert Wilders Compared', *Perspectives on European Politics and Society* 11 (1), pp. 22–38.

Vromen, A. 2005. 'Who Are the Australian Greens? Surveying the Membership'. Paper presented to the TASA Conference, University of Tasmania, 6–8 December 2005.

Wangnerud, L. 2009. 'Women in Parliaments: Descriptive and Substantive Representation', *Annual Review of Political Science* 12, pp. 51–69.

Ware, A. 1979. *The Logic of Party Democracy.* London: Macmillan.

——2002. *The American Direct Primary: Party Institutionalization and Transformation in the North.* Cambridge: Cambridge University Press.

——2003 Book Reviews. *Party Politics* 9 (4), pp. 523–5.

Wauters, B. 2009. 'Intra-Party Democracy in Belgium: On Paper, in Practice and Through the Eyes of the Members'. Paper presented at the 37th ECPR Joint Sessions, Lisbon, 14–19 April.

——2010. 'Explaining Participation in Intra Party Elections: Evidence from Belgian Political Parties', *Party Politics* 16 (2), pp. 237–59.

——2011. 'Why Did They Do It? Motives for Introducing Party Leadership Elections in Belgium'. Paper presented at the ECPR Joint Sessions, St. Gallen.

Webb, P. 1997. 'Attitudinal Clustering within British Parliamentary Elites', *West European Politics* 20 (4), pp. 89–110.

——2000. *The Modern British Party System.* London: Sage.

Weber, M. 1919. *Politik als Beruf.* Stuttgart: Reclam Verlag.

Weldon, S. L. 2002. 'Beyond Bodies: Institutional Sources of Representation for Women in Democratic Policymaking', *The Journal of Politics* 64 (4), pp. 1153–74.

Weller, P. 1985. *First Among Equals: Prime Ministers in Westminster Systems.* Sydney: George Allen and Unwin.

Whiteley, P. 2009. 'Where Have All the Members Gone? The Dynamics of Party Membership in Britain', *Parliamentary Affairs* 62 (2), pp. 242–57.

——2010. 'Is the Party Over? The Decline of Party Activism and Membership across the Democratic World', *Party Politics* 17 (1), pp. 21–44.

——H. Clarke, D. Sanders et al. 2001. 'Turnout', *Parliamentary Affairs* 54 (4), pp. 775–88.

——P. Seyd, and A. Billinghurst 2006. *Third Force Politics: Liberal Democrats at the Grassroots.* Oxford: Oxford University Press.

————and J. Richardson 1994. *True Blues: The Politics of Conservative Party Membership.* Oxford: Clarendon Press.

Widfeldt, A. 1999. *Linking Parties with People? Party Membership in Sweden 1960–1997.* Aldershot: Ashgate.

Wiliarty, S. E. 2010. *The CDU and the Politics of Gender in Germany, Bringing Women to the Party.* Cambridge: Cambridge University Press.

Williams, R. and A. Paun 2011. *Party People: How Do—And How Should—British Political Parties Select Their Parliamentary Candidates?* London: Institute for

Government <http://www.instituteforgovernment.org.uk/publications/49/> [accessed 12 January 2012].

Wintour, P. and D. Hencke 2008. 'Hain Failed to Declare £100,000 of Donations', *The Guardian Online* <http://www.guardian.co.uk> [accessed 10 January 2011].

Wolinetz, S. 2002. 'Beyond the Catch-all Party'. In: R. Gunther et al. (eds.), *Political Parties: Old Concepts and New Challenges*. Oxford: Oxford University Press.

World Movement for Democracy. *How to Strengthen Internal Party Democracy* <http://www.wmd.org/assemblies/third-assembly/workshops/political-parties-and-finance/how-strengthen-internal-party-demo> [accessed 6 June 2012].

Wright, W. E. 1971. 'Party Processes: Leaders and Followers'. In: W. E. Wright (ed.), *A Comparative Study of Party Organization*. Columbus: Charles Merrill.

Young, L. 2000. *Feminists and Party Politics*. Ann Arbor, MI: University of Michigan Press.

——2008. 'Women (Not) in Politics', Unpublished paper, University of Calgary.

——and W. Cross 2002a. 'Incentives to Membership in Canadian Political Parties', *Political Research Quarterly* 55 (3), pp. 547–69.

————2002b. 'The Rise of Plebiscitary Democracy in Canadian Political Parties', *Party Politics* 8 (6), pp. 673–99.

——and J. Everitt 2004. *Advocacy Groups*. Vancouver: UBC Press.

——n.d. 'Women's Representation in the Canadian House of Commons', IAPR Technical Paper Series, No. 041006, University of Calgary.

Zariski, R. 1972. *Italy: The Politics of Uneven Development*. Hinsdale, IL: Dryden.

Index

Note: Page numbers in *italics* indicate illustrative material.